Risk Accounting and
Risk Management
for Accountants

Risk Accounting and
Risk Management
for Accountants

Dimitris N. Chorafas

AMSTERDAM • BOSTON • HEIDELBERG • LONDON • NEW YORK • OXFORD
PARIS • SAN DIEGO • SAN FRANCISCO • SINGAPORE • SYDNEY • TOKYO
CIMA Publishing is an imprint of Elsevier

CIMA Publishing is an imprint of Elsevier
Linacre House, Jordan Hill, Oxford OX2 8DP, UK
30 Corporate Drive, Suite 400, Burlington, MA 01803, USA

First edition 2008

British Library Cataloguing in Publication Data
A catalogue record for this book is available from the British Library

Library of Congress Cataloguing in Publication Data
A catalogue record for this book is available from the Library of Congress

ISBN: 978-0-7506-8422-4

For information on all CIMA publications
visit our web site at http://books.elsevier.com

Typeset in 10/14 pts Melior by Charon Tec Ltd (A Macmillan Company), Chennai, India
www.charontec.com
Printed and bound in Great Britain

08 09 10 11 12 10 9 8 7 6 5 4 3 2 1

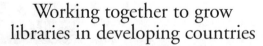

Working together to grow
libraries in developing countries

www.elsevier.com | www.bookaid.org | www.sabre.org

ELSEVIER   BOOK AID International   Sabre Foundation

Contents

Preface

The champions of tennis tournaments are those who play every point *as if* it is a match decider. If we were to describe in one brief sentence the core functions of *risk accounting* and of *risk* management, then this is it.

This book has been designed and written for accounting professionals who are increasingly confronted with challenges associated with the control of exposure. The text is based on extensive research in the United States, England, Germany, France, Italy, Switzerland and Sweden. Its orientation is practical; therefore, it includes plenty of case studies, which help in guiding the hand of the reader in the new realm of accounting functions.

Because the best weapon one has against any type of risk is knowledge of what is happening in business today, the text starts with two fundamental factors underpinning risk: volatility and uncertainty. Then, in a comprehensive way, it presents how and why accounting, auditing and risk control correlate.

The themes covered in Part 1 include what the accountant needs to know about risk and risk management, as well as duties and responsibilities associated with risk accounting. One of the focal points is business risk; another is a comprehensive presentation of correlation coefficients, confidence intervals and dynamic financial analysis – enriched with case studies.

The text outlines the reasons why risk accounting and risk management are forward accounting functions, whose exact design varies with their implementation. Therefore, they must be examined within the perspective of each company's business challenges.

The themes included in Part 2 are credit risk, stress testing of credit risk, credit risk mitigation through credit derivatives and swaps, market risk, stress testing of market risk, position risk, and issues beyond credit risk and market risk. The latter include liquidity risk, event risk, legal risk and payments risk.

The reason for taking this holistic view, which has been a deliberate choice, is that risk accountants and risk managers must look for smoke at many areas of operations – and they should do so almost at the same time. *If* smoke indicates fire, *then* delays in damage control may confront them with a four-ring alarm blaze. Risk management is not child's play.

Part 3 addresses Basel II, risk-based pricing, and the need that members of the board of directors understand and appreciate risk accounting. The models promoted by Basel II are, in essence, risk accounting tools, expressed in a general form, and need to be personalized by every institution because averages are very bad advisors.

The text critically examines the results of recent quantitative impact studies (QIS 4 and QIS 5) and finds them wanting. It also focuses on the aftermath of current mispricing of credit risk, and on problems connected to marking to market and marking to model. With this background, it emphasizes the guidelines top management needs to establish, and the role of internal control in assuring that limits to exposure are observed:

- With any trade or investment
- With any counterparty
- At any time, and
- Anywhere in the world.

One of the challenges present in every company, and most particularly a financial institution, is that most directors are not intimate with the issues connected to a galloping exposure due to novel derivatives and risk-mitigation instruments. This issue is addressed by the last chapter of the book, with advice given on how to be a devil's advocate through risk accounting facts and figures.

Unlike fishermen who talk about the one that got away, risk accountants and risk managers prefer stories about the risks they landed. Risk control is not a matter of avoiding exposure. If so, it would resemble suicide for fear of death. Instead, the very core of risk accounting and risk management is to be at all times in charge of exposure.

I am indebted to a long list of knowledgeable people, and of organizations, for their contribution to the research that made this book feasible. Also to several senior executives and experts for constructive criticism during the preparation of the manuscript.

Let me take this opportunity to thank Mike Cash for suggesting this project, Claire Hutchins for seeing it all the way to publication and Geoff Crane for the editing work. To Eva-Maria Binder goes the credit for compiling the research results, typing the text, and preparing the camera-ready artwork and index.

Dimitris N. Chorafas

Part 1

Risk and the Accounting Profession

Volatility, Uncertainty and Non-traditional Risks

1. Risk defined

Risk is the chance of injury, damage or loss. Typically it is a hazard, but errors in judgement and incorrectly kept accounting books also lead to assumption of unwanted exposure. In finance, risk is usually, though not always, related to the volatility of the future value of a position due to changes in creditworthiness, market behaviour or, more generally, uncertain events, unexpected happenings and other outliers.

Evidently enough, risk is not specific to finance and accounting; it is present in all professions and often seen as closely related to expected or projected benefits. As Max Planck, the physicist, once said: 'Without occasional venture of risk, no genuine effort can be accomplished even in the most exact sciences.'

In banking and accounting, risk is expressed quantitatively as the probability or degree of loss. Mathematically, probability is a quantitative measure. Assumed risk, however, is not just mathematics but also a function of qualitative factors, such as the nature of the counterparty (a person, company, government or other entity), characteristics of the transaction and specifics of the exposure:

- Default (Chapter 5)
- Interest rate and exchange rate risk (Chapter 7)
- Type of accident (in insurance), or other.

The quantitative expression of risk is the measure of variance around an expected value, which is often the mean value of a distribution. Because each type of risk involves a significant amount of judgement – and even the best judgement is subject to vagueness characterizing a certain issue and of uncertainty surrounding it – qualitative factors are very important in risk:

- Measuring
- Monitoring, and
- Controlling risk (more on this in Chapter 3).

Measuring, monitoring and controlling are also key activities in accounting and auditing. Luca Paciolo, the father of what is today known as *accounting*, was an analytically oriented mathematician (and Franciscan monk). He was also a researcher. Leonardo da Vinci and Paciolo were part of a circle of intellectuals who, in their time, explored the frontiers of knowledge.

Like Euclid, the ancient Greek mathematician who established the system of geometry bearing his name, Luca Paciolo was widely travelled and a very versatile person. He taught mathematical sciences in many Italian cities as well as abroad, prior to producing in 1494 (with a second edition in 1521) his most notable work, *Summa de Arithmetica Geometrica Proportioni et Proportionalita*. This title reflected the work Paciolo did with da Vinci on divine proportion and the golden cut.

One chapter of Paciolo's book, entitled 'Tractatus de computis et scripturis', is wholly dedicated to *accounting*. Rules aside, Paciolo also gave advice on sound accounting practice. Not only do the terms *general ledger* and *balance sheet* find their origin in his work, but he also contributed the vital concept of the *accounting period* when he wrote that: 'Books should be closed every year, particularly in a partnership, because frequent accounting makes for long friendship.'

While the accounting rules and methods we have today reflect the imaginative work of Paciolo and da Vinci five centuries ago, there is absolutely no reason why these accounting rules cannot be extended and made more sophisticated. In fact, they have been subject to adaptation as new requirements develop:

- The early part of the 20th century saw the emergence of *cost accounting* as a new discipline.[1]
- At the beginning of the 21st century, with IFRS, IAS 30 and IAS 39, *risk accounting* was integrated into accounting procedures and practices.[2]

In many countries not only professionals but also legislators and regulators have been at the forefront of this adaptation. In August 2006, in Paris, the Minister of Justice established two requirements for professional accountants: (i) understanding the entity (for which they work) and its environment; (ii) evaluating the risk of material anomalies in the accounts.

Clauses of the same law address the work of auditors, emphasizing the likelihood of risk and asking for procedural tests. The new law stipulates that auditors must submit their conclusions on the outcome of the above-mentioned tests, linking them to the risk evaluation and level of material anomalies that they have found. This essentially addresses the notion of *accounting risk*.

As these examples demonstrate, qualitative issues to which accountants and auditors must now respond go well beyond Paciolo's mathematics, bringing accountants' expertise into new domains alongside those of risk managers. This change can be seen as the aftermath of deregulation, globalization, innovation and rapid technological advances that affect market behaviour. In the modern economy:

- Risk is uncertainty about future profits, losses and ultimately solvency, and
- Such uncertainty reflects our lack of knowledge about some future events and their impact.

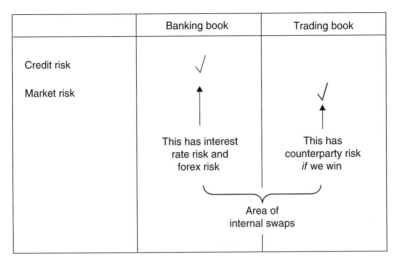

	Banking book	Trading book
Credit risk	✓	
Market risk	↑	✓ ↑
	This has interest rate risk and forex risk	This has counterparty risk *if* we win

Area of internal swaps

Figure 1.1   Internal swaps help in separating credit risk from market risk

To overcome uncertainty and manage risk, we must make *hypotheses*, or tentative statements. The challenge with hypotheses and their underlying assumptions is that they are usually subjective, and their aftermath cannot be easily measured in advance. This is particularly true of a class of exposures known as *non-traditional* risks (section 2).

Accountants are also confronted with the after-effects on the general ledger and income statement of internal transactions accepted by regulators for internal *management accounting*, but not for regulatory reporting (Chapter 2). An example is internal swaps, which sweep out of the banking book market risk (allowing it to concentrate on credit risk), and bring it into the trading book, where it will be handled. Figure 1.1 provides an example.

Among other major challenges to classical accounting that surfaced during the last ten years is special reserves made by commercial banks at upswing of the business cycle. Some central banks, for instance the Bank of Spain, require them but accounting rules have not changed to accommodate them in a satisfactory way. This is a regulatory reporting challenge.

2. Non-traditional risks

Major banks are increasingly focusing on what they consider to be non-traditional risks, such as: strategic, business risk (Chapter 3); event risk and legal risk (Chapter 9); and reputational risk (Chapter 12). Because all of them are rapidly increasing, financial institutions have stepped up efforts to qualify them, quantify them and possibly control them. Over the last two decades they have become part of a more comprehensive effort intended to improve:

- Corporate governance, and
- Risk control systems.

Traditional exposures are usually (though not always) *expected risks* characterized by relatively high frequency but low impact. They are typically covered by profits resulting from current operations and through regulatory capital. *Unexpected risks* are of lower frequency but higher impact. They also involve many unknowns and exhibit a pattern that is non-traditional.

This distinction is reflected in the risk distribution presented in Figure 1.2. In lending, *expected losses* (EL) are traditional risks. On the contrary, *unexpected losses* (UL) incorporate many non-traditional type exposures whose aftermath must be covered through reserves (economic capital) and/or a credit risk transfer mechanism (Chapter 6).

Economic capital is allocated to business units to provide financing for unexpected losses. The spikes in Figure 1.2 are higher impact events found at the right leg of a risk distribution. To independent credit rating agencies, which are concerned about an entity's creditworthiness, economic capital provides a guarantee of solvency.

The higher the rating targeting by a credit institution, the higher must be the *level of confidence* in the bank's ability to confront adversity with its own capital; hence the smaller the α shown in Figure 1.2. (The meaning of level of confidence and of α are explained in section 5, Chapter 4.)

Non-traditional risks don't need to be totally new in nature; they may differ from traditional risks because of their complexity and intensity. Credit risk (Chapter 5), as it has been known since *circa* 1700 BC with the Code of Hammurabi, the great emperor of the First Babylonian dynasty, is traditional. Counterparty risk embedded in credit derivatives and other credit risk transfer instruments (Chapter 6) is non-traditional. Behind the latter can be found complex queries:

- Are the markets only an expression of other, more fundamental factors which propel risks?
- What are these factors and how do they relate to each other?
- Is risk only really recycled between different types of instruments, or does it aggregate?

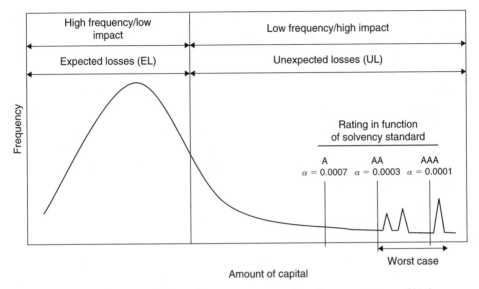

Figure 1.2 Expected losses and lower impact events correlate. The same is true of higher impact events and unexpected losses

These types of queries confront a growing number of bankers, investors and analysts confronted by credit risks arising from adverse changes in the creditworthiness of counterparties, and by market risks that are the result of adverse changes in interest rates, currency exchange rates, equity prices, commodity and other prices, leading to major position risks (Chapter 8).

In a manner similar to credit risk, there has always been *liquidity risk* due to the fact that an entity is unable to fund assets, face debt obligations or meet at a reasonable or even high price its assumed responsibilities. With globalization and deregulation, however, the old concept of liquidity risk has taken a new and much wider dimension because:

- A major liquidity crisis in a big bank risks snowballing through the financial industry, and
- A liquidity crisis in one market is exported the world over, as First World economies and emerging markets are financially interlinked.

Operational risk resulting from inadequate or failed internal processes and people, or from external events impacting upon operations, has been classically conceived as a case of fraud or of interruptions in the payments and settlements system (Chapter 9). Today, several of the origins of operational risk are viewed as non-traditional, and for good reason.

A non-traditional type of operational risk is *management risk*, expressed in the different scandals such as the bankruptcy of Enron, Global Crossing, Adelphia Communications, WorldCom and many others – which led to the Sarbanes–Oxley Act of 2002. More recently, non-traditional management risk has been the backdating of options at Broadcom, Apple Computer and other firms.

Business activities that are subject to legal proceeding or failures in compliance involve both management risk and legal risk. Legal risk also exists in cases other than plain theft. For instance, they arise because of breakdown of the law enforcement industry (judiciary and police), political greed, corruption, occult interests and exploitation of different loopholes existing in the letter of the law.

Like credit risk, legal risk has existed for a long time. Unlike credit risk, whose origin is the counterparty's inability or willingness to perform, the origins of legal risk are infinite and each has its own characteristics. In the past, legal risks have been more or less contained in terms of financial impact, while today they have:

- Multiplied in frequency
- Increased in amplitude, and
- Involve inordinate compensation.

Examples of non-traditional legal risk are compensations awarded by juries to plaintiffs, which amount to billions and quite often to more than the market value of the firm being condemned. Tobacco cases have become a classic, but other industries too face major legal risk. In the first years of the 21st century, a jury ordered Lucent Technologies to pay $2 billion to plaintiff shareholders. The judge reduced this to $500 million, because that was the maximum the company could afford to pay without going bankrupt.

Whether traditional or non-traditional, all risks confronting an entity must be identified, measured, evaluated and managed – including the risk of misjudging our opponent. 'We have reckoned without the energy and guile of the old warrior. Perhaps we were unlucky, perhaps maladroit [clumsy],' said Jean Monnet, the French financier, after he and Dillon lost the fight for control of the Bank of America to Amadeo P. Giannini.

Non-traditional risks see to it that the doors of risk and return, which have always been adjunct, become more indistinguishable. There is no significant gain without taking risks; provided that these risks are commensurate with our ability to overcome adversity, they are understood in terms of their nature, analysed for their impact and carefully watched for timely corrective action.

3. Volatility patterns

Well-managed companies are keen to detect the prevailing *pattern of risk* for each class of their exposure. Knowledgeable executives focus their attention on patterns of risk concentration. Good governance requires that as soon as a pattern is established, it becomes the subject of both quantitative and qualitative evaluation. As section 1 brought to the reader's attention, while numerical information is very important, equally vital is its interpretation, a task accountants and auditors are more and more being asked to perform (Chapter 2).

Interpretation requires solid knowledge of the business, which guides one's hand in reasoning and provides hypotheses necessary to proceed with evaluation of risk. Fairly often, a careful qualitative and quantitative analysis establishes that uniform treatment of exposure is unwarranted. Instead, it is wise to distinguish between:

- *Specific risk*, which has to do with individual characteristics of an entity, and
- *Systematic risk*, which tells how exposure connected to a certain variable, such as equity prices, is geared to general market movements.

For example, growth shares feature low yields but offer higher risk and return, because they can rise more in a bull market but drop further than other shares in a bear market. Theory says that in the long term, if these shares continue to grow the reward will be greater, but buying at the wrong time widens the investor's exposure – and nobody *really* possesses expert timing.

Along this track, analysts use empirical research approaches for risk estimation, while market professionals tend to concentrate on issues related to pricing. Financial research and development (R&D) laboratories address the pricing of options, measure volatility and try to understand differences between various option pricing models. Four patterns of risk underpin a large number of these studies:

1. *The risk of asset loss.* For instance, the possibility that mortgages, corporate loans and debt instruments may go into default. In the general case this is credit risk, an issue addressed by the 1987 Capital Accord by the Basel Committee on Banking Supervision (Basel I) and Basel II (Chapter 10). Both targeted capital requirements for credit institutions.
2. *The risk of wrong pricing of financial instruments.* This may be due to plain error, but a more frequent reason is wrong estimates of market

volatility, sometimes due to conflicts of interest. Pricing risks, which cause significant capital losses to the bank, are those connected to instruments that have not been thoroughly analysed, or whose expected volatility has been poorly estimated.

3. *Loss embedded in financial derivatives* (section 3). To a significant amount this loss is the result of high leverage, which typically accompanies derivative products and investments. Another reason is that exposures associated with new financial instruments are not well known; however, they may be associated with high-impact events and non-traditional risks.

4. *Loss due to interest rate, currency exchange, equity prices and index volatility.* In its simplest form, *market risk* is loss resulting from movement in market prices or rates. It exists because all commodity prices are volatile. *If* there was no movement of substance in market prices, *then* there will be no concern over market exposure – a utopian notion.[3] (The 1996 Market Risk Amendment by the Basel Committee addresses this risk – see Chapter 7.)

As the pattern of volatility in Figure 1.3 suggests, this is never stable, though there are periods sustaining a relatively low volatility. For instance, measured by the historical 30-day standard deviation, the volatility of the DAX, the Frankfurt equity index, amounted to approximately 20% per year in the 2004 to 2006 timeframe, which is well below the figures of mid-2002 to mid-2003, when it peaked at over 60% per year.

Far from being negative for financial markets, volatility is a precondition for their dynamic behaviour. It also helps in price discovery, but also results in disruption of various functions in the financial system. From an investor's viewpoint, volatility is an approximation of the prevailing uncertainty in the market:

- In rising markets it is a reason for euphoria
- In falling markets it is perceived as generating stress, and
- In several cases it may result in liquidity and solvency problems.

The analysis of monthly realized volatility of a typical enterprise listed in the stock exchange is done through bifurcation into *a company-specific* component and one reflecting *systematic* risk, as discussed in the opening paragraphs of this section. Such an approach helps in documenting whether market volatility has risen or fallen for the entity itself and for the market as a whole.

If market (systematic) volatility has risen more than the company-specific component (expressed as *beta*), *then* even broadly diversified investments in

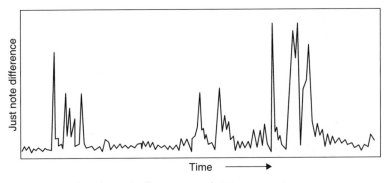

Figure 1.3   A pattern of market volatility over nearly 20 years

stocks are exposed to a higher volatility risk. Further indications as to whether the development of volatility might cause disruptions to the financial markets may be gained from expected future volatility.

Not only structural but also cyclical factors influence the change of volatility patterns in financial markets. Empirical studies have demonstrated that stock market volatility is negatively related to overall economic activity, raising the question of what implications an unexpected weakening of global growth would have on stock market volatility. The level of implied equity market volatility is closely related to the correlation between returns on:

- The equity market, and
- The government bond market.

The *leverage hypothesis* states that if an entity's stock market value falls, the equity's share in capital decreases and correspondingly leverage rises. Volatility usually rises as share prices fall and falls as share prices rise. Empirical evidence suggests that the drop in 2004–06 stock market volatility and rising share prices have led to a significant decline in credit premiums on corporate bonds. In contrast, growing volatility leads to wider risk spreads.

Investment decisions can benefit from the use of trade Volatility Index (VIX) by the Chicago Board of Trade. The relative return of higher quality stocks are positively correlated with VIX and those for lower quality stocks are negatively correlated. More defensive sections of the economy tend to perform better when overall equity market volatility increases, while higher volatility (beta) sectors tend to underperform as volatility rises.

While the relationship between VIX and most asset classes is not statistically significant, changes in the VIX have an important negative relationship to the short-term performance of equities, but a positive relationship to the short-term performance of cash – even if over the long term the correlation between VIX and cash is not statistically significant.

4. Financial derivatives

The *perfect market* hypothesis states that all players share the same information and act rationally. Both suppositions have little to do with reality. Even markets exposed to traditional risks are not rational, just as there exist no perfect financial instruments. This statement becomes so much stronger with non-traditional risks.

If new information was indeed generally available to all players and immediately factored into the prices of financial instruments, *then* there would have been no arbitrage. Other impossibilities supported by perfect market theory are that:

- All desired payment flows can be replicated from a combination of traded instruments, and
- *Derivatives* would have no impact on spot markets, because their value can be computed explicitly from the value of the underlying asset.

(For starters, derivative financial instruments are characterized by an *underlying*, which may be the price or rate of an asset or liability, but not the asset or liability itself. Examples of underlyings are interest rates, currency exchange rates, share prices, other commodity prices, an index of prices or some other variable that is used in conjunction with the notional principal amount of the derivatives contract.)

Usually, although not necessarily always, derivatives represent future obligations – examples are forward rate agreements (FRAs) and options (more on this later). The term *notional principal amount* is borrowed from the swaps market, where it signifies the contractual quantity of money, never actually to be paid or received. An example is interest rate swaps (IRSs).

(Etymologically, a *swap* is a contractual agreement to exchange, or swap, assets or payment obligations. Foreign exchange swaps, for instance, are the simultaneous spot sale and forward purchase of foreign currency, or simultaneous spot purchase and forward sale of foreign currency. The most important category of swaps is the interest rate swap, followed by foreign exchange contracts, equity-linked contracts and commodity contracts.)

Whether we talk of derivative financial instruments or spot commodities, like equity and debt, financial markets are not characterized by instantaneous information for all players; the players themselves are not necessarily rational and complex money flows are not easily replicated. These and other facts demolish the market hypothesis. Moreover, there exist transaction costs, trade restrictions and changes in market liquidity, which means that effects may well be totally different from ideal.

This is by no means unwanted, because while it involves risks it also provides for better than average returns. To implement their strategies investors generally use both spot and derivatives markets, their choice often depending on several factors including those of lighter legislation, greater leverage and relatively lower transaction costs for derivative instruments – counterweighted, however, by greater non-traditional risks.

Assumed risk left aside, it is usually easier to implement fairly complex strategies in derivatives markets than in spot markets. Today, with derivatives liquidity is ample, market access is unrestricted and instruments are quickly tradable. The problem is that risks and returns are very often asymmetric.

Theoretically, one may sell a future on a stock index which replicates the equities in his or her portfolio. Theory says that gains on stocks are offset by losses from the sale of the futures, and losses on stocks by gains from the futures position. In practice, there is no ideal offsetting. One leg of the transaction might be much shorter than the other, as ultimately many investors found to their surprise.

Options are the oldest derivative product on record, invented in ancient Greece by Thales of Militos, one of the seven sages. They are contracts that give the purchaser the right, but not the obligation, to buy (call option) or sell (put option) a specified quantity of a financial instrument, commodity or other asset, at a specified price (strike price), during (American option) or at the end (European option) of a specified period of time. The purchaser of the option pays the writer (seller) a premium to compensate the risk taken under the option.

Forwards are contracts to purchase or sell a specific quantity of a given financial instrument, commodity or other asset at a specified price determined at the outset, with delivery or settlement at a specified future date. At maturity, settlement is by actual delivery of the item specified in the contract, or by means of a net cash settlement.

Futures are similar contracts to forwards but they are standard and exchange traded, while forwards are individually tailored and treated over the counter (OTC). Also contrary to forwards, futures are generally settled through an offsetting trade. (OTC contracts are typically bilateral agreements and represent more than 75% of all derivatives trades.)

Futures and forwards markets enable the transfer of market risk between different players, and they make possible hedging against spot price risks. For instance, by taking a futures position, buyers know in advance the price at which they can buy an underlying asset later on, while writers freeze the price at which they will deliver the underlying asset.

Caps and floors are contracts resembling interest rate options. An interest rate cap will compensate the purchaser of the cap if interest rates rise above a predetermined rate (strike price). An interest rate floor will compensate the purchaser if rates fall below a predetermined rate. A combination of the two is provided by an interest rate *collar*.

FRAs, IRSs, futures, forwards, put and call options, caps, floors and collars are useful instruments, and – when traded in connection with commercial transactions – help the counterparties in keeping a tap on their exposures. This is not true, however, when trading:

- Is done for purely financial gain
- Is long maturity, and
- Involves large amounts of money.

An example is interest rate swaps with 30-year maturity. How banks can know the interest rates three decades down the line falls in my knowledge gap, said a central director of the Bank of England. They don't, and at maturity 30-year interest rate swaps will hold many surprises for one of the counterparties.

An inordinate amount of risk also comes from *exotic* derivatives, like complex swaps and a swarm of sophisticated options. Examples are: all or nothing, knock-in/knock-out, barrier, binary, complex choser, nested, embedded, look-back, one touch, outperformance, step-lock and plenty of others, since new instruments are designed every day. This statement is also valid about trading credit risk exposure.

Credit derivatives (Chapter 6) are contracts used to hedge against credit risks. They also permit exploitation of changes in creditworthinesss by enabling credit risks to be traded individually. Theoretically, this happens at low transaction costs and without major restrictions. In practice, risk should always be counted in transaction costs (section 5) and restrictions to the trade must be clearly established by the firm.

In conclusion, at the positive end of the financial derivatives equation is the fact that they are versatile instruments subject to steady innovation. Their major negative comes from the amount of assumed non-traditional risk, which is not always understood, let alone under control. One of the reasons is that non-traditional risks create novel exposures; another is that in many enterprises risk management is not at its best and even the concepts underpinning it are wanting.

5. Risk is a cost

Risk is no alien concept in banking. However, globalization, deregulation, technology and a golden horde of new financial instruments convinced clear-eyed bankers that, more than ever, transactions made and positions taken must be fully understood and rigorously controlled. Innovation, leverage, volatility, liquidity and lack of it combine to increase the risk of major exposures, which has the potential to destroy a financial institution or any other entity.

A sophisticated approach to risk control is to look at *risk as a cost*, like every other cost registered on accountant records. We must stop talking of assumed exposure as being balanced by return. Risk is the:

- Cost of yesterday when the commitment was made, and
- The cost of tomorrow revealed at the transaction's maturity.

A statement made a few years ago by Dr Alan Greenspan, then chairman of the Federal Reserve, helps to better appreciate the principles underpinning a dual approach to risk and cost. On 29 August 2003, at the annual meeting of the Federal Reserve Bank of Kansas City, Greenspan defined the Fed's role in interest rates as *risk management*. He said risk management is a combination of:

- Judgement, and
- Analytics.

Hence, the setting of interest rates by the central bank must account for *probable* evolution in economic growth, and *improbable* outcome in inflation, deflation and economic collapse. This is precisely the principle that should underline the accountant's approach in costing, therefore *monetizing*, assumed exposure.

During the same Fed annual meeting, Greenspan also underlined that Federal Reserve members and economists may have different opinions because of different types of economic outlook, and projections on inflation and its aftermath. This strengthens risk management by making the approach to it more polyvalent. Precisely the same principle is valid with *costing risk*:

- No two accountants would probably come up with exactly the same numbers in risk monetization

- However, this is not a serious problem because what is most important is order of magnitude and direction of the monetized exposure.

To converge in their estimates regarding the costing of risk, accountants and risk managers must constantly monitor performance by instrument and counterparty anywhere in the world. And, as with every scientific discipline, they must use precisely the same method for each client and class of instruments. The underlying principle is best expressed in two bullets:

- Monetization makes it possible to better appreciate the impact of assumed exposure
- When the magnitude of risk is shown in real money, everybody gets to realize the consequences.

Monetization is like looking at risk through the mind's eye at a time when person-to-person contact is no longer what it used to be. Here is what Bryan Burrough says about Jacob Safra's advice: '[He] taught his son that the essence of money lending was a borrower's character, and he drilled young Edmond in the ways to deduce character by reading a man's face. "Look him in the eye," he would say, "for eyes tell more than balance sheets." '[4]

Safra was not alone in this policy. Benjamin Franklin walked around town to see if those to whom he had lent money were at work or in the tavern, and J.P. Morgan greatly valued character. This indeed is the best policy when the banker knows his clients person to person, which is far from being the case in today's impersonal society. *If* the counterparty's character is opaque, the proxies are:

- Risk, and
- Cost.

A well-designed system should establish warning signals on risk/cost overruns, for all activities under its wings, while the people manning it show decisive action as soon as such signals are detected. Just like the Fed does in connection to interest rates, the setting of risk/cost limits must account for:

- Probable evolution of credit risk and market risk by instrument, counterparty and area of operations, and
- Improbable outcome due to unexpected risks, credit deterioration, liquidity squeeze and event risk (Chapter 9).

Some of the variables connected to these outcomes will be *exogenous*, generated by the market or by legislation and regulation. Others will be *endogenous*, under management's authority but requiring identification diagnosis, evaluation of risk factors, prediction of their impact, analysis of likely results, and decision on repositioning or other control action.

To calculate the risk inherent in a financial instrument, or generally in a given banking operation, we must identify fundamental factors of exposure, determine their linkages, establish appropriate metrics, take measurements and reach conclusions. Three classes of professionals are necessary to put in place such a system. One is expert bankers who contribute not only know-how on instruments, counterparties and transactions, but also their insight gained through long experience. Another is accountants of the new culture described in Chapter 2. Their contribution will go well beyond recording numbers, returning to the origins of the accounting profession at the time of Luca Paciolo and his inquisitive approach to facts and figures (section 1).

In this effort, the accountants will be assisted by the third group of professionals – the *rocket scientists*. Rocket scientists have entered banking practice since the late 1980s.[5] They are applied mathematicians, physicists, engineers, mathematical economists, experimental psychologists and system experts who came into finance from the aerospace, missiles, computers and communications industries. Their presence serves two purposes:

- Opening up new business opportunities, and
- Developing powerful analytics for the control of risk.

The rocket scientists' background and training assists accountants in providing tools that can act as *magnifying lenses* in the cost side of risk. In the banking business, R&D has become indispensable because of its contribution in determining the exact nature of links and nodes of a system, which can keep exposure and the cost under lock and key, in spite of increasing frequency of non-traditional risks and magnitude of their impact.

6.   The science of risk management

The evidence provided by the preceding five sections leads to the conclusion that the able management of exposure has a long list of prerequisites that must be fulfilled. Its exercise also needs a rigorous methodology; which is a basic characteristic of any science. Another 'must' is steady practice to learn how the system ticks.

This concept has been superbly phrased centuries ago by Roger of Hourden. Changing only one term, it reads: 'The science of risk management, if not practised beforehand, cannot be gained when it becomes necessary. Nor indeed can the athlete bring high spirit to the contest, who never has been trained to practise it.'[6] Training is the key word in any science, and accountants are well placed to train themselves in the control of risk.

Learning risk management is so much more necessary because of the strong anchoring of risk-taking policies in modern business, growing leverage in the economy and the inescapable macroeconomic shocks in the globalized land-scape. All this explains why accounting practices must respond to the need to focus on, and register in no uncertain terms, every signal connected to exposure.

Additionally, accountants constantly have to calibrate their tools to keep risk managers aware of the state of the art in their assessment of exposure. Accountants should also appreciate that the proper definition of risk taken by their firm through its financial instruments and counterparties requires a value differentiation provided by the perspective of the executor:

- Traders
- Loans officers
- Risk managers, and
- Senior executives of the firm.

A comment I have heard quite often in my research is that there is no real awareness of risk among accountants, and not only among accountants. Evidence provided for this statement has included the overly simplistic notions sometimes adopted for risk assessment. One of the knowledgeable persons who contributed valuable concepts to this book argued that *risk control activism* is comparable to monetary policy assessment, which must demonstrate the:

- Determination with which a central bank tries to enact its statutory objectives
- Basic features of the macroeconomic environment in which monetary policy is made, and
- Frequency and amplitude of policy moves over a period of time as captured, for instance, by interest rate volatility.

Up to a point, policies connected to effective control of credit risk and market risk, and those targeting exposures associated to systemic factors, correlate. In fact, the most interesting, and important, developments in risk management science are not those associated with phenomena of a smoothly running economy, but those of practical breakdown.

In the case of economic and financial crises, the very essence of applying scientific method is an effective response to the need of focusing attention on the nature and likelihood of previously unencountered states of a system, particularly states beyond its original scope, or issue under investigation.

Based on principles of scientific analysis, this approach contrasts with opinion surveys, which sometimes include bias. For instance, a mid-December 2006 survey of oil analysts and traders asking for assessment of whether crude oil futures are likely to rise, fall or remain neutral in the coming weeks gave the following result: Rise 12, Neutral 6, Fall 8. 'Fall' represented just 30% of opinions, but as the oil market of January 2007 demonstrated, the minority carried the day.

A scientific process of prediction studies interrelationships between critical factors, some of which are only partially known. An analytical approach like input/output protocols assists in identifying, and sometimes projecting, critical points of convergence and divergence, also in assessing the significance of changes of direction presented at crucial junctures.

This type of research often focuses on the specificity of future *branching points*, which are built into the system under investigation – whose definitions, axioms and postulates are all man-made. Accountants have the mission to provide accurate, timely and analytical data; rocket scientists labour to torture this data (noun, singular) and make it reveal its secrets.

The message to the reader distilled from these references is that, as well-managed entities appreciate, the concept of risk is broadened and deepened at the same time. By contrast, the laggards lack both policies on risk control and tools permitting the investigation of complex situations involving:

- *Volatility*, and the correlation it generates between markets and instruments.
- *Uncertainty*, about high-frequency/low-impact expected events and most particularly low-frequency/high-impact unexpected events.
- *Liquidity*, both market-wide and specific to the firm, given prevailing volatility and uncertainty.
- *Solvency*, including the possible reasons for insolvency, ways and means for fast realization of assets, and default point (DP) characteristics.

The ability to define, model and analyse complex situations is core to any scientific risk management approach. The increasing depth and breadth of financial studies suggests that more intellectual effort has to be organized around the problem to be solved than in connection to traditional functions served by classical accounting. This is a basic premise in science, which now mutates into finance and accounting.

Notes

1 D.N. Chorafas, *Operational Risk Control with Basel II: Basic Principles and Capital Requirements.* Butterworth-Heinemann, London, 2004.

2 D.N. Chorafas, *International Financial Reporting Standards and Corporate Governance: IFRS and Fair Value Impact on Budgets, Balance Sheets and Management Accounts.* Butterworth-Heinemann, London, 2005.

3 D.N. Chorafas, *The 1996 Market Risk Amendment: Understanding the Marking-to-Model and Value-at-Risk.* McGraw-Hill, Burr Ridge, IL, 1998.

4 Bryan Burrough, *Vendetta: American Express and the Smearing of Edmond Safra.* Harper Collins, New York, 1992.

5 D.N. Chorafas, *Rocket Scientists in Banking.* Lafferty Publications, London, 1995.

6 Jonathan Phillips, *The Fourth Crusade and the Sack of Constantinople.* Pimlico, London, 2005. Roger of Hourden had spoken of 'the science of war'.

Risk Management and the Accountant

1. Beyond classical accounting

Successful companies use financial information technology to transform accounting's role from what has been called, in a diminutive way, 'bean counting' to full partner in the way the business is run. Part, but only part, of this transformation is due to quantum leaps in computer technology. The bigger part has to do with policy change. Finance departments are no longer preoccupied with bare bone numbers. They are now concentrating on analysing information.

Accountants turned financial analysts are slicing, dicing and investigating elements included in masses of information from all over the company on everything from accounts receivable to inventories. Individual customer-by-customer profit and loss statements have given senior management ammunition to:

- Renegotiate unfavourable contracts, and
- Be more selective in choosing business partners.

A major breakthrough in the bank's quality of management is the production of real-time virtual financial statements, which allow one to be ahead of the curve in evaluating risk and return, and make critical capital allocation decisions earlier than ever before; this also slashes thousands of hours of grunt work, which has been classically required to close the books.

Information technology has enabled the accountancy profession to focus on strategic issues hidden behind warehouses of data. This is restructuring the profession of accountancy and fostering a sea change in the way companies assess their business prospects. The most savvy managements appreciate that rigorous analysis of accounting information helps them to:

- Discover new customers
- Wring more revenue out of existing ones
- Lower financing costs by optimizing assets and liabilities, and
- Control their exposures in a proactive way.

Companies that are leading in this ongoing effort have cost compression and risk management as guidelines. Their management realizes that the real potential is in deepening and augmenting customer relationships while keeping costs and risks behind bars (see Chapter 1 on the monetization of risk).

It is not by accident that the chief financial officer (CFO) has emerged as the central player in modern management practice. Finance gathers a company's most critical data in overseeing functions such as customer accounting, supplier records, billing, accounts payable, general ledger, and P&L. Clear-eyed CFOs are spearheading the shift from legacy systems, which cranked out lots of data but little useful information, to integrated and interactive systems that have made possible added value applications.

There exist, however, an awful lot of laggards. Many companies are still mucking around with their old transaction systems and have not yet ventured into the new age of accounting. Yet, their managers must have heard that in some of their competitors new technologies are producing not only dramatic cost savings, but also radical changes in the way they do business internally and externally. Proactive entities have realized gains by:

- Integrating and standardizing a mismatch of traditional procedures such as accounts payable, general ledger and payroll, and
- Discarding legacy systems entirely in favour of highly competitive solutions, which cost less and provide more deliverables.[1]

Additionally, CFOs worth their salt have, for more than a decade, used the internet and *intranets* to collect and deliver financial information. One of the earlier intranet applications allowed employees to view their payroll information online any time they want; another has enabled companies to significantly reduce paper-based transactions.

High technology is vital, but it is not the only ingredient in achieving these results. Another important element is organization-wide *cultural change*, and the need that the company's accounting and financial reporting system reflect an advanced business model. Sound governance requires timely estimates and judgements on assets, liabilities, revenues and expenses, and disclosure of contingent assets and liabilities in a more exact and more analytical manner than ever before.

The management of companies who hold leading positions in their industries has decided to spend more time looking forward than backwards, and wants the accountants to also work in this direction. This is done in appreciation of the fact that whether we look at risks, costs, sales or any other key factor of business, the forward examination of problems and positions holds the keys to success.

This is also the way the auditors' monitoring system works in order not only to flash out cases but also, and most importantly, to prevent offenses such as accounting fraud – which is a global problem. Investigations have to be carried out both forward and backward in order to establish whether employees and managers have been cooking the books.

The safe bet is that many of the findings brought up through rigorous investigation are of a critical nature, but *if* this is the case *then* so be it. 'Be nice, feel guilty and play safe. If there was ever a prescription for producing a dismal future, that has to be it,' Walter B. Wriston, the former chairman of Citibank, once said. The aphorism applies hand-in-glove to all matters concerning accounting and auditing, as well as the management of the enterprise as a whole.

It is always rewarding to examine ways and means of improving the safety of an enterprise by identifying and correcting its weakest links, because that's where the highest risk lies. Automotive engineering offers an example. Experts advise that nearly half of accidents occur at the front end of the vehicle on a straight road in daylight and good weather, at less than 80 kilometres per hour.

Just like in finance, where the result of running into an ill-studied transaction can be deadly, running into the car ahead accounts for 25% of all accidents. Moreover, an estimated 95% of all road accidents are caused by human error. In the majority of products and systems, the weakest link is the human factor.

The importance of an engineering example like risk control in automotive design is that it opens a different window to problem-solving because it involves analytical thinking. It also documents that every profession has its challenges. Sometimes solutions to what appear to be totally unrelated problems are not as different as they might seem at first sight.

Since it is not possible to design a different control system for every driver, and moreover the driver's habits change over time, the best solution is an adaptive design. The same approach works well in risk management. In automotive engineering, for example, a generic restraint system can be adapted to a specific vehicle by updating the control algorithm.[2] At the same time, however, while most of the building blocks are in place for real-time control of restraint systems, there are still some significant challenges – just like in the case of real-time risk control.

2. Thinking out of the box

Reasoning by analogy from a different field of endeavour than the one in which we are presently submerged (as section 1 has done) is one of the best ways of thinking 'out of the box' of legacy approaches that quite often lead to sub-optima and dead ends. Here is another example, this time from medical science. 'The belief is growing on me that the disease is communicated by the bite of the mosquito,' suggested Ronald Ross, a British doctor in India. That insight won him a Nobel prize.[3]

Defying age-old notions that malaria was caused (as its name suggests) by foul air, Ross showed how it really spread. Unfortunately, those who succeeded him in the task of fighting malaria have been short of imagination as well as of accountability for results. This should not happen with risk management.

Once we know the causes, the application of effective solutions can limit expected losses and provide better insight into unexpected losses caused by counterparties, financial instruments, the business environment and/or a failure in the institution's internal control system. Some of the ingredients of continuing effective risk control are:

- Rigorous auditing
- Better performance measurement
- Appropriate capital allocation, and
- Realistic pricing of financial products.

In all these cases, thinking out of the box improves the accountant's ability to gauge additional risk factors that exist outside the immediate trading and back-office functions. Regrettably, this is not common practice. In the course of the research project that led to this book, experts in financial analysis, trading, treasury operations and the control of risk commented that in a large number of institutions current risk management systems cannot cope with the explosion in types and severity of exposures because they are too much tuned to what has happened in the past.

The inadequacy of current approaches has been caused by a variety of factors, chief among them being traditional thinking and the fact that members of the board of directors seldom have direct experience of risk management (Chapter 12). Still another factor is that the institution continues using obsolete and incompatible information systems:

- Designed to address simpler business activities
- Using a variety of heterogeneous design methodologies, and
- Handling incompatible data formats, on different technical platforms and with a variety of programming languages.

All this is part of traditional thinking. Organizations that have done their homework in restructuring their risk management solutions have come to the conclusion that there is an overwhelming need for homogeneous systems and approaches able to provide any-to-any immediate consolidation, calculation and presentation of limits, positions and risks (section 5) – as well as opportunities to trade.

New strategic-level departures to risk management are vital because mammoth financial institutions and the so-called 'non-bank banks' challenge the traditional domain of a credit institution's activity. They also overrun the classical risk control concept and, by extension, bank regulation, which is typically based on the notion of firms with specialized activities. To be in charge in this fact-changing environment, management needs to:

- Introduce a broader mix of risks originating in diverse business lines, and
- Provide a comprehensive but flexible risk control approach that take a view of the firm as a whole.

An example of this broader mix is the sale by insurance companies of credit risk protection through credit derivatives (Chapter 6). The contracts straddle the investment and underwriting activities of insurers, which are conventionally managed separately. By so doing, large and sophisticated entities increase de facto their risk appetite because of an excessive concentration of most diverse financial activities; hence, they need a vastly strengthened system of risk control.

Accountants, auditors and internal control specialists are key to this system, because they both provide inputs to it and use its outputs. Thinking out of the box suggests that these inputs must be redesigned to serve the needs of both the more classical analysis of exposure and a discipline known as meta-analysis.

Meta is a Greek word meaning a level higher than the one we have been classically working. Meta-knowledge is knowledge about knowledge; *meta-accounting* is accounting analysis beyond filling pigeonholes in accounting books. The concept of meta-analysis has existed for six decades, but it has grown over the last 20 years. Originally invented in 1948, it blossomed with expert systems and knowledge engineering[4] as a way of:

- Extracting statistically meaningful information from lots of small accounting entries or results of trials, and
- Reaching far-sighted conclusions even if trials have been conducted, and accounts written in ways that make it difficult to compare the results.

Notice that the conclusions of meta-analysis are only valid if the outcomes of both positive and negative trials are included in the study. *If* the negative trials are left out *then* the results may be too optimistic, as often happens with the interpretation of experimental outcomes that are screened to weed out what is (wrongly) considered to be irrelevant outliers.

The science of risk management, whose conquest was introduced in Chapter 1, requires that nothing is discarded *a priori*. Every information element counts. Outliers are a means of thinking out of the box. High-impact risks are often hiding at the long leg of the distribution of exposures, and it is the duty of the analyst to flash them out and put them in perspective.

3.   Case studies: GE and Amaranth

Case studies are one of the best ways to exercise analogical thinking. Properly chosen, they constitute astute analyses of how a company has tried to outthink and outmanoeuvre its competition only to find out through shocks that this has involved an unaffordable amount of risk. Alternatively, case studies can teach how well-managed companies are able to regularly reinvent their business and stay alive.

Here is a practical example on a company that has been able to reinvent itself. When during his tenure Jack Welch, then chairman of General Electric, foresaw that the profitability of aircraft engines and appliances was falling, he moved the company into new profit zones:

- Financing
- Servicing, and
- Maintenance.

As the value chain of the globalized market moved from producing manufactured goods to services, GE was there to capture it. This business foresight and windfall of profits that came along with it should be compared to the case of less discerning executives who never tried to make up for lower profit margins, either because they lacked foresight or because they were too timid to take needed measures, including:

- Turning inside-out of product lines
- Using cash cows to finance new departures in a changing market.

Experts attributed Jack Welch's timely response to the fact that he saw faster than his competitors that, for any product on the market, there exists a larger economic equation of which the product itself is only a subset. Moreover, once he fixed his sight on that market, Welch moved to capture it while other CEOs were undecided and waited until the market passed them by.

Foresight is what risk management needs not just once or twice, but all the time. Lack of it leads to disaster, as the case of Amaranth Advisors demonstrates. This Greenwich, Connecticut-based hedge fund's mark of distinction is that, in just three weeks (30 August to 20 September 2006), it lost $6 billion by speculating on the price of gas. That loss represented two-thirds of the $9 billion it had under management.

As Amaranth's capital submerged under a torrent of red ink, several analysts suggested that the creation of new instruments, such as complex derivatives, probably makes the financial system stronger in the long run (by seeing to it that risks become better priced and more widely distributed), but in the short run companies are subject to extinction when:

- The quality of their risk control is not commensurate to their exposure, and
- Their leveraged instruments have yet to be tested by a severe recession, a big corporate default or sudden market change.

Other experts pointed out that if many companies active in derivatives markets had made the same bet, and it proved wrong, the market may have descended to the abyss. In late 2006, a wrong bet has been that risky assets will outperform and volatility will stay low for a long period of time.

This has not been the right hypothesis. On 20 September 2006, in a letter to investors, Amaranth said its losses could reach 65% of its funds. Withdrawal by investors hurt it more, and the same has been true of an exodus by managers deprived of their bonuses. The pension fund of 3M, a manufacturing firm, and the San Diego County employees' retirement fund, were among those exposed to Amaranth's sea of red ink.

In Wall Street, a wide-signed opinion has been that since many hedge funds are financially interlocked, the money in hedge funds run by Goldman Sachs and Britain's MAN Group was also at stake. Acting as investors in Amaranth, funds managed by Crédit Suisse and Morgan Stanley were also hit.

Not to be left behind, investment banks have been assessing their losses as a result of lending to hedge funds through their prime-brokerage firms. Moreover, this $6 billion black hole unsettled regulators. Christopher Cox, head of the Securities and Exchange Commission (SEC), said that substandard risk management has been at the origin of the debacle. 'I've never seen a hedge fund so highly leveraged in energy,' commented Peter Fusaro of the Energy Hedge Fund Centre. He reckoned that Amaranth held about 10% of the global market in natural-gas futures, adding that: 'Somebody was not monitoring this correctly.'[5]

After the loss, Amaranth stated that it had reached agreement to transfer its energy portfolio to J.P. Morgan Chase and Citadel, another hedge fund. Financial analysts were surprised by the choice of the second player, noticing that Citadel had lost a fortune by short-selling natural gas in 2005 and was still rebuilding its gas-trading business.

Neither were Amaranth and Citadel the only hedge funds to suffer from wild swings of natural gas price. In August 2006, MotherRock, a smaller entity, collapsed after big losses. Some experts suggested that as of September 2006, hedge funds had $67.4 billion invested in the energy sector, up from $30 billion in 2004.

While this was a small share of the $7 trillion global energy market, the combination of:

- Volatility in energy markets, and
- The growing pool of investment in energy

meant an increasing number of investors had been exposed – many of them institutional – without really knowing the size of the risk they assumed. This is precisely what Chapter 1 has stated should never happen. There is no excuse for lapses in risk control; when they occur, the main background reason is lack of quality management.

4. Newton's principles in analytics

Meta-analysis and meta-accounting use several century-old principles characterizing physics and scientific research at large. Therefore, accountants who want to be ahead of the curve in their profession would be well advised to read the biographies of great physicists and study the way their minds worked.

Because of his polyvalent background, Sir Isaac Newton provides one of the best case studies. Most people think of him as the physicist who established the law of gravity, which is true. Few people, however, appreciate that Newton spent more of his career as a central banker (first Warden and then Master of the Mint) than as a physicist at Cambridge University. Indeed, he was the first rocket scientist ever (Chapter 1).

One of the stronger points of Newton's personality, of which the reader should definitely take notice, is that he stepped away from what he was taught, what he saw as routine and what by all likelihood seemed to be 'obvious' (see also the case of Ross in section 2). His second most important characteristic was that in his work he provided focus.

- He was an analytical scientist who primarily worked on his own, and
- His conceptual abilities permitted him to draw together the many facts that led from ancient times to modern science.

This is precisely the concept underpinning meta-analysis. Newton's study involved both mathematics and thoroughly documented experimental evidence, in appreciation of the fact that both are fundamental ingredients of the work of every scientist – and, in fact, of every accountant and every risk manager. The risk protection strategy, discussed in section 5, is based on these principles.

Newton's approach can be instrumental in deciding how successful the control of exposure will be, as well as the quality of results obtained. This is direct reflection of one of the strengths of Isaac Newton's personality: the ability to ask penetrating questions that led to the heart of the matter he was investigating. By all evidence, he appreciated that lack of focus produces a distorted picture of reality.

To appreciate what motivated this great mind, we must keep in perspective that the late 17th/early 18th century was (like today) one of rapidly changing social and scientific environments. What were conceived at the time as 'tomorrow's' demands were not the same as 'today's' or 'yesterday's' – and people had to think out of the box to reach conclusions meaningful for the future.

The principles of scientific analysis established by Newton can serve risk managers, traders and the new generation of accountants because what lies between them is intent and an inquisitive approach. Among enlightened people, *intent* follows fairly closely the philosophy of John Locke, which was based upon the concept that all our knowledge derives from experience. In Newtonian thinking, knowledge comes from two sources of experience:

- *Sensation*, which is the gateway for the external world's input, and
- *Reflection*, which is the output of the work of one's own investigative mind.

Like Locke, Newton ascertained that because we do not perceive an object but only an idea of it, the true nature of the world around us can only be studied and ascertained through mathematics. I have found no better statement to describe the work of accounting and of accountants. After all, Luca Paciolo, who founded accounting, was a mathematician (Chapter 1).

Additionally, the fact that in his career Isaac Newton moved from physics to economics and finance provides evidence of another basic principle of meta-analysis. Key questions in Newton's mind when he and Charles Montague, the Chancellor of the Exchequer, confronted British finances were:

- For how long will the growth of the economy be sustainable?
- Which economic factors help intensify competition against the French?
- Is the divergence of resources to the war effort against Louis XIV likely to persist for some time?
- What are the best opportunities for the enhancement of commerce and financial might?

Subconsciously at least, these queries had their roots in a deeper background, which made use of the principles of scientific investigation and led to questions such as:

- How important are assets and liabilities management?
- How could the Mint best handle interest rate risk?
- Is there something that should be done to strengthen the unofficial regulatory system?

Even enlightened minds, however, may fail in prognosticating oncoming risk. Isaac Newton did fall victim to a famous scam. History books say that he lost £20 000 (a large amount at that time) in the financial hecatomb of the South Sea Company, which was established in 1711 in the illusory hope that it would solve the problems of a growing national debt resulting from a succession of wars engaged by England and Holland against the expansionary designs of Louis XIV of France.

5.   A risk protection strategy

The British South Sea Bubble – which came upon the steps of the French Mississippi Bubble and Royal Bank scam – has remained as one of the greatest Ponzi games in financial history. It engulfed some of the best-known politicians and financiers of its time, and in its way demonstrated that one cannot be too careful in accounting for and controlling risk.

When new risks arise, as in the case of financial derivatives, or old ones grow in importance, people and companies confront novel types of exposure with which they are little or not at all acquainted. For instance, interest rates, which had long been stable, rose sharply in the 1970s and became volatile for more than a decade.

By the late 1980s, companies that were not prudent enough to hedge their positions, like the savings and loans (building societies) companies in the USA, came under great pressure to liquidate mortgage loans on their books, and some of them collapsed. The silver lining has been that their bankruptcy stimulated the development of a market for mortgage-backed securities.

Interest rate risk is, to a significant extent, a *normal risk* attached to the bank's classical line of business: deposits and lending. But as we saw in section 4, there are also *higher order risks* associated with new financial industries like complex derivatives and/or big bets.

A steady and persistent rise in exchange rate may turn into high risk. An example is the autumn 1998 global crisis, when big hedge funds speculated against the yen with huge financial bets. In only four days the dollar plunged by 18% against the yen. By contrast, in 1980–85 the dollar had appreciated by nearly 50%, undermining the international competitiveness of American firms.

To confront major persistent risks, some of which are due to speculation, management must consider likely developments and plan meticulously for them. When the yen was rising at stratospheric levels against the dollar, Japanese companies that depended heavily for their exports on the US market developed and implemented risk control scenarios with 75 yen to the dollar when the exchange was still $1 to 100 yen.

Fundamental to effective risk management is the establishment and maintenance of a sound system of *risk limits* to provide barriers against an accumulation of exposures inherent in ongoing business activities. Experts suggest that the size of these limits reflects the entity's *risk appetite*, given the:

- Market environment
- Business strategy, and
- Financial resources available to absorb losses.

Sound governance requires that business units are restricted by specific limits with respect to trading exposures, the mismatch of interest-earning assets and interest-bearing liabilities, equity investments, emerging markets exposures and other critical factors. These risk limits must be allocated to lower organizational levels, which have to be steadily supervised in terms of compliance.

Closely associated with decisions concerning risk limits is the entity's ability to confront liquidity and funding risk. Policies provided in this regard should sustain a tailored approach to individual cash flow structure within the business units and for the group as a whole.

As a matter of principle, funding requirements must be based on projected business needs expressed in terms of economic capital, regulatory capital rules, rating agency criteria and other considerations specific to the firm. Additionally, structures and processes must be in place at the legal headquarters and business unit levels to:

- Manage the relevant liquidity risks, and
- Assure appropriate liquidity profiles under various stress scenarios.

Economic capital, though a relatively new term in accountancy,[6] is fundamental for reasons of risk protection. Essentially, the term represents a current best practice for solvency assurance, established after having measured all quantifiable risks. This is done in terms of economic realities rather than regulatory or accounting rules.

While economic capital is forward looking, position risk (Chapter 8) is the result of past commitments. As such, it constitutes a direct and significant source of exposure. Its computation should take account of direct and indirect risks, some of which may not be easy to quantify.

An economic capital model should also take account of the fact that financial institutions are not just warehouses of assets but also act as originators and distributors of financial services. Moreover, although there is widespread recognition that the risk and return characteristics of new financial instruments and business lines have important implications for economic capital and the capacity to bear risks, there exists no industry consensus on how to handle them.

Where an industry consensus can be found is in the fact that compliance risk should definitely be avoided. *Compliance risk* is the risk of legal or regulatory sanctions, resulting in reputational damage (Chapter 12), or financial loss because of failure to comply with applicable laws, regulations, codes of conduct, standards of good practice and generally accepted ethical values. The £17 million ($30 million) penalty by the FSA and $120 million penalty by the SEC to Shell Oil Co. in late July 2004 for having misrepresented its oil reserves is an example of compliance risk.

Because Basel II (Chapter 10) includes a focused supervisory review of compliance to the rules of the new capital adequacy framework (Pillar 2), by all likelihood, compliance risk will increase. The safe bet is that at least the supervisory authorities of the major economies will like to have an input on risks to financial stability, which include:

- Bankruptcies
- Financial crime
- Market abuse
- Market malfunction, and
- Mismanagement of companies.

Some bankers are of the opinion that compliance will extend its sphere of authority into consumer protection, like adequate understanding by consumers of the risks involved in financial products and services.

Issues connected to compliance become more complex because both financial stability and consumer-oriented risks can arise not only from individual firms, but also from worldwide economic trends, developments in social policy, changes in consumer behaviour, new technologies and introduction of new products that are only partially understood or lead to unintended consequences. Hence the importance of risk monetization as a basic indicator that is easily understood.

6. Pareto's law in management accounting

The preparation of reliable financial statements requires not only the use of thorough accounting records, but also of judgements and estimates. Because of this, critical accounting policies must be regularly reviewed and properly described to provide a better understanding of how assumptions and judgements about future events are made, as well as how they can impact on the company's finances.

By definition, a critical accounting estimate is one that requires fairly difficult, subjective or complex assessments that fundamentally interpret results of operations. For a construction company, for example, these include: percentage-of-completion accounting for contracts to provide design, engineering, construction and supporting services; allowance for bad debts; legal and investigation matters; and forecasting effective tax rate, including future ability to utilize foreign tax credits and deferred tax assets.

To do so, companies base their estimates on historical experience and on various other hypotheses they believe to be reasonable, according to current facts and circumstances. For instance, for regulatory financial reporting the measurement of current and deferred tax liabilities and assets is based on provisions of the prevailing tax law – while the effects of potential future changes in tax laws or rates are not considered.

Management accounting, on the other hand, has different rules because its objective is to present decision makers with the true picture of projects and processes, thereby allowing corrective action. All issues *material* from a managerial, as opposed to a regulatory, viewpoint must be reflected; the effects of projected future changes in tax laws for each tax-paying component and jurisdiction *are* material. Equally important is:

- Identifying types and amounts of existing tax law differences
- Measuring the deferred tax assets for each type of tax credit carry forward, and
- Increasing or reducing deferred tax assets by a valuation allowance.

Regarding percentage of completion, this is a method of accounting that can benefit significantly from computer graphics and computer-aided design (CAD) software. The focal point is cost and revenue from ongoing contracts as regards the established plan and current evaluation of performance, including estimates of:

- Total cost to complete the project
- Project schedule and completion date
- Percentage of the project that has been completed in good order, and
- Amounts of any unapproved claims, as well as change orders included in revenue.

Sweden's Securum has been one of the first financial organizations worldwide to apply this method. Its implementation requires, at the outset of each contract, a detailed analysis of estimated cost to complete the project milestone by milestone. Time, cost and quality should be part of this analysis.

Risks relating to productivity, service delivery, usage and other factors are integral parts of the estimation process. Inspectors evaluate planned costs, current claims, effect of change orders and percentage of completion at each project milestone. This requires accounting for anticipated profits and losses on contracts, recorded in full in the period in which they become evident.

This interactive approach to a managerial (as contrasted to regulatory) income statement – used at every milestone or section of it – makes it possible to be in charge of P&L by knowing where and when to apply controls. The downside is the increase in accounting information elements in order to reach a meaningful level of detail. This problem can be effectively solved by applying Pareto's law (Vilfredo Pareto was Professor of Economics and Mathematics at the University of Lausanne, in the late 18th century).

In brief, *Pareto's law* states that a small amount of a variable A which correlates with variable B accounts for a large amount of the latter. A *Pareto diagram* shows the relative frequency or size of events. For instance, 10% of the drivers cause 80% of the accidents on the road.

A Pareto diagram is shown on the left side of Figure 2.1. Practically every business makes the larger part of its profits from a relatively small number of clients. In a credit institution, the top 2% of clients tends to bring in up to 50% of profits and the top 20% brings in 80% of profits. High-end clients, however, are always very demanding and can be satisfied only by the best.

The application of a versatile tool like Pareto's law varies widely. When he was Defence Secretary, Dr Robert McNamara asked his assistants to identify how many of all wares of the American military were *mission critical* and

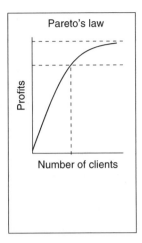
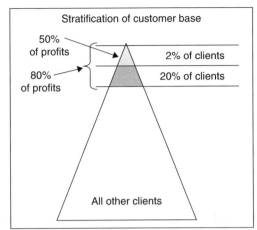

Figure 2.1   Pareto's law implies a stratification according to criteria, with emphasis on a given variable – for instance, profits

how many represented more than 80% of total weapons costs. The answer was that:

- 4% were mission critical, and
- 4.5% stood at about the 80% total cost level.

Because many items belonged to both classes, in total some 6% of all defence wares were mission critical and represented the largest amount of invested funds. These were the items that had to be managed in the most careful manner – a principle that can be very well applied in detailing, applying and safeguarding mission-critical accounting information elements, and those which can be given less attention.

Here is another application of Pareto's law. According to published statistics, in the 1985–2005 timeframe the income share of the top 1% of the American population has roughly doubled. A conclusion reached by economists is that since the supply of prestige assets must be, by definition, limited, the price of such assets is sure to rise. Ajay Kapur of Citigroup has described in the following terms America's current Pareto distribution:

- The top 20% account for nearly 60% of all consumption
- Spending by the bottom one-fifth stands at only 3%.[7]

Here is another example. In 2003, legislators in the state of Arkansas passed an act, the first of its kind in the USA, to measure the body mass index of the state's schoolchildren. This produced most comprehensive data on child obesity, revealing that:

- More than 40% of Arkansas children are obese or at risk of becoming so, and
- This 40% compares poorly to the national average, which hovers around 30%, which is in any case too high.

Moreover, children are not alone in obesity. More than 60% of Arkansas adults are overweight, adding to the state's chronic health ailments, induced obesity and smoking – and from there to high health costs. This accounting led Mike Huckabee, the Governor of Arkansas, to a meta-investigation that is statistically an application of Pareto's law: 5% of the state's Medicaid cases use up 50% of the state's Medicaid budget, standing at $3 trillion per year.

These references find a vast domain of implementation in accounting and in risk management. Applied to compliance, Pareto's law assists in fine-tuning risk strategies within the letter of the law.

7. Using the cash account for risk control

The lesson taught by section 6 is that, as far as management accounting is concerned, accountants would be well advised to shift their focus from treating all accounting elements as equal in weight, to *prioritizing* them according to their impact. Prioritizing helps professional accountants in getting more information from their analysis of the firm's books. An example is the search for concentration of risk across the institution's divisions and subsidiaries. Reasons contributing to risk concentration include:

- Fierce competition for new clients
- Hot business sectors that 'we have to be in'
- Markets that are 'truly different this time'
- The managers' and traders' distaste to warning signals on concentration.

Yet, a company's ability to be in charge of its exposures is in direct proportion to the sophistication of a system able to detect and identify every risk, as well as to measure it, compare it to limits (section 5), and alert senior executives who were responsible for what takes place and confront the risk manager with the facts.

For better risk-based decisions, the adopted solution should be supplemented by knowledge artefacts able to establish whether exposures in the portfolio have been authorized by the board, and if they conform to regulatory guidelines. Much can be learned on the origin of risks by data-mining years of:

- Balance sheets, and
- Income statements.

Available in real time, enriched with assumed risks and projected rewards, reflecting prevailing macroeconomic conditions, and incorporating selected market indicators, balance sheet and P&L data, as well as client and other counterparty accounts, have revealed lots of secrets. Successful efforts along this frame of reference have used cash as the pivot point, defining short term for cash in a way distinct from the short term for other investments.

Cash and cash equivalents include cash on hand, amounts due from banks, money market instruments, commercial paper and other investments having maturities of three months or less at date of acquisition; these are reflected in reporting cash flows. Cash equivalents are stated at a cost that (given the short term) approximates fair value.

Several banks have found that using the cash and cash equivalents account is a good way of exercising control over rogue traders. It is relatively easy for a trader to conceal a loss-making deal on paper, by faking the records or making up another position that hedges it. But it is much more difficult to come up with the cash to pay the counterparty to the trade.

- Cash enables risk management to detect from the cash outflow that something is wrong
- This, however, requires the cash account to be re-established as the king of the bank, and its ultimate safeguard.

Nick Leeson sold options contracts to generate cash, but his losses eventually got to the point where he gave himself away by demanding huge sums of cash from headquarters. That pattern was repeated at the American-Irish Bank (AIB), where John Rusnak managed to keep his trading losses hidden until the end of 2001. The head of treasury at Allfirst was then alerted by the big cash calls the trader was making.

As these examples suggest, the challenge is to increase by more than an order of magnitude the sensitivity of senior management to the institution's cash position, by using cash as the messenger. Indeed, one of the crucial questions debated with participants in the research project that led to this book was whether top management should be alerted when traders offset their losses in cash markets with paper gains on other holdings.

The majority opinion has been 'yes'. Financial history shows that, in many blow-ups, people in positions of responsibility were not watching the cash. In other cases, accounting cash data were available, but management was too slow to react to danger signals. Both cases can lead to disaster.

Alfred P. Sloan, the legendary chairman of General Motors, gives an excellent example on the need to be ready and react quickly, when he describes how his company avoided the aftermath of the 1929–32 Depression suffered by other companies:

> 'No more than anyone else did we see the depression coming ... We had simply learned how to react quickly. This was perhaps the greatest payoff of our system of financial and operating controls.'[8]

The reader should also pay attention to Andrew Carnegie's dictums on risk management: 'Many men can be trusted, but a few need watching.' On another occasion the well-known industrialist, investor and philanthropist stated: 'Everything I saw tended to convince me that, on the Darwinian principle of survival of the fittest, you have no reason to fear the future.'[9] The 'need for watching' and the application of the 'Darwinian principle' correlate.

Notes

1　D.N. Chorafas, *The Real-time Enterprise*. Auerbach, New York, 2005.

2　*European Automotive Design*, September 2006.

3　*The Economist*, 9 December 2006.

4　D.N. Chorafas and Heinrich Steinmann, *Expert Systems in Banking*. Macmillan, London, 1991.

5　*The Economist*, 27 September 2006.

6　D.N. Chorafas, *Economic Capital Allocation with Basel II: Cost and Benefit Analysis*. Butterworth-Heinemann, London, 2004.

7　*The Economist*, 18 November 2005.

8　Alfred P. Sloan, *My Years With General Motors*. Sidgwick & Jackson, London, 1965.

9　Peter Krass, *Carnegie*. Wiley, Hoboken, NJ, 2002.

Duties and Responsibilities in Risk Accounting

1. The accountant's mission in risk control

A basic law of capitalism is that money will migrate to the environment it considers to be more secure, and/or the highest return is to be had. The pressure is relentless on money managers to care for the assets entrusted to them, and to do so better than they have done in the past.

Also, there is a parallel pressure on the most successful companies to continue their fast growth performance, despite their increase in size following years of rapid growth. Along with expanding business opportunities, two types of controls contribute to better results:

- Cost control, sustained through *cost accounting*, and
- Risk control, promoted by means of *risk accounting*, as we saw in Chapters 1 and 2.

Reporting along the risk accounting and cost accounting lines of reference is necessarily based on both qualitative and quantitative criteria, for which the accounting component must provide metrics. An additional requirement is that of dependable information on the monetization of risk exposure and on projected and realized returns for risks taken – which must be performed in a most disciplined way under company-wide standards.

Discipline is always a key factor to success, even more so when volatility and uncertainty increase the demands posed on risk control procedures. Therefore, management must encourage a disciplined accounting culture by promoting integrity, high ethical standards, segregation of duties, clear lines of responsibility, appropriate supervision and a clear set of standards.

Because in all issues related to risk control (and cost control) accounting acts as a registration and monitoring system, another important ingredient of sound management is comprehensive internal controls, with activities such as approvals, authorizations, compliance checks and follow-ups on non-compliance clearly defined at every level of activity.

- If the entity is to achieve sustained success, then confidence and trust, built up over many years, are most vital, and
- Reputation, expertise, experience, integrity and intellectual honesty – not just profits – are crucial elements that contribute to growth and survival.

To effectively contribute in controlling exposure, accountants must understand the risk universe of *their firm*, its flow of business and the accompanying flow of risks. This means that their systems and procedures must clearly delineate (and follow up on) risk elements, allow efficient management of the limits system, keep close track of counterparty and financial market risks, and manage assets and liabilities in a consistent and secure manner.

Prerequisites to doing so go well beyond the availability of a system of accounting and of technology for data capture, mining and reporting. Peter Drucker is credited with the principle that every policy, every programme, every activity and the people responsible for its execution, as well as record keeping, should be controlled with a number of critical questions:

- What is your mission?
- Is it still the right mission?
- Is it still worth doing it?

Drucker's principle defines a procedure that permits critical examination of the accountant's responsibilities associated with the management of risk. Have we considered each major risk individually? Did we set margin of error on major risks (see Chapter 4)? Have we tested correlations among major risks? Have we established the correlation prevailing between first-order and second-order (major and secondary) risks?

The answers to be provided to these questions must be given in the most disciplined and well-documented manner. One of the experts who contributed to this book suggested that the accountant's action in this regard presents several characteristics of an officer's duty in battle. The function of disciplined movement is to produce:

- In the minds of friends the assurance that they cannot lose, and
- In the minds of foes the conviction that they cannot win.

Certain practices, like *creative accounting* (section 2), and those who practice it are the accountant's foes. Industrial engineering provides a lesson on how to control such deviations. Productivity standards specify that in work on the production floor performance typically varies between 80% and 220% of a given standard. The reason for performing below this may be loafing and above it might be some sort of cheating.

Because nothing proceeds in a straight line, productivity varies from person to person and workpost to workpost – but there are limits. This is a basic principle in cost accounting. Likewise, risks follow a distribution characterized by a main body and outliers. To learn about what underpins exposure, including unusual cases, every risk connected with our business should be tested under three conditions:

- Normal, within 2.9 standard deviations of the mean
- Tail, which may correspond to 4 or 5 standard deviations
- Stress, where the processes or product's behaviour are examined under extreme conditions, often 10–15 standard deviations from the mean.

Stress conditions must be studied through *stress testing*,[1] which is one of the pillars of risk accounting. A major contribution of stress tests, which became popular during the last ten years, is that they are instrumental in flushing out weak spots in the armoury of an instrument, process or institution.

Evidently, if one is worried about something going wrong, the best thing to do is to correct it and get back to the work as usual. The prerequisite, however, is to identify what is wrong, which is not always possible under 'normal conditions'. Stress tests help in this identification, which is why they are now one of the most powerful weapons of risk controllers and accountants.

Failure to use the best possible tools may result in major losses and very costly settlements. *If* the exposure data the accountant presents to senior management and risk controllers is opaque, *then* the fault falls squarely on his or her shoulders. In contrast, *if* the data being considered is thoroughly researched – but top management makes no decision and keeps it in the closet – *then* the fault is with the CEO and the board.

Because of the importance of stress testing in risk accounting, reference will be made to its notions and procedures in several chapters of this book. Chapter 5 explains stress testing for credit risk, Chapter 7 presents practical examples on stressing for market risk, while on other occasions stress testing is viewed from the perspective of its more general contribution to sound governance.

Stress testing is, by necessity, a defensive weapon. As General James Burns advised President Truman in answer to his query about the hydrogen bomb: 'It's a fundamental law of defence that you always have to use the most powerful weapons you can produce.'[2]

2. Creative accounting

After an investigation that lasted from 2003 to 2006, US regulators concluded that *Fannie Mae*, which underwrites American mortgages, had indulged in *fraudulent accounting*. For this it had to pay $400 million, but its former executives may still face charges for misreporting profits so as to supplement their bonuses. These ill-gotten gains should be reclaimed by the company, Fannie Mae's federal regulator said.[3]

A few months after that 2006 announcement, two former foreign-exchange dealers at National Australia Bank received prison terms for a scandal involving rogue trading that led to the resignations of both the chairman and chief executive of Australia's biggest bank. The dealers, along with two colleagues who were sentenced earlier, had tried to conceal losses after the Australian dollar appreciated in 2003.[4]

The same year, the American International Group (AIG), one of the world's largest insurers, agreed to pay more than $1.6 billion to settle US government and New York state charges that it had engaged in fraud, bid-rigging and improper accounting. Of that total, $800 million were to go to investors:

- $375 million were earmarked as repayments to policyholders, and
- $344 million were destined for states harmed by the company's actions.

Moreover, New York state was also scheduled to collect a separate $100 million penalty, while the US government received $25 million. AIG also agreed to reduce commissions to brokers and agents for steering insurance contracts to different companies, and said it would support laws banning certain kinds of 'contingent commissions'.[5]

Creative accounting and opaque financial disclosures are business risks (section 3). They expose the accounting profession to the worst perils and they are not just limited to a couple of companies or to one country, even if occasionally a company is singled out for accounting malpractice, like Arthur Andersen. Creative accounting is the name given to widespread policies and practices that stand high in the list of charges made by supervisory authorities against:

- Private
- Public, and
- Government-controlled firms.

Neither are people practising creative accounting any more than members of a group of Mafiosi or Ponzi-game specialists. Kenneth Lay, the man who made and then destroyed Enron, had a doctorate in economics from the University of Houston, and learned his business in the booming Texan oil industry at Humble Oil and Refining.

Under Lay's watch, Enron transformed itself from a dull gas pipeline outfit into a trading firm that was more of a hedge fund than an energy producer. It also ventured into foreign energy markets, though its enterprises in Britain, Brazil and

India generated the first cracks in its all-powerful image – an image that in the late 1990s had made it:

- One of *Fortune*'s most admired companies, and
- A darling of the stock market.

It was all smoke and mirrors, even if to the American public, Kenneth Lay's greatest crime was to advise employees, as the firm crashed, to keep their Enron shares, or even to buy more, while he was selling his own. This showed creative accounting's most ugly face, because it involved breach of confidence. Many Enron employees lost their jobs, their pension funds and their savings, as bankruptcy left their shares worthless.

Japan has had more than its share of creative accounting scams. In an effort to stamp out this practice, a new law that came into effect in July 2006 doubled the maximum jail sentence for fraud to ten years and increased the ceiling on fines to 700 million yen ($6 million). The law also gave extra power and broader authority to the Financial Services Agency (FSA), Japan's financial regulator, to crack down on such practices.

Among Japanese banks, the third largest was clobbered after another regulator complained that it had coerced some small and medium-sized companies into buying interest rate swaps (Chapter 1) – a rather complex financial product they did not understand. And on 1 July 2006, three days before the new law came in, ChuoAoyama PricewaterhouseCoopers, a leading auditor, began a two-month abstention from the banking business, an unprecedented penalty, for its involvement in accounting fraud.[6]

But even if the application of the law leaves a footprint, all over the globe companies continue to invent new creative accounting practices. A now famous example has been the so-called *prepays*, a triangular deal between Enron, two big banks and several major insurers, which permitted Enron to claim as income and profits future receivables discounted by banks – which guaranteed themselves against potential losses by buying insurance protection.

Table 3.1 shows who the main players were. That deal ended in court after Enron defaulted and the banks asked the insurers to cover their losses. A settlement was finally reached out of court, with the banks absorbing 60% and the insurers 40% of Enron's huge prepay losses. Experts said that these percentages roughly represented the chances each party had of winning the court case.

This was creative accounting at its best, in a cocktail with derivatives. Precisely because many derivative financial instruments are opaque, doubtful accounting and derivatives exposures correlate. To make matters worse, to reduce

Table 3.1   Insourcing/outsourcing with the prepays

Outsourcer	Insourcer
In invention of the prepays	
Enron	J.P. Morgan
	Chase Manhattan
In assurance of capital	
J.P. Morgan	AIG
Chase Manhattan	and other insurers

losses on their securities portfolios, some of Japan's largest banks are employing an accounting technique banned by international standards.

This is a creative accounting approach that seems to be permitted, although not recommended, under Japanese rules. It entails using the average price of share holdings during March (the Japanese accounting year ends on 31 March) to calculate their value, rather than the internationally accepted method of using the closing price on the last day of the financial year. The decision to use such derivative accounting gimmicks by Sumitomo Mitsui Banking Corporation, UFJ and Mizuho – starting in the first years of the 21st century – highlights the stark difference in corporate governance between:

- Japan's then troubled credit institutions, and
- Their global counterparts in commercial banking.

By means of not-so-orthodox accounting practices, which included an inordinate amount of deferred tax assets (DTAs), Japanese banks sought to offset the twin pressures of charges for non-performing loans and securities losses. The bending of accounting principles has been promoted by the fact that Japan's banks hold huge portfolios of securities, the values of which have been severely undermined by the decline in the Nikkei 225.

New mark-to-market regulations by the Basel Committee (Chapter 10), of which the Bank of Japan is a member, meant that these portfolios have to be booked at market value. Yet, even with creative accounting, *Nihon Keizai*, Japan's financial daily, reported in April 2001 that losses at Japan's main banks as a result of their non-performing loans was likely to be 1.9 trillion yen ($14.5 billion), much higher than originally forecast. Apart from violating business ethics, creative accounting has its limits.

3.   Business risk

Creative accounting is far from being the only practice that brings with it business risk and reputational risk, but it is one of the most widely spread.

Business risk is the risk that a firm's revenues could fall short of ongoing expenses for reasons that range from major market contraction, to management weaknesses, product shortcomings, a reputational after-effect of malpractice and other issues. The company may be losing its market or the market might have moved away.

While capital requirements for credit risk, market risk and operational risk have been regulated by supervisory authorities, there is no regulation regarding reserves for business risk. Many commercial banks, however, put aside capital for this eventuality. Crédit Suisse allocates 60% of its goodwill as a cushion for business risk.

Another characteristic of business risk is the lack of a generally acceptable definition. Each bank tends to identify business risk in its own way. Jos Wieleman, of ABN Amro Bank, defines *business risk* as that caused by uncertainty in profits due to changes in the competitive environment that damage a company's franchise of operational economics. As such, business risk:

- Relates to the volatility of the operational earnings of a bank, driven by changes in revenues
- Reflects changes in operational earnings, as a consequence of fluctuations in volume and prevailing margin, and
- Is affected by the structure of both *cost base* and *risk base*, the latter sometimes leading to reputational risk (Chapter 12).

Credit risk, for example, impacts on business risk as demonstrated by *Japan premium*. Following the debacle of the Japanese banking industry in the 1990s in the aftermath of a huge amount of non-performing loans, Japanese credit institutions found it difficult to borrow in the global interbank market without paying a special premium.

This and similar premiums are part of risk accounting, because they reflect changes in the bank's expense base after adverse events. Japan premium, for example, has been crucial to an orderly continuation of the Japanese banks' activities. While many economic capital models do not include this type of risk, sound governance requires that it is considered when assessing:

- Capital needs, and
- Financial staying power.

As this example demonstrates, business risk is linked to price and activity levels in financial markets. Relevant references are deposits, loans, trading, fees and commission income derived from the management of clients' investment portfolios. Activity level is the key driver for brokerage commissions, underwriting commissions and advisory fees. Events connected to business risk may affect:

- Stability of the revenue stream
- Ability to reduce expenses in a major downturn, and
- Penalties the bank may have to pay, which morph into business risk.

Section 2 provided several examples whose origin has been creative accounting, a major contributor to business risk. Legal risk, too, can turn into business risk because it may keep away clients or have other negative after-effects, including major costs.

In mid-July 2004, J.P. Morgan Chase, the second largest American bank, set aside $2.3 billion to cover the possible costs of litigation arising from the Enron and WorldCom affairs. Two months earlier, Citigroup paid $2.7 billion to settle a class-action lawsuit related to WorldCom's troubles, and put aside even larger provisions for Enron-related and other court actions.

The case of Parmalat, Europe's most major financial scandal so far, has seen a storm of lawsuits as new management tried to save the hedge fund from bankruptcy with a dairy products line on the side. The company sued its bank for having allegedly misled it. Two of the lawsuits were seeking $10 billion in damages against Deloitte & Touche and Grant Thornton, the certified public accountants (CPAs) that for years oversaw the accounts of the bankrupt firm.

The legal action undertaken by Enrico Bondi, then special administrator of Parmalat, accused both CPAs of improper auditing that allowed huge sums to be allegedly stolen, squandered or wasted by former managers. This legal action, which has been bad news for the auditors, came only days after launching lawsuits against three banks: Citigroup, UBS and Deutsche Bank – all of these and others were involved in financial dealings with Parmalat before the massive fraud that caused its bankruptcy.

The threat for Deloitte & Touche was the possibility that the Parmalat case could become what Enron was to Arthur Andersen – a huge business risk and reputational risk, which led to the disappearance of the auditor. Some analysts expressed the opinion that Bondi's move was shrewd. He made all parties to lawsuits filed by Parmalat in America jointly liable for the damages the company asked as compensation. As a result, even by winning one case he stood a chance of recovering an impressive amount of compensation.

Trading, too, has joined creative accounting and legal risk as a source of business risk problems, all the way to the demise of a firm. In mid-May 1996, ex-star bond trader Joseph Jett went on trial in Manhattan. Two years earlier, in 1994, Jett was dismissed by Kidder Peabody, the investment bank, amid allegations that $350 million of profits reported by his trading desk never existed.

In the legal case against Jett, Kidder Peabody stated that, as a trader in securities, he exploited a loophole in the bank's accounting system, which had failed to keep pace with the complex trading strategies used in modern markets. In fact, that brokerage had disappeared from the radar screen because in 1994 the losses incurred by this wrongdoing led General Electric, Kidder's parent company, to dispose of the Wall Street firm.

According to his accusers, Jett's scheme involved entering more than 60 000 trades in the bank's books. He bought a number of stripped bonds – where the interest and principal payments have been separated – and then sold them individually. Subsequently, he recorded his intention of:

- Recombining the pieces of these bonds, and
- Handing them back to the US Treasury when they matured.

The backward-looking Kidder accounting system enabled Joseph Jett to report a profit between the price he paid and the price he would get back, even though, in reality, no such profit ever existed. This is a prime example of the need for risk accounting and for a first-class general accounting system.

Most of Jett's $11.4 million salary and bonuses for 1993–94 were based on this fake profit performance. This case involved different creative accounting gimmicks from those of Nick Leeson, who brought down Barings in February 1995, and those of Toshihide Iguchi, who lost more than $1 billion for Daiwa Bank.

An irony attached to the exploitation of accounting loopholes is that while Kidder Peabody, the broker, went down the tubes, Joseph Jett did not face criminal charges and he did not even appear in court. Instead, he appeared before an administrative law judge employed by the Securities and Exchange Commission (SEC), which brought civil fraud charges against him. Critics said that the SEC's decision to:

- Stick to civil, rather than criminal, charges, and
- Use an administrative law procedure rather than one in federal court

reflected a soft approach that might have been motivated by political factors, rather than the difficulty of explaining complex financial cases before a jury. Another irony is that this soft handling brought protests from Jett and his lawyers because, in their opinion, 'he will not face a fair hearing' for the demolition work he had done at the investment bank that employed him.

4. Business risk factors: an example

Within the framework provided by section 3, we can identify a number of risk factors that contribute to the business risk assumed by a firm. We will take as an example a telecommunications equipment company that is still reeling from the aftermath of the internet and telecommunications sectors bubble of 2000/2001. Here is how its annual report identified the business risks with which it was confronted.

'Our sales levels are unstable and we are not currently profitable'

As a result of continuing unfavourable business conditions, the firm's sales declined significantly from historic levels, and management has been unable to predict future sales accurately or to provide long-term guidance for future financial performance. This created uncertainty regarding the company's capital spending plans, further affected by its clients' continued reduction in inventory levels in order to rebalance excess fibre and channel capacity, particularly in the long-haul market.

'Our customers' businesses have been harmed by the economic downturn'

According to the senior management of the telecoms equipment firm, this morphed into business risk because turnover has been largely dependent upon product sales to telecommunications systems and services entities – who in turn are dependent for their business upon sales of fibre-optic systems to telecommunications carriers.

As a result of the bubble's long-lasting effects, many of these companies have been operating at losses and they were unable to make meaningful long-term predictions for their recovery. Hence their forecasted requirements for telecommunications gear have been conservative.

'Our realignment programme may be unsuccessful in aligning our operations to current market conditions'

This realignment programme aimed to eliminate some product development projects, consolidating or curtailing others in order to focus research and development investments on the most promising projects. It also targeted consolidating the

manufacturing facilities from multiple sites into single locations, as well as consolidating sales and administrative functions.

'Interruptions affecting our key suppliers could disrupt production, compromise our product quality and adversely affect our sales'

The company obtained a significant number of components, included in the
manufacture of its products, from single or limited source suppliers. A disruption or
loss of supplies from these companies, or price increases for their components,
would materially harm its results of operations, and may even affect product
quality and customer relationships. Currently the firm did not have alternative
sources for such materials and components.

'If our customers fail to meet their financial obligations to us, our business will suffer'

Although the firm performed ongoing credit evaluations of its customers and monitored balances owed by counterparties, management was not able to predict changes
in its customers' financial condition during a recessionist economic environment.

Based on its estimates as to the quality of its accounts receivable, the firm maintained allowances for doubtful accounts for estimated losses resulting from the
inability or unwillingness of its customers to make required payments. The annual
report added that continuing economic slowdown in the telecoms industry exacerbated vulnerabilities to demand fluctuations for communications products.

'Average selling prices have been declining'

Prices for telecommunications products generally decline over time as new and
more efficient components and modules with increased functionality are developed,
manufacturing processes improve and competition increases. But the business
risk faced by this company exacerbated the general trend – as declining sales
forced telecommunications carriers and their suppliers to reduce costs, leading
to increasing pricing pressure on both themselves and their competitors.

'If we fail to attract and retain key personnel, our business could suffer'

Every company's future depends, in part, on its ability to attract and retain key
personnel. Competition for highly skilled technical people has become extremely

intense, and the company continued to face difficulties in hiring qualified engineers in many areas of its business. If management is not able to hire and retain such personnel at compensation levels consistent with competitor compensation and salary structure, because of reduced income, the firm's longer-term business will suffer.

'Our intellectual property rights may not be adequately protected'

A high-technology company's future depends in a significant way upon its intellectual property, including patents, trade secrets, know-how and continuing technological innovation. Management was concerned that because of personnel turnover, an after-effect of business risk, the steps taken to protect intellectual property may not adequately prevent misappropriation, or assure that others will not develop competitive technologies or products. Moreover, any patent issued to the firm may be challenged, invalidated or circumvented.

'Recently enacted and proposed regulatory changes may cause us to incur increased costs'

New legislation and regulation tends to increase expenses, as the company evaluates implications of new rules and devotes resources to respond to these new requirements. In particular, the firm expected to incur additional expense as it implemented Section 404 of the Sarbanes–Oxley Act, which requires management to report on, and independent auditors to attest to, internal controls.

'If we fail to manage our exposure to worldwide financial and securities markets successfully, our operating results could suffer'

Every company is exposed to financial market risks, including changes in interest rates, foreign currency exchange rates and marketable equity security prices. The primary objective of most of a company's investment activities is to preserve principal while at the same time maximizing yields without significantly increasing risk. Though the firm utilized derivatives to confront such risks, management underlined that hedging is not fail-safe.

The company's international presence, too, exposed it to business risks, including its ability to comply with the customs, import/export and other trade compliance regulations of the countries in which it did business, together with any unexpected changes in such regulations, tariffs and other trade barriers, political, legal and economic instability in foreign markets, particularly in those markets in which it maintains manufacturing and research facilities.

The telecoms equipment manufacturer's annual report also pointed out that other business risks resulted from challenges associated with the integration of foreign operations, currency fluctuations, potential adverse tax consequences, greater difficulty in accounts receivable collection, as well as difficulties in staffing and management in some foreign countries.

5. Monitoring assets and liabilities

Each of the business risks outlined in section 4 leaves a footprint on accounting books, either on the assets or on the liabilities side. Therefore, it must be steadily monitored according to the principle of materiality. The same is true of all other variables tracked through accounting practices whose effect must be studied proactively, particularly in terms of costs and risks.

For instance, with an IFRS balance sheet, interest rate risk must be monitored and managed primarily based on marking to market, along with hypotheses on rising and falling interest rates, for prognostication purposes and stress testing reasons. Attention should also be paid to the prevailing and projected business environment.

Ironically, because many companies tend to pay lip service to limits, there is more credit risk being assumed in benign business environments than in a recession, or when the cost of capital is high. When capital is virtually free because of low interest rates, it is usually:

- Poorly allocated
- Subject to lax credit criteria, and
- Easy to spend, feeding a bubble.

For instance, in the second half of the 1990s equity capital, as measured by astronomical price/earnings ratios, has reached for the stars. While most internet companies had no earnings, investors filled in the blanks. Capital was virtually free and therefore was inefficiently allocated. However, there had been a lesson in the technology bubble from Japan of the 1980s and it should have been used to advantage.

Risk accounting should pay attention to the Rogers principle[7] that 'market corrections go down long enough to scare everybody out and make sure they give up; then they turn around.' In mid-May 2006, the stock market went through a severe correction. Then, in mid-January 2007 crude oil fell 33% in total to a 19-month low after its peak at a record $78.30 a barrel in July 2006.

One does not need to be too smart to appreciate the volatility underpinning all commodities. In the early years of the 21st century, nearly free-of-cost money led to a mortgage bubble, as rules were bent to produce more business and higher profits. Because large portions of the retail portfolio of a commercial bank consist of non-maturing accounts like fixed rate mortgages and variable-rate savings, this eventually resulted in mismatch risk. Hence it is wise to model sensitivities on the basis of effective repricing behaviour of non-maturing accounts.

To improve assets and liabilities (A&L) management, following the deep crisis of the US Savings and Loans (S&Ls, thrifts, building societies) industry, the Office of Thrift Supervision (OTS) required all thrifts under its authority (some 1100 of them) to submit each day their exposure based on:

- Prevailing interest rate
- 100, 200, 300, 400 basis points (bp) up
- 100, 200, 300, 400 bp down.

The ± 200 basis points were the test OTS used for its evaluation of the S&L staying power, while ± 400 basis points constituted the stress test. All these tests have been based on accounting data and on hypotheses made on the longer-term interest rate behaviour. As such, they constitute a good example of risk accounting for market risk *and* credit risk exposure.

A different procedure is followed with risk accounting for market exposure regarding positions in the trading book. In accordance with regulations, many commercial banks see to it that, for asset and liability management purposes, value at risk (VAR; see Chapter 7) is calculated at the 99% confidence level (Chapter 4) over a 20-day holding period. Two years of underlying data are used to derive the market movements used for this calculation.

This is what the 1996 Market Risk Amendment specifies but, while necessary, it is not enough. A 99% confidence level means that 1% of all cases will be left out of risk evaluation – and the largest exposure with the highest impact lies exactly at the long leg of the distribution. Therefore, when rating agencies examine capital adequacy they look not at 99% confidence but at the 99.97% one-year level – which is nearly two orders of magnitude higher. They also:

- Perform an aggregation using conservative correlations, except for trading, which is based on historical simulation, and
- Make rather conservative scaling assumptions while imposing model uncertainty add-on, to get from 99% to 99.97%.

In addition, risk accounting should carefully map contingent liabilities and irrevocable commitments. Contingent liabilities include: credit guarantees in the form of avails, guarantees and indemnity liabilities; delivery and performance bonds; letters of indemnity; irrevocable commitments in respect of documentary credits; and other performance-related guarantees. Each of these references:

- Reflects itself in accounting books,
- But, generally, is not thoroughly analysed even if it can be a source of exposure.

Sound governance can always be found in the background of risk control and of cost swamping, while time and again poor management proves to be a more frequent reason for company failure than poor assets. Table 3.2 presents in a nutshell the

Table 3.2   Why banks fail: findings of a research project by the Bank of England

Identifier of institution	Mismanagement	Poor assets	Liquidity problems	Secrecy and fraud	Faculty structure	Dealing losses
I	X			X		X
II	X				X	
III	X	X		X	X	
IV	X	X		X		
V	X			X		X
VI	X	X				
VII	X	X	X	X		
VIII			X		X	
IX	X	X	X			
X	X	X	X			
XI	X	X	X	X		
XII			X			
XIII	X	X	X			
XIV	X	X	X			
XV	X	X				
XVI	X	X				
XVII	X	X				
XVIII		X	X			
XIX	X	X				
XX	X	X				
XXI				X	X	
XXII	X	X				

conclusions of a very interesting study by the Bank of England, where misman-agement is the main cause of company failure.

Measurement and monitoring are the pillars of risk accounting. Roger Lowenstein says that Benjamin Rosner, the man who built up Associated Cotton Shops, the US dress shop chain, is rumoured to have once counted the sheets on a roll of toilet paper to avoid being cheated. And when Warren Buffett stayed with his wife at the New York Plaza, he would ring up a friend and ask: 'Big boy, could you bring over a six-pack of Pepsi? You can't believe what room service charges!'[8]

Based on these premises, we can come to the conclusion that modern profes-sional accountants should acquaint themselves with the linkages that exist between their job and control of exposure, appreciate the inputs and outputs con-nected to the basic missions of risk management, and proactively exploit what in the past has mainly been used as post-mortem evidence. This ongoing process of making accounting figures reveals that their secrets rest on:

- *Monitoring the performance of critical functions, including marketing, trading and sales.* Beyond recording all transactions, this requires: testing interest rates, currency exchange rates and other trading exposures; mark-ing to market or to model securities positions and other assets; and prepar-ing management accounting reports – beyond the more classical compliant regulatory reports.

- *Assessing uncertainty about future values of assets and liabilities associ-ated with transactions and positions.* This, too, is a steady process closely linked to accounting but going much further than classical chores. To be accomplished in a dependable manner, it requires expertise in interactive computational finance, modelling and stress testing.

- *Expanding the horizon of accounting input that impacts the balance sheet.* As a matter of ill-conceived cost trade-offs, many institutions tend not to monitor every critical function and its after-effect on cost and risk. This is counter-productive, because at the same time they take an inordinate amount of risk while costs resulting from poor management hit the profit and loss statement.

Another flaw in risk control practices is that to limit the extent of risk assessment some institutions make judgements about when certain types of market risk can be ignored and when positions in related securities can be aggregated together. This reduces transparency and leads to situations where the bank suffers sub-stantial losses from events not anticipated within a given framework; therefore, it is a very bad practice.

6.   IFRS, accounting standards and transparency

Outside the USA, where GAAP has been for many years the accounting standard, the establishment of a network of links and nodes between accounting and risk management started on 1 January 2005, when all companies listed in the European Union are required to comply with the International Financial Reporting Standards (IFRS).[9]

This was a positive development that increased transparency and made possible comparability of financial statements in the EU.[10] The IFRS accounting and financial reporting standards have been issued by the London-based International Accounting Standards Board (IASB). Among the areas where IFRS differ from the previously prevailing national standards are:

- Reclassification of instruments as debt or equity
- Accounting for business combinations
- Hedge accounting, standards concerning the recognition and measurement of financial instruments (IAS 39)
- Valuation of financial instruments, including the recognition of derivatives, available-for-sale securities, hedging provisions, share-based payments and more.

In terms of reclassification of certain debt and equity instruments, IFRS require that specific capital instruments, such as preferred shares that were previously treated and recognized as equity, are reclassified as liabilities. An example of risk accounting promoted by IFRS is that it distinguishes equity from non-equity preferred shares on the basis of whether the dividends paid out on the share are mandatory or discretionary.

IFRS requires that all derivatives are recognized on the balance sheet and measured at fair value. Gains and losses from changes in the fair value will flow through the income statement (P&L), with the exception of derivatives qualified for hedging. Moreover, derivatives that are embedded in hybrid financial instruments, but with economic characteristics and risks that are not closely related to those of the underlying, must now be separated from the hybrid instrument:

- Valued at fair value, and
- Recognized on the balance sheet on a stand-alone basis.

As with US GAAP, under IFRS available-for-sale securities must be recorded at fair value. Experts note that the increased use of fair value for such securities may result in an increase on the overall asset size of the balance sheet, as well as in higher volatility of the equity.

One of the most important impacts of IFRS is on hedge accounting. IFRS distinguish between two main types of hedges: *cash-flow* hedges and *fair-value* hedges. To qualify for hedge accounting, under IFRS companies must provide:

- Documentation of the hedging and hedged instruments
- Identification of the exposure being hedged, and
- Effectiveness testing of the hedge procedure itself.

Through the principle of risk accounting, fair-value hedges are closely connected to risk management. This is an integral part of overall risk control incorporating the use of derivative instruments. Interest rate derivatives may be, for instance, used to minimize fluctuations in earnings that are caused by interest rate volatility. In a similar pattern, most financial institutions and other companies use:

- Foreign currency forward contracts to hedge the foreign currency risk associated with available-for-sale securities, and
- Cross-currency swaps to convert foreign currency denominated fixed-rate assets or liabilities to floating-rate functional currency assets or liabilities.

Cash-flow hedges are used to mitigate exposure to variability of cash flows on loans, deposits and other debt obligations. This is done by employing interest rate swaps to convert variable-rate assets or liabilities to fixed rates, or cross-currency swaps to convert foreign currency denominated fixed- and floating-rate assets or liabilities to fixed-rate base currency, assets or liabilities.

The hedge accounting rules of IFRS allow the hedging item to follow the accounting treatment of the hedged item. The gain or loss on the hedging instrument is recognized in the income statement along with the offsetting gain or loss on the hedged instrument.

In short, strict requirements need to be complied with in order to qualify for hedge accounting, to prevent income manipulation through creative accounting practices. Companies assess the effectiveness of hedging relationships:

- Prospectively, and
- Retrospectively.

A prospective assessment is made both at the inception of a hedging relationship and on an ongoing basis. This requires that management justifies its expectation that the relationship will be highly effective over future periods.

The retrospective assessment is also performed on an ongoing basis, requiring management to determine whether or not the hedging relationship has actually been effective. *If* through a retrospective evaluation it is concluded that hedge accounting is appropriate for the current period, *then* the company measures the amount of hedge effectiveness to be recognized in earnings.

It needs no explanation that IFRS accounting rules have been written to promote *transparency* and a rigorous way of financial statement presentation. Those who develop them at the IASB appreciate that the solvency of enterprises, and of the financial system as a whole, is based on two pillars:

- Each credit institution's ability to sustain risk, and
- The overall stability of the banking sector.

Precisely for this reason, both IFRS and Basel II (Chapter 10) emphasize prime transparency and accuracy in financial reporting. The Basel Committee on Banking Supervision defines *transparency* as the disclosure of information that allows market participants to make an informed assessment of a bank's:

- Financial position
- Performance
- Risk exposure
- Risk control practices, and
- Business strategy, with its associated business risk (sections 3 and 4).

Transparency in financial statements can be achieved only if the information provided through them is timely, accurate, relevant, comprehensive and based on sound measurement principles applied consistently.

Assumed exposure becomes more transparent to the market and regulators through *risk-oriented* reporting, which, with Basel II and IFRS, represents an important addition to standard disclosure requirements. With the new rules, credit institutions must not only explain their assets, finances and earnings position, but also outline:

- Their specific risk situation, and
- Their ability to manage risks they have assumed.

This makes transparency a fundamental tool of market discipline. *Market discipline* is a cause-and-effect mechanism in which market participants – for instance, creditors, bondholders, shareholders, depositors and other players – have an incentive to monitor risk taking and react to the information they receive through their investment decisions. All this, however, is valid only when there exists personal accountability.

7. Personal accountability

To paraphrase an old real estate property maxim, the three most important things in picking the right company for investment are management, management and management. Other than knowing something of the company's track record, the clearest indication for a prospective investor is the quality of the board of directors and most particularly of the CEO, as well as the personal accountability assumed by directors and senior managers.

In the light of many corporate collapses and alleged top management fraud, it proves rewarding to assure that: the company has independent-minded, non-executive directors who seem both qualified and respected in their field; the board's members have a reputation for integrity, honesty and business acumen; and there has been instituted board committees for auditing and risk management (more on this in Chapter 12).

Both performance and personal accountability are important, though from time to time the chairman or president may make a mistake in the direction he or she chooses. One of the most hilarious things happened on a misty night in 1920. The guard of a rail crossing in Seine-et-Marne (near Paris) heard somebody knocking on his window. There was a man in pyjamas who said: 'I am the president of the Republic.' After this first surprise came the second. The pyjama man was indeed Paul Deschanel, who fell from the presidential train having mistaken the door of the men's room for that of the exit from the wagon.[11]

The man who never made a mistake has not yet been born, but it is no less true that the decisions and behaviour of directors, presidents, managers, traders, accountants and other professionals is a most critical factor in effective management, which tends to diminish if:

- The company's internal controls are found wanting, and
- Management standards are lax.

CEO malfeasance unveiled through a wave of prosecutions in the first years of this century by the Attorney General of New York state and the Securities & Exchange Commission (SEC) is an example of lagging personal accountability.[12] Other examples are: poor risk management, which has turned several companies belly up; failure in compliance to rules and regulations; and superficial strategic decisions that damaged the company's competitiveness and ended in business risk.

The fate of Equitable Life, the venerable life insurance company, provides an example of failed personal accountability, that of Barings another. Equitable's troubles called into question the supposed security of certain life insurance policies, of an accumulated value of over £300 billion. This has been a distinctive product in Britain with few parallels in other countries:

- Theoretically, it offered a way of getting returns from equities and bonds supposedly without direct exposure to the financial markets
- In practice, as the 1 million savers who put their faith in Equitable's with-profits fund have learned, these policies can be very risky.

Contrary to the accounting principles advanced in section 6, the transparency of these instruments is low. A key problem with many investments sold to the general public is that 'what you see is not necessarily what yet get'. Investors are often unaware of the instrument's charging structure, which typically front-load expenses on to the initial payments. Another issue is the way investment returns accrue, still another the level of fees and the way these are charged.

Lack of personal accountability sees to it that misappropriation of funds is a major woe. The USA is not immune to such cases. To improve the level of senior management responsibility, in October 2003, an advisory panel urged the US Sentencing Commission to hold directors and executives in leadership posts at companies and government agencies fully responsible for overseeing programmes to prevent white-collar crimes.

According to this advisory group, sentencing guidelines should directly address violations of compliance programmes that companies and government agencies set up to swamp unethical behaviour. The advisory panel said those overseeing programmes against white-collar crime should not be treated leniently if they don't bother enforcing their own rules.

In response to the wave of management scandals in the early years of the 21st century, the advisory panel recommended that an entity's governing authority is held responsible for its lack of anti-crime initiatives, and for failure to put in place internal controls able to detect, capture and handle the wrongdoer's indiscretion. Dr Richard Feynman, the nuclear scientist, gave this advice on personal accountability:

- The core duty in a tough mission is that of weighting uncertainties
- Catastrophes happen when we ignore statistical science and use a vague style of risk assessment.

Feynman's comments on the tragedy of the *Challenger* space shuttle, which he investigated as a member of a blue ribbon committee, are eye opening:

> 'A kind of Russian roulette ... (The shuttle) flies (with O-ring erosion) and nothing happens ... Then it is suggested that the risk is no longer so high for the next flight. We can lower our standards a little bit because we got away with it last time. ... You got away with it. But it should not be done over and over again like that.'[13]

Notes

1   D.N. Chorafas, *Stress Testing for Risk Control Under Basel II*. Elsevier, Oxford, 2007.
2   George Bailey, *The Making of Andrei Sakharov*. Penguin, London, 1988.
3   *International Herald Tribune*, 10 February 2006.
4   *The Economist*, 27 May 2006.
5   *The Economist*, 8 July 2006.
6   *The Economist*, 8 July 2006.
7   After Jim Rogers, the oil expert, who predicted the start of the commodities rally in 1999.
8   Roger Lowenstein, *Buffett, The Making of an American Capitalist*. Weidenfeld & Nicolson, London, 1996.
9   D.N. Chorafas, *IFRS, Fair Value and Corporate Governance: Its Impact on Budgets, Balance Sheets and Management Accounts*. Butterworth-Heinemann, London, 2005.
10 Regulation 1606/2002/EC concerning the application of IFRS was adopted by the European Parliament and the EU Council on 19 July 2002.
11 Jean Egen, *Messieurs du Canard*. Stock, Paris, 1973.
12 D.N. Chorafas, *Management Risk: The Bottleneck is at the Top of the Bottle*. Macmillan/Palgrave, London, 2004.
13 James Gleick, *Genius: The Life and Science of Richard Feynman*. Pantheon Books, New York, 1992.

Accounting for Total Exposure:
A Case Study

1. Understanding total exposure

As defined in Chapter 1, financial risk is a potential negative change in a person's or entity's assets, income or other crucial variable, as a consequence of volatility, uncertainty, unexpected or uncontrollable events. The safe bet is that the more active a person or entity is, the greater will be the number of its exposures and, quite often, their magnitude. These exposures will then have to be added up to give a total risk figure.

Accounting for total exposure is a challenging job that often presents surprises, because the sum of exposure is not a matter of arithmetic addition. Many people incorrectly believe that cost and risk can be added linearly, probably misguided by the way the supermarket bill is added up – provided, of course, that there are no volume-based discounts. This wrong thinking leads firms to the belief that when summing up their exposures:

- Correlations among risk factors can be ignored
- Real-time technology is unnecessary, and
- There exists some magic formula that provides a realistic simplification of the computation of total risk.

All three bullets are very misleading and believing in them can be highly damaging, as the case study in section 2 documents. To a significant extent, these and similar lightweight assumptions are ingredients of a classical Greek tragedy where the principal character rises by dint of talent and energy to the pinnacle of society, *then* is brought crashing down by inner flaws or demons that cannot be controlled.

In the case of modern financial institutions and other entities, the demons are uncontrollable risks. What many companies perceive as 'simplification' in measurement of their exposure is meaningless (and often misleading) in regard to determination of the entire amount of *risk capital* that becomes necessary because of assumed exposure. Also at a disadvantage are:

- Risk and return evaluation of business strategy, and
- The allocation of risk capital to individual risk categories.

Rather than being reduced to some bits and pieces, the overall exposure tracking system should be global, counting everything on and off the balance sheet, including both derivatives traded on the futures and options exchanges and over the counter (OTC), counterparties, countries, and every other factor on which the entity's business strategy rests.

Risks that have to be aggregated largely fall into three categories: *credit exposure*, including counterparty risk (Chapter 5) and country risk; *market risks* (Chapter 7), including interest rates, currency exchange, equity price and commodity price risks; and *operational risks*, including legal risk. The case study in section 2 will demonstrate how other risks tend to morph into legal risk (which is examined further in Chapter 9).

Wrong hypotheses about transacted and inventoried exposure work to the detriment of risk management. An example is the statement: 'Derivatives do not really add risks to the financial system, and all they do is to provide the ability to identify, price and transfer risks.' Plenty of evidence documents that time and again this sort of assumption has proved to be utterly wrong, because derivatives:

- Add enormous risks to the bank holding them, and
- Have both mass and momentum to destabilize the global financial system.

The careful reader will recall from Chapter 1 that while, in general, derivatives can be useful instruments, leveraging sees to it that they carry with them plenty of unwanted consequences. Therefore, they have to be most carefully watched.

To test how well they positioned themselves in terms of their survival, some institutions are using a method known as *Time Until First Failure* (TUFF). In this, a sequence of days is plotted and the outlier is the occurrence of a loss exceeding a predetermined value or limit. This method is interesting because it permits the use of techniques and mathematical models already popular from statistical quality control (SQC) and reliability engineering.

As shown in Figure 4.1, a statistical quality chart has upper and lower tolerance limits, and within them upper and lower quality control limits. As long as the sample measurements are kept within the quality control limits, the process is *in control* because the engineering specifications (tolerances) are being observed.

This concept of limits applies to many financial issues as well (see the discussion of credit limits in Chapter 5). A chart showing the trading range is not quite the same as a statistical quality control chart, but it is one familiar to bankers and, as far as visualization is concerned, its effects are positive.

A 'plus' of statistical quality control charts is that they are flexible. The one shown in Figure 4.1 has been designed to track currency exchange rates. Statistical theory says that *if* there are three points in a row, *then* there is high probability a fourth one will follow in the same direction. Indeed, point P shows a bifurcation.

- *If* the curve had a bend upwards, *then* the process would have remained in control

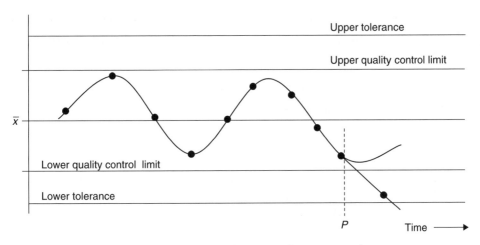

Figure 4.1   Using a statistical quality control chart to track currency exchange rates

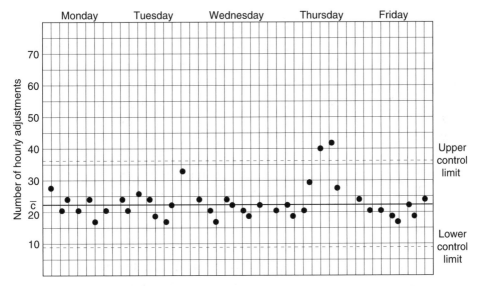

Figure 4.2   Quality control chart for number of defects per unit in a week on an hourly basis

- Since it continued downwards, the currency concerned had to be immediately supported or fall out of tolerance – as happened in the early 1990s with the British pound.

Other quality control charts are by *attributes*. Something either happens or it does not. These are most suited to lower impact risks, as they help to bring them in control by tracking a specific operation. An example is given in Figure 4.2.

An extra reward from the implementation of quality control charts by variables and by attributes is the possibility of post-mortem evaluations. In my experience, post-mortems are critical in:

- Building a risk awareness culture, and
- Providing consensus on risk control policies.

Developed in connection with the Manhattan Project during World War II and thoroughly tested for nearly 70 years in the manufacturing industry, quality control charts have a significant role in the financial industry. Graphics help to convey to board members and senior management the seriousness of an exposure, and they also facilitate the task of:

- Setting guidelines, and
- Assuring these are enforced.[1]

One of the best scenario analyses that I have seen makes good use of SQC charts, within a pattern of sound risk control policies. This financial institution treats unexpected losses as a matter of *volatility* of expressed losses beyond a predetermined threshold. *Then* it charges the consolidated profit and loss statement with an amount that corresponds to the statistically derived expected losses beyond that threshold. Information is obtained from the bank's credit portfolio:

- Loss expectation is based on assumptions about developments over the medium term, covering a full economic cycle, and
- This amount is credited in the balance sheet as credit risk reserve for unexpected losses (UL), beyond expected loss (EL) provisions.

The annual amounts being charged fluctuate depending on the economic cycle and occurrence of actual losses beyond the aforementioned threshold. Outliers in actual losses are posted as events, an exceptional reserve that directly impacts the bank's economic capital base.

A scenario associated with the output of this model documents for members of the bank's executive committee, and of the board, why such amounts are necessary to assure that spikes in loss volatility can be taken care of (with the exception of catastrophic losses), and how reserves and capital needs could balance each other out over a longer time horizon, on which is based the bank's economic plan.

2.   A real-life case study on total counterparty risk

The principles guiding the computation of total exposure reviewed in section 1 are equally applicable to counterparty assumed risk with a major client, including credit, market and legal risk. The added flavour in this case is that an integrative approach for a single client requires a high degree of coordination between the bank's departments. Lack of it can lead to disaster.

The institution involved in this case is one of the better-known European investment banks, whose management has been (overall) fairly successful. What it lacked, until a major failure occurred and the whole risk control system was revamped, was an integrative approach to the management of the counterparty relationship. Its existence would have allowed it to bring onto the radar screen the cumulative exposure assumed by the bank in its transaction with the client.

Here are the facts. Back in the early 1980s, a 'dear client' deposited in the bank 10 million Dutch guilders.[2] At the same time, he borrowed US $6 million, converted them to Canadian dollars and bought a convertible Canadian dollar bond in a Canadian company.

These were four practically simultaneous transactions. In all of them, the bank was only too happy to oblige. Three different departments acted independently of one another and made good business: deposits, foreign exchange (acting twice) and securities. Since the client had made a cash deposit, apparently there was no risk connected to these transactions.

But the client did not stop there. Shortly thereafter he wrote a call option on the shares of the Canadian company, and the next day he switched his US dollar loan to a Swiss franc loan, while he also bought a put option on the US dollar against the German mark. Subsequently, he wrote a call option on the US dollar because he still had his Canadian dollar bonds.

Taken together, these transactions didn't add up; department by department, however, was a different matter. The bank's treasury department, which handled the derivatives transactions, saw nothing wrong with them, and the same was true of forex:

- Call option
- Currency exchange (third in a series)
- Put option
- Second call option.

Only in an integrative way were the operations, briefly described in the preceding paragraphs, added to the bank's exposure with this 'dear client', who allegedly asked his account manager if all these transactions were possible. Looking at all these fees generated by the transaction, the account manager had no objection. Neither did he object when the next day the 'dear client' wanted to withdraw 5 million guilders, since the client had by then accumulated impressive paper profits.

As far as classical accounting procedures were concerned, these had correctly recorded the client's position. However, as so often happens with banks and other companies, this was done in a matter-of-fact fashion by recording each transaction in the books without consideration of:

- The risk the institution had assumed in this tandem of transactions, and
- The after-effect of volatility, which could have been easily mapped by considering the trend line and confidence intervals (section 6) rather than a scalar quantity of P&L.

Not so long thereafter the market moved south, turning the 'dear client's' significant paper profits into a torrent of red ink. The bank too was losing money and, since this account was deeply in the red, it decided to keep the collateral. The client objected, requesting that the bank should 'not only give me back my collateral but also pay me damages because you advised me wrongly'.

Not surprisingly, the case went to court. The judge of the first instance found the 'dear client' to be right. The Court of Appeal reversed this decision, but only partly. It rejected the claim for the collateral while confirming that the bank must pay damages, because at no time did it make its client aware of the risks he was taking with this rapid succession of transactions that were ill-documented with regard to their rationale.

This is a real-life case: court proceedings began in 1982 and ended in 1988. The investment bank had to pay damages because the court said it allowed its client to go that far that fast, instead of advising him to stop, because the risks he was taking added up to a sky-rocketing, unsupportable exposure.

An internal project subsequently found that, at that time, the bank's information system was not able to assess the risks involved on an integrative basis, evaluate the overall exposure and set limits. Transactions were authorized by various departments based on *their* assessment of the situation, not on a bank-wide perspective.

This is an excellent example of both management and system shortcomings, but it is by no means an exceptional case. Such conditions continue to prevail in many credit institutions and investment banks. There exist hundreds of different events like this, where the bank turns out to be wrong not because the original risk assessment was wrong, but because transactions were carried out afterwards without:

- Continuously assessing the risks involved, in an integrative manner, and
- Contemplating the resulting exposure by taking account of previous transactions already inventoried, and of market trends.

In a 1989 discussion, the CEO of the bank in question stated that in the previous five years Dutch banks had to provide for losses twice as great as their net profit and, in a relatively small country like the Netherlands, banks had to reserve for losses over 5 billion dollars (value in 1989).

In a general sense, this picture is no different in other countries because the banks' senior management and regulators don't pay enough attention to the problem of total exposure that is being assumed counterparty by counterparty.

Basel II (Chapter 10) intended to correct this situation by requiring individual integrative exposure measurements and financial reports for large counterparties – but existing evidence suggests that only US regulations really stand by this principle.

To be in charge of integrative single-party risks, the investment bank which was the subject of this case study built a system that continuously assesses all risks by transaction desk, instrument and counterparty – individually and collectively. At some point down the line, however, it also found that it still incurred integrative-type risks due to human interference with the system.

Although the computer gave a warning not to authorize these transactions, the account manager overrode it on the grounds that the model is not able to handle complex transactions, and anyway the safety margins were too severe. This became a case beyond accounting, information systems and trading – one where internal control and auditing had to intervene, as happens with many other banks.

3. Understanding where the risks really lie

A project aiming to correct the failure of evaluating total exposure by counterparty, instrument, business unit and the institution as a whole must start by addressing a number of critical queries. Their intent is to make sure that both senior management and project members understand where the risks really lie and how they correlate with one another.

Because, as we have just seen, the human element is the weakest link in the chain, the project should start not with questions relating to tactical issues and mechanics, but with those of strategic importance: the overall concept, quality of internal controls and trading system dynamics. The first issues that should attract management's attention are:

- Why is *this* counterparty dealing in options? Swaps? Forward rate agreements?
- Is the counterparty a steady user of OTC, or does it balance its business with exchange traded products?
- What's the net and gross exposure with this counterparty? How does it compare with limits during the last three years? Five years?
- Is the account executive aware of total exposure? What has he or she done about the exposure? What's the frequency of inputs to the client?

A suitable answer to these questions cannot be expressed in just a few numbers, the way the old culture has worked with 'vanilla ice-cream'-type banking products. Contrary to this short-sighted approach, banks should be keen to *merge* trading and analytical skills to better understand where precisely the risk occurs. Nobody can say 'what has happened to others couldn't happen to us'.

The best way to develop and implement a rigorous system of internal controls is to be specific. Many people understand that no two banks have the same requirements, and what may be good for one institution could be substandard for another. But few people appreciate that major cultural differences can exist within the same institution, and that these differences have a significant impact on risk control.

Speaking from professional experience, it has been a fairly frequent finding that even within the same financial organization different divisions have a hetero-geneous appreciation of exposure and incompatible systems of internal controls. In many cases these divisional internal controls short-circuit the corporate-wide system. Divisions justify them as 'better fit for their type of business', but that's nonsense.

A specialization of internal controls might be sufficient in single-product finan-cial institutions, but parochial systems are a disaster in conglomerates of products and services. Holistic results in risk management require total homogeneity of metrics, systems and procedures. Without them, it is not possible to understand where the risk occurs.

A crucial question to be asked when we structure or revamp internal controls is the diversity of the product lines they will be supporting, with emphasis on those instruments and product lines contributing the most to income and levels of exposure. An internal control system must be personalized to the institution that implements it. The structure of risk accounting, auditing, risk management and internal control must also observe the principle that organizations are staffed by people, and people:

- Create complex networks of power, and
- Stonewall information gathering and corrective action.

Every senior manager gathers about him or her trusted subordinates, who are in turn loyal to their own boss and work to that agenda. When in the Nixon years James Schlesinger became CIA director, he announced on arrival, 'I am here to see that you guys don't screw Richard Nixon!' To underscore his point, Schlesinger told the CIA top brass he would be reporting directly to White House political advisor Bob Haldeman and not to National Security Advisor Henry Kissinger.[3]

As with any other system, internal control and the organization at large work as long as all these centres of power share a common vision and aim. When disputes arise, whether professional or personal, each power centre defends its own turf and the arteries of the organization clog. This becomes a contest of wills, and it may well damage the survival of the institution.

To overcome stonewalling, the better managed banks have sought out more rigorous control schemes. One of the evolving models is that of a centralized risk management function, which assumes primary responsibility for entity-wide risk control and establishes strict guidelines for operating units. Centralized risk management:

- Reports to a senior executive of the institution, and
- Works in association with the board's risk management committee (Chapter 12).

Whether the centralized or distributed approach is chosen, clearly defined risk internal control and management processes must assure a system of personal responsibility and accountability (Chapter 3). They must also reduce the possibility that some risks will escape detection and control because one or more power centres make them opaque.

Along with the establishment of the appropriate structure, a crucial factor influencing the assignment of responsibility for risk control is the ability to qualify and quantify all dimensions of risk, including the personal dimension. A good example is the necessary separation between risk taking and risk evaluation, which must be clear-cut in all areas of activity.

Such separation seeks to assure that the originator of a given position cannot also be in charge of risk evaluation and of the trader's performance measurement.

It also helps to prevent price manipulations arising from conflicts of interest, which are boosted when the compensation of staff is directly linked to the performance of:

- Positions taken, and
- Commitments made on behalf of the bank.

Both have to be measured in a dependable manner, and *confidence intervals* should be established for both, as section 5 explains. 'If you cannot measure it, you can't manage it!' is a new motto in the financial industry, and at the same time it symbolizes one of the main challenges in building risk accounting systems robust enough for new financial instruments.

In the case study of the 'dear client', which we examined in section 2, the first risky situation occurred when the client borrowed US dollars, switched his US dollar position to a Canadian dollar position and bought Canadian debt. A subsequent internal study has shown that at that moment the client should have been stopped.

However, the loan department authorized the US dollar loan based on his original deposit of 10 million guilders. The forex department authorized the switch from US dollars to Canadian dollars because it estimated the risk on Canadian dollars as not being that much different as on the US dollar, and the client said 'it was only for a short period'. The securities department also made a good profit, and after all the client possessed Canadian dollars.

The court did not buy these arguments. Instead, the judge said: 'Being a bank you should have known there were risks involved and you should have warned your client. Since you have not warned your client, you are liable and you have to pay your client a damage.' The risks embedded in a tandem of transactions amplified one another.

Prices characterizing each of these positions change, in a gradual fashion, and this weighs heavily on total exposure. This lack of integrative risk control brings to mind the story of two bankers. One said: 'I can't sleep any more.' The other stated: 'I sleep like a baby.' The first one asked: 'How come?' 'Well,' the second one answered, 'every other hour I wake up and I have to cry.'

4. Correlation coefficients

Computing the right correlation coefficient (ρ)[4] is one of the challenging problems in establishing a system of total risk control for each major counterparty, instrument, product line, business unit and the institution as a whole. For starters, the relationship between two variables – such as risk type A and risk type B – may be described by a single value known as *covariance*, which is a symmetrical function of the observations.

In the early years of this century, Alan Greenspan had said that the science of covariance in finance is still in its early stages. This, however, should not discourage one from trying to perfect the method. If S_A denotes the standard deviation or risk A and S_B that of risk B, and S_{AB} the covariance of these two risks, then their correlation coefficient is equal to:

$$\rho = \frac{S_{AB}}{S_A \cdot S_B} \tag{4.1}$$

Correlation coefficients vary from +1.00 to −1.00. A zero correlation would mean that there is no relationship between the sets of scores belonging to risk type A and risk type B. In general, the lower the absolute value of ρ, the poorer the relationship. In banking, extreme values such as $\rho = +1.0$, $\rho = 0.0$ or $\rho = -1.0$ are very rarely observed.

A positive correlation means that when the scores of one variable increase, those of the other will too. The correlation of Figure 4.3 is roughly equal to +0.7, a relatively high correlation, which generally denotes that the two variables are characterized by a close relationship. But there may be exceptions to this statement. In science we are generally more certain when we reject a hypothesis than when accepting it.

Many derivative instruments are correlated, some being explicitly designed in that way. A differential swap, for example, is often termed a *correlation product*,

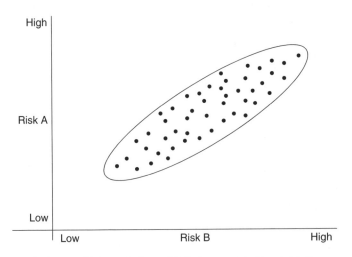

Figure 4.3   A correlation coefficient of about 0.7 between risk A and risk B

since its payout is modified by relevant currency exchange rates and interest rates in the transaction. Even if the instruments are different and conditions underpinning the transactions are diverse, the exposure tends to be correlated. But by how much?

A good way to judge the quality of governance of an institution is by observing how it computes (or chooses) correlation coefficients. Poorly managed banks pick out at random the value of $\rho = 0.40, 0.30, 0.20$ or simply 0.0. Those that are better managed try to compute the real value, and they don't accept $\rho = 0$ because one never knows if there is a hidden correlation. Rather, they use $\rho = 0.15$ as a proxy. Well-managed banks:

- Establish rich databases that permit more accurate measurement of ρ, and
- Continue testing their correlations, because they know that these change over time.

A prudent policy is that when in doubt, better use a higher correlation; this avoids bad surprises and unexpected consequences in financial exposure, which sometimes may be serious. Sound governance requires the upper range of ρ to be computed through analytics, rather than assuming low values of ρ because capital requirements become lower (Chapter 10).

Additionally, a pragmatic policy demands regular revalidation of correlation coefficients. It is always wise to remember that an institution's regulatory capital and economic capital are conditioned to a most substantial degree by correlations.

To face the challenge associated with capital calculations, many banks put rocket scientists to work. This is good practice, as long as they work in close collaboration with the institution's accountants and bankers. A fact that should never be lost from sight is that the calculation of correlations:

- Is only 20% a mathematical problem, and
- 80% of it involves management, accounting numbers and assumptions.

Here is an example from credit risk correlations presented in a recent study by the Research Task Force of the Basel Committee. This is a simple but illuminating case of a portfolio consisting of only two types of credit with similar unconditional probabilities of default, but each driven by different systematic factors.[5]

This portfolio contains a large number of small exposures to each type of credit, so that specific risk has been diversified. Figure 4.4 presents in a nutshell the research project's findings in regard to capital required with different mixtures of type A and type B credits. Assumptions characterizing the asset correlation between these two credit risk types range from $\rho = 0$ to $\rho = +1.0$ in steps of 0.25.

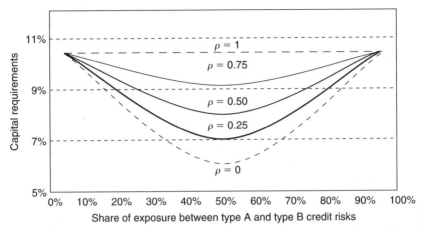

Figure 4.4   Capital requirements in function of correlation coefficients. (Findings of the Research Task Force, Basel Committee on Banking Supervision, Working Paper No. 15, 'Studies on Credit Risk Concentration'. BIS, Basel, November 2006)

- The ordinate scale is capital requirement (%)
- The abscissa is the share of exposure in different ratios between type A and type B credit risks.

At 50% share of type A and type B, the two credit exposures have equal weight; at 0%, either type A (left) or type B (right) has no weight, which means that the other type of credit risk has a 100% share. Leaving out $\rho = 1.0$ and $\rho = 0$ as unrealistic in the real world, the study of the other three curves with correlations $\rho = 0.75$, 0.50 and 0.25 presents an interesting insight:

- When there is concentration of risk (A or B), capital requirements are higher, and
- The greater the correlation coefficient, the more important the corresponding capital requirements.

Even with perfect diversification between type A and type B credit risk, a correlation of $\rho = 0.75$ exceeds the level of 9% capital requirements. Under the same conditions, $\rho = 0.25$ leads to only 7% capital requirements – which is a simple and powerful way to explain how, with A-IRB of Basel II, banks managed to reduce their regulatory capital well below 8%.

It is also appropriate to notice that most likely a credit risk portfolio containing a mix of exposures from only type A and type B will require lower capital than one with a greater number of exposures. As the Research Task Force points out, a single-factor model cannot be expected to capture all aspects of credit risk in a multi-risk factor environment, even if its parameters are calibrated so that the model delivers capital estimates to be used as proxy to those derived from a richer, more complex model.

Similar conclusions characterize correlations in market risk. As soon as we move into assumptions regarding correlations prevailing between instruments and exposure, we find too many issues to address and there is no industry-wide frame of reference to be followed, let alone a standard. There are also many specific risks that are situational, causing spikes at the tail of the risk distribution.

In the case study on the European investment bank (section 2) and its 'dear client', for example, all foreign exchange transactions were highly correlated because they involved five different hard currencies that related among themselves – even if each had its own forex risk distribution. The same is true about call and put options US $/DM, as well as Canadian bonds and call options on Canadian bonds.

Additionally, such correlations change over time because volatility, liquidity and risk appetite also change. Risk correlations are dynamic and new ones are generated, as practically every risk factor might prove down the line to have an unsuspected correlation with another risk factor, which was not perceived earlier on. After WWII, the American and European equities markets were not correlated. A couple of decades later, however, they moved in unison. In the 1970s and early 1980s, western and developing countries' stock markets were not correlated. Today they are.

5. Correlations are specific to the institution

Risk control and risk-based pricing of financial products are meaningless without accounting for correlations. Furthermore, experience in the banking industry shows that when senior management is unwilling or unable to study and document correlations in exposure, the bank's risk management system is worse than half-baked.

Any exposure may be characterized by correlations that are unsuspected or opaque at first sight. Here are some examples of correlations prevailing between credit risk and operational risk:[6]

- Balance sheet analysis leaves fraudulent claims undetected
- A credit rating procedure leads to approval of loans that should not be granted
- Account officers do not detect early enough changes in client behaviour, or information on missed payments is skipped, due to information technology error.

These kinds of failures are everyday happenings. Operational risk management, after all, is about avoiding such nasty surprises – a reason why Basel II (Chapter 10) has upgraded the notion of operational risk requiring capital adequacy to confront it. The fact of having capital reserves, however, does not cancel out operational risk and its impact on correlations.

Because every financial institution has its own risk profile, it must compute its own correlations, subject to control by supervisory authorities. Contrary to what many bankers, including central bankers, believe, correlations are not transferable from one institution to another. 'There is no sharing of correlation coefficients,' said Eugen Buck, of Rabobank, adding that 'Correlation factors must be computed in conjunction to diversification and they are very specific to an institution.'[7]

Other senior bankers, too, stated that every bank has its own portfolio pattern and therefore its own correlations. Among cognizant executives, the general consensus has been that in regard to correlation coefficients much depends on:

- The type of bank
- Its business, and
- The risks that it assumes.

Past correlations as well as references to what other banks are doing might be interesting, but they are not a way to run one's own business. Past correlations may well be obsolete because globalization continues to change the prevailing correlation between capital markets of the USA, Europe and Asia. At the same time, however, the detection of correlation changes requires:

- A high degree of granularity, and
- Sensitivity to the effect of underlying evolution to exposure.

Speaking from past experience, a sound way of looking at correlations is that they usually come in fuzzy sets. For instance, $\rho = 0.15$ may mean $\rho = 0.10$ or 0.20. Therefore, it is wise not to look only at a correlation's mean value, but also at its variance (more on this in section 6 on confidence intervals).

Another criterion that should be used in judging correlation coefficients is that they must be reasonable. In the large majority of cases, $\rho = 0.9$ or 1 is way too high and $\rho = 0.1$ or 0 is much too low, even for major, apparently correlated events in the first case and those that seem to be uncorrelated in the second.

In an effort to establish the impact of assumed correlations on *unexpected losses (UL)*, the German Banking Association worked with Deutsche Bank, Dresdner Bank, Commerzbank and Hypovereinsbank to evaluate UL eigenmodels. The results on unexpected losses were not comparable because of major differences in correlations:

- Under similar conditions, the lowest and highest UL estimates have differed by up to 500%
- But *if* the same value of ρ was used with all eigenmodels, *then* this difference is reduced to between 2% and 12%.

According to expert opinion, the 500% difference arises from the fact that some banks rely on CreditRisk+, others on KMV, still others on CreditMetrics, and each of these commercially available credit risk models has its own correlation coefficients. With CreditRisk+ the estimates of ρ are low. With KMV they are relatively high, leading to:

- A higher capital charge
- But also greater dependability that the estimated capital level will be able to confront adverse conditions.

It is not surprising that different correlations are derived from eigenmodels. Because they are based on equity prices, option-type models like KMV have a high asset correlation, often at the 50% level. However, asset volatility can be as much as five times higher than default volatility.

Default-based models lead to low ρ, at the 10–15% level, for a couple of reasons, the major one being that databased default information is much poorer than asset information. The downside of default-based estimates is that real-life correlations are much more dynamic than default data suggest:

- It helps precious little to use static correlations
- It is like reading last year's newspaper to learn about the most recent news.

There are also other irrationalities as far as correlation coefficients are concerned, superficiality being one of them. Confronted with this huge difference in estimates of ρ, in the range of 10–50%, a major bank decided to settle for a correlation of 25%. This is a low average and a 'guestimate'; as such, it provided a weak basis for computing capital requirements.

6. Confidence intervals

The concept of confidence intervals is new in accounting, but it is rapidly increasing in importance. Whether in physics, engineering or financial analysis, a considerable number of problems involve the estimation of variables of a given population distribution, which is often assumed on the basis of sample(s). In estimating the behaviour of a given variable, the analyst will be typically concerned with obtaining from the sample under study:

- One single value, usually the *mean*, $\bar{x}$, which is the best estimate of the variable's central tendency, and
- A measure of dispersion characterizing the range within which would fall other values of the variable under study (more on this later).

The mean, also known as the expected value, is just a *point estimate*; it is a statistic inadequately fulfilling the analyst's objective to learn about the variable's behaviour, because nothing travels in a straight line. At best, the area under the curve from one leg up to the mean represents 50% of values. And the other 50%?

By itself, the *expected value* gives us no indication about the range within which we have a certain confidence that the different values of the variable will be included, nor does it provide any evidence about the shape of the distribution. In fact, this point estimate may be the *arithmetic mean* of the values in the distribution, or the *mode* (point of highest frequency), or the *mid-range* (halfway between the higher and lower value).

Mathematically speaking, one way to proceed with a study of the distribution of events (or values) is through the method of *maximum likelihood*. Under fairly general conditions, this works on the assumption that for relatively large samples the obtained estimates will be approximately *normally distributed*, and that the higher frequency events (and their estimates) will be closer to the mean value.

Another way to proceed is the method of *moments*. With this, we obtain estimates of the population parameter(s) by equating a sufficient number of sample moments to the population moments – the mean being the first moment of the distribution. Notice, however, that these approaches still leave open the need to estimate the distribution's dispersion – which has been classically done through the *variance*, the second moment of the distribution (the standard deviation s is the square root of the variance).

The mean and standard deviation are shown in Figure 4.5, which represents a normal distribution. One of the problems with this approach with respect to risk management is that while we assume that values and events are normally distributed (which is itself an approximation), we also concentrate on values or events of higher frequency – though we know that risk events at the long leg of the distribution have low frequency but high impact.

A realistic distribution of risk events is shown in Figure 4.6. While the main body is assumed to be normally distributed (it is leptokyrtotic rather than normal), it would be a mistake to end our analysis at $3s$, within which lies a little over 99% of the area under the curve. This will leave out the spikes at the right leg, representing risks of major impact.

Moreover, because we want to do a solid job, we would like to have an estimate of how many values from the risk distribution are included in our study. This is provided by *confidence intervals*, which have become a key element in research and analysis. From physics and engineering to finance, this concept is important in all statistical studies:

- Values falling outside the confidence interval are not relevant in our study, though their after-effect can be significant
- Those values falling within the confidence interval are characterized by a margin of uncertainty commensurate to their frequency (or distance from the mean).

In simple terms, the confidence interval presents an estimate of how many values around the mean are likely to be included in the study, and must be taken into account in the evaluation of results. A confidence level of 95% means that 5% of all values are likely to fall outside its borders.

This statistic is called a *confidence interval* because we can be reasonably confident that the population mean and other values fall within that interval, even if not all values are included. *Confidence limits* are the end lines of the interval in question, as can be seen in Figure 4.7 through an example on the spillover of market volatility in the 1990–96 timeframe (notice that at any particular time the distribution of yield is not normal).

This approach provides commendable results if the estimates of a population's parameters through the proxy of sample statistics are accurate enough. Approximations derived from samples should be close to the mean value, and if repeated approximations are made these should cluster together about their own mean.

Here, in a nutshell, is how the level of confidence is chosen, keeping in mind that in every statistical reference there exists variation. We can say that in lieu of determining from the sample one single value as an estimate of the unknown parameter k, we determine two values less than and more than k:

$$K' \leq k \leq K'' \tag{4.2}$$

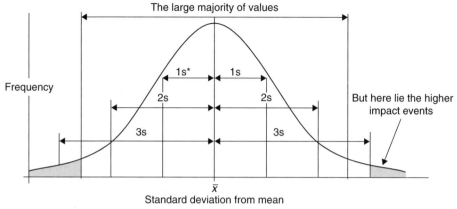

Figure 4.5   We assume risk events are normally distributed, but this is not always true

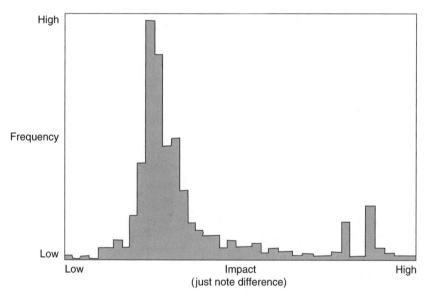

Figure 4.6   A practical example from real-life risk analysis: distribution of risk events with long leg and spikes

This is done in such a way that there exists a given probability $1 - \alpha$, that $K' \leqslant k \leqslant K''$:

- The interval between K' and K'' is known as the *confidence interval*, and
- These two values, K' and K'', are the *confidence limits* of the given parameter.

Statistically speaking, we do not know whether this particular interval covers k, but we do know that the probability of having drawn a sample interval which

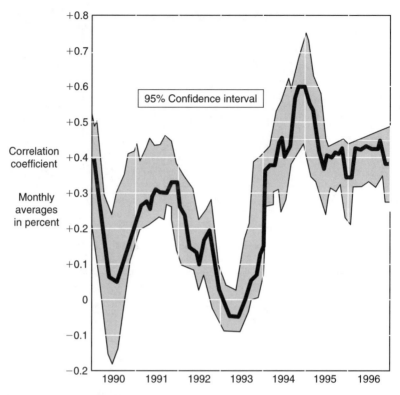

Figure 4.7   Spillover of yield volatility from the American debt securities market to the German market (*Source*: Deutsche Bundesbank, by permission)

does not cover k is α (also known as the *level of confidence*, producer's risk or Type I error). In the example with yield volatility confidence intervals $\alpha = 0.05$, and this corresponds to a confidence level of 95%.

In the *operating characteristics (OC) curve* in Figure 4.8, we also observe a Type II error, consumer's risk, or β.[8] Let's take credit rating as an example: β would stand for the probability the bank would give a loan when it shouldn't, given the borrower's low creditworthiness. By contrast, α would be the likelihood of rejecting the loan requested by a creditworthy borrower.

Given a certain sample and its statistics, in a wide number of applications we can determine the limits that may be expected to contain the values of the creditworthiness parameters of the population. Here the word 'expected' includes in itself a certain risk – namely, the risk that some values of the parameter considered at a certain test would not be included within the computed range.

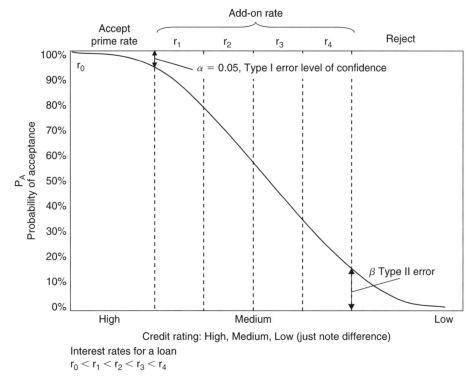

Figure 4.8   Accept or reject: using an operating characteristics curve in deciding on a loan

- *If* $\alpha = 0.05$, as in the preceding example,
- *Then* chances are that 5% of the parameter values would fall outside the confidence limits and 95% would fall within.

For $\alpha = 0.01$, the corresponding chances are 1% and 99% respectively. Other things being equal, a confidence interval calculated with $\alpha = 0.01$ is much broader than the one calculated with $\alpha = 0.05$; the latter, too, is broader than one computed with $\alpha = 0.10$. A higher level of confidence means a smaller α. Entities that choose a higher confidence level are essentially more conservative because they want to be sure their confidence limits will not be exceeded by real-life events.

In conclusion, *operating characteristics curves*, like the one in Figure 4.8, are at the root of the process of inference and, at the same time, map the fact that statistical inference involves risks. Risks taken with statistical techniques is the price we pay for the use of analytics. This price is much less than the one we will be eventually paying by using rule of thumb and speculation.

7. Dynamic financial analysis

An effort to control total exposure will find it difficult to achieve results if not assisted by the best tools mathematics and technology can provide. Correlation coefficients and confidence intervals are only two examples of analytical assistance. Others are the Monte Carlo method, fuzzy engineering, genetic algorithms, etc.[9]

Additionally, it should always be kept in perspective that many of the inputs into models and simulators come from accounting records. Therefore, other things being equal, the more efficient the accounting system and the more accurate the data it provides, the better will be the results of analytics.

A relatively recent example of a fairly powerful study tool is dynamic financial analysis (DFA). This is a method in which a model is developed of the entire institution's operations, according to both current plan and alternative plans. The complexity of the model depends on the market parameters chosen and the nature of the entity's operations. A sophisticated DFA model will incorporate modules focusing on:

- Product channels
- Cash flow
- Credit risks
- Interest rates
- Exchange rates
- Market prices
- Customer claims
- Costs and expenses
- Profit margins
- Likelihood of catastrophic events.

Dynamic financial analysis models are used to project operating results, in conjunction with a set of scenarios about the future. Challenges include: the fact that projected results are assumption driven; the consistency of such scenarios; pre-estimates of future correlation between financial risks; and a relatively high level of confidence, by choosing $\alpha = 0.01$ or less.

Moreover, a DFA policy should progressively address all risk functions. Banks with experience in this process say that because input data will come from accounting and other operating departments, all their members must be convinced of the importance of risk. This will have a triple effect:

- More attentive data collection
- Appreciation of what is represented by models, and
- Better day-to-day execution of risk management duties.

It should be noted that the policy of indoctrinating and gaining the collaboration of everybody in the organization on risk control is relatively new in business. It also demonstrates that the way in which risk management policies are determined and implemented has undergone marked changes, with risk awareness becoming a 'must'.

While, in the past, risk management was often left at the discretion of trading units, as we have seen on several occasions the better managed financial institutions have already put in place a central risk management unit that:

- Controls the observance of board-established limits
- Draws up common risk evaluation strategies, and
- Executes dynamic financial analyses regarding exposures that can be incurred in various product lines and trading desks.

This requires that each business unit develops more, not less, risk control skills to be able to stand up to central risk management. The business units must also become more investigative than in the past, able to analyse cause-and-effect in exposure and in discovering risk factors that may not be detectable at first sight.

Even enlightened minds might fail in this task. Reportedly, Francis Bacon once stated that the three things that made his world different from that of the ancient Greeks and Romans were: the printing press, the compass and gunpowder. He did not mention the water pump, yet it was more critical to the advancement of agriculture and commerce than gunpowder.

Well-managed banks also point out that compliance to internal rules and regulations and compliance to rules advanced by supervisory authorities correlate. And the former, like the latter, are greatly assisted through analytical approaches – because they contribute to a cultural change that facilitates the intellectual acceptance of credit risk and market risk controls, in terms of:

- Context analysis, and
- Aggregation of exposure.

This goes back to the principle that the control of risk should be everybody's responsibility, and this must be a strategic choice. Results can be enhanced by the right communications policy, including feedback on risks involved and corrective action that has taken place. One challenge is to remove the fear to report errors, another to do away with complacency after the first positive results.

Notes

1 D.N. Chorafas, *Reliable Financial Reporting and Internal Control: A Global Implementation Guide.* John Wiley, New York, 2000.
2 The exact amount of the transaction has been changed.
3 *EIR*, 16 July 2004.
4 More precisely, this correlation coefficient is r_{AB}, a statistical sample estimate of the population correlation coefficient ρ that is unknown. Such a distinction, however, is outside the scope of the present book.
5 Research Task Force, Basel Committee on Banking Supervision, Working Paper No. 15, 'Studies on Credit Risk Concentration'. BIS, Basel, November 2006.
6 D.N. Chorafas, *Operational Risk Control with Basel II: Basic Principles and Capital Requirements.* Butterworth-Heinemann, London, 2004.
7 Reference made in a personal meeting.
8 Not to be confused with the β that denotes volatility.
9 D.N. Chorafas, *Risk Management Technology in Financial Services.* Elsevier, Oxford, 2007.

Part 2

Risks to be Kept Under
Close Watch

Credit Risk

1. Credit risk defined

Credit risk is the risk that a counterparty – borrower, or participant to a trade or other type of transaction – is unable or unwilling to meet its financial obligations. In the event of a default, a bank generally incurs a loss equal to the amount owed by the borrower, less a recovery amount resulting from collateral (if available), as well as possible gains from foreclosure, liquidation or restructuring of the company.

This is the reason why the creditworthiness of the borrower is so important, leading credit institutions to classify current clients and prospects along criteria able to provide a certain assurance that the counterparty will not default until maturity of the loan. Banks have traditionally used five, six or seven thresholds in creditworthiness, which is looked on today as being a coarse approach.

The recent trend, promoted by the advanced internal ratings-based method (A-IRB) of Basel II, as well as by independent rating agencies, is a scale of 20 thresholds. This is practised by Standard & Poor's (S&P), Moody's Investors Service, Fitch Ratings and other agencies – and by a growing number of banks. These 20 thresholds range from AAA (the highest) to D (for default), and can be classified into two major groups:

- AAA, AA, A and BBB correspond to investment grade
- BB, B, CCC and below are non-investment grade.

Each of these thresholds, both investment grade and non-investment grade, is subdivided into three: for instance, AA+, AA, AA−. In a nutshell, the definition of each major threshold is:

- **AAA** – best credit quality and lowest expectation of credit risk
- **AA** – obligor's ability to meet financial commitments is very strong
- **A** – obligor's ability to meet financial commitments is strong, but less so than AA
- **BBB** – obligor has the ability to meet financial commitments, but adverse economic and financial circumstances are likely to weaken counterparty performance
- **BB** – obligor has speculative characteristics and is subject to substantial credit risk
- **B** – obligor's financial circumstances are weak, resulting in inadequate debt-servicing ability.

However, even if the counterparty is characterized by a high level of creditworthiness, this may be adversely affected by future managerial, business, financial and economic events. Hence the need for an outlook in the direction of rating over one-, two-, five- and ten-year periods. Notice that:

- A positive or negative rating outlook does not necessarily imply a rating change is inevitable, and
- Ratings for which outlooks are stable could be upgraded or downgraded in the aftermath of unexpected circumstances.

Analysis of creditworthiness is typically done through metrics and ratios applied to balance sheets and income statements of the company seeking a loan. Ten years of B/S should be a minimum; 20 years is better. Moreover, numbers alone will not reveal all the secrets. A sound methodology demands answers to several other critical queries, some of which are:

- How many new products are in the pipeline?
- Can we prognosticate future product performance?
- Is the company diversified or concentrated in its products pallet? In its customer base?
- What's the company's market appeal? The strengths of its brand?
- Has the company a history of weak credits?
- Is the company confronting a concentration of risks?
- What's the evidence about its ability to control its exposure?

Other critical qualitative questions concern: the performance of the company's management; general discipline; functioning of its internal controls; any abnormal losses; a worrying pattern of short-term loans; precedence of creative accounting; cases of illiquidity that might have been in the past; information about failures in compliance; and the prospective borrower's cost structure. *Costs matter.*

Based on counterparty rating as well as on aforementioned qualitative factors and on evidence about concentrations in exposure – currency risk, country risk and other factors – banks establish a system of individual credit limits. Credit limits are one of the traditional means of managing credit risk and of providing for diversification. Its pillars are:

- Establishing individual credit limits by country and counterparty
- Accounting for economic conditions and the business cycle
- Applying a proper credit risk providing methodology, and
- Steadily updating the credit risk pricing structure through feedback.

As the careful reader will recall, exposure due to credit risk can be grouped into two major categories: expected losses (EL) and unexpected losses (UL). Neither of these is steady. Expected losses that occur in any one year may be higher or lower than those of previous years. In any year, the amount of expected losses depends on:

- The quality of the credit analysis that preceded them
- Management's ability to account for the macroeconomic environment
- Changes taking place in interest rates, and other factors.

The charge-offs, or write-downs, for expected losses are also subject to volatility, though they are a reflection of credit quality. Zero charge-offs are unheard off, which means that banks know in advance that some of their clients will be unable or unwilling to perform. Charge-off rates up to 2% are generally considered as 'normal'. Figure 5.1 presents two decades of statistics of charge-off rates at US commercial banks. Write-offs are a lagging indicator of the condition of borrowers' balance sheets.

During this period, the borrowers' weak balance sheets show in the 1987, 1992 and 2002/2003 peaks in charge-off rates. The strengthened financial conditions of American corporations are reflected in the low charge-offs of 1994–99, as well as 2005/2006. Further evidence is provided by the very low default rates on corporate bonds.

The downside of 'good time' is that when delinquencies on business loans extended by commercial banks fall to very low levels, the credit institutions tend to reduce their credit quality watch. This becomes a big negative in the next change in the business cycle, when economic conditions deteriorate and weak borrowers are unable to meet their obligations.

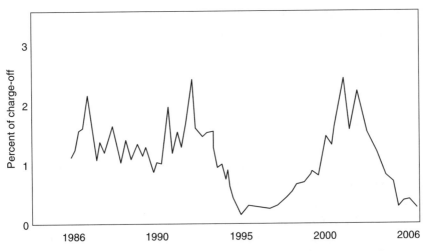

Figure 5.1   Two decades of charge-off rates at US commercial banks: 1986–2006

Under certain circumstances, a bank may decide to maintain potentially bad loans with specific provisions on its balance sheet. This is usually done as long as the debtor is in a position to redeem part of the loan, even if this is only interest. The bank will typically record a loan as *non-performing* before it finally writes it off. Many non-performing loans are in arrears for some months.

Only when the credit institution actually removes all or part of this bad debt from its balance sheet is the loan deemed a *write-off*. However, write-offs may also occur in the context of *securitizations*, as banks sell their bad loans to third parties to recover some of their capital, and/or as a way of financial restructuring.

In conclusion, credit risk must be studied through quantitative and qualitative means. Credit rating is quantitative. The behaviour of the borrower CEO, and that of his or her immediate assistants, is qualitative. Are they over-rewarding themselves with stock options, morose or bad-tempered even when making money, antisocial and introverted, or status symbol conscious?

It is also wise to ask other, more personal questions. Are the CEO, Chief Finance Officer (CFO) and the heads of Accounting and Auditing heavy drinkers? Do they have large mortgages on large houses? Are they removing floppy drives for 'security purposes'? Using a maze of passwords? Is the CEO refusing to talk to the auditors or the regulators?[1]

2. Counterparty risk

The term *counterparty* denotes an entity or person to whom the bank or any other entity has an on-balance sheet and/or off-balance sheet credit or market exposure, or a potential exposure of this or some other type. For example, such an exposure may take the form of a loan, commodities contract, real estate deal, derivatives transaction or other commitment.

The clauses of a commitment are observed when both parties perform according to the responsibility they have assumed. As we saw in section 1, in a narrow sense, credit risk refers to the risk that a borrower will not fulfil a contract. For instance, they will forego payment obligations on time because of default. *Counterparty risk* has a broader sense denoting more than exposure to deterioration in a borrower's creditworthiness, with some of the reasons, like country risk, possibly being out of the counterparty's control.

Counterparty risk leads to losses if the transaction is not concluded in conformance with all of the agreed upon terms. Bank management usually says that its willingness to take on risk in credit-related operations is limited, and credit risks are assumed only when:

- Collateral is offered, and
- Margins are adequate.

This statement, however, looks at the relationship from the narrow sense of credit risk, rather than from the broader one of counterparty risk. Apart from the fact that credit risk is always present, because even first-class counterparties may fall from high credit standing, there exist other risks that are more difficult to diversify.

For instance, guaranteed municipal bonds involve direct credit exposure to municipalities, corporations and reinsurers, as well as to various deals involving structured financing. Exposures involved in structured 'asset-backed' securities (ABSs, a derivative instrument) include:

- The risk that collateral will prove to be illiquid or inadequate, and
- Performance risk relating to sellers and servicers for assets funding the insured obligations.

Another important type of counterparty risk, as contrasted to pure credit risk, is total exposure connected to a single counterparty or group of connected counterparties – including settlement risk as well as country risk and cross-border problems.

Shocks may affect cross-border counterparties because of a sudden ban to big money transfers or critical market events affecting a country's financial system. By means of a rigorous analysis based on historical happening and plausible hypotheses, every institution should classify the types and degrees of counterparty risks.

A major counterparty-by-counterparty analysis of exposure allows premiums to be applied in the banking relationship. Whole industries may become subject to extra fees, as happened in the 1990s with the *Japan premium* paid by Japanese banks to borrow money in the global interbank market.

The term *counterparty credit risk* (CCR) denotes the bilateral credit risk of transactions with uncertain exposures that can vary over time with the movement of underlying market factors. CCR also refers to the likelihood that the counterparty to a transaction could default prior to final settlement of the transaction's money flows, as was the case with the Herstatt bank in the early 1970s (*Herstatt risk*).

As the preceding examples have demonstrated, another reason why counterparty risk contrasts with the credit institution's exposure to a loan is because in that case credit exposure is unilateral and only the bank faces a risk of loss. With CCR, the risk of loss is bilateral, and the market value of the transaction can be positive or negative to either counterparty.

An important case of counterparty credit risk is that of derivative financial instruments traded over the counter. These are largely custom-made bilateral agreements and their treatment has been set forth in an amendment to the 1988 Basel Accord. Basel II updated the handling of OTC derivatives transactions, and it advanced clauses for counterparty credit risk imbedded in repo-style and other deals.

The prior treatment of OTC derivatives, known as the current exposure method (CEM), reflected potential future exposure calculated by applying a weighting factor to the notional principal amount. Because the risk sensitivity of this treatment appeared limited, particularly with regard to the internal ratings-based (IRB) methods, supervisors enhanced it by introducing a new treatment for securities financing transactions (SFTs).

All these references point to the fact that counterparty risk is attracting increasing interest from regulators, because large and complex financial institutions and the transactions they bring forward play a major role in the international financial system as intermediaries in the:

- Interbank, and
- OTC derivatives markets.

They also contribute a great deal to the generation and reallocation of risks. Moreover, the increasing rate and size of transactions between large financial institutions is an indicator that they are exposed to similar risks. *If* the value at risk (VAR; see Chapter 7) in the trading book of global credit institutions is taken as proxy of their risk appetite, *then* assumed counterparty exposure increases rapidly, with the result that an abrupt spike in market volatility could result in:

- Liquidation of trading positions, and
- Significant amplification of market trends.

In conclusion, because of counterparty risk, the increasing dependency of earnings on investment banking and proprietary trading is making financial intermediaries more vulnerable to adverse market developments. As we will see in section 3, unfavourable trends in the hedge fund industry can also engender direct counterparty and investor risks, creating serious conditions for the global financial industry.

From a 2007 perspective, the good news is that in the 2003–06 timeframe, the economic climate has improved and company probability has risen, while expected default frequencies (EDFs, as defined by Moody's KMV) were significantly reduced. As shown in Figure 5.2, the confidence interval EDF mean value and the

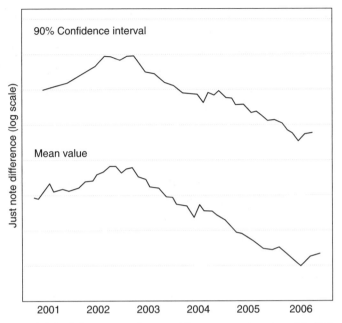

Figure 5.2   Expected default frequency of quoted European enterprises. (Statistics from Deutsche Bundesbank)

90% confidence level have not changed over the years, but the trend has been downwards, with a minor pick-up in 2006.

3.   Counterparty risk with hedge funds: a case study

With an estimated $1.5 trillion under management and a leverage ratio that sometimes exceeds 50, hedge funds amplify market dynamics, especially when they adjust their portfolios quickly and collectively as in the case of homogeneous trading strategies. Hedge funds are major counterparties of many credit institutions, but contrary to many commercial banks their risk appetite and investment behaviour cannot be directly observed because of their limited transparency.

While correlations between hedge fund returns are taken as indicators of possible movement of hedge fund portfolios, it is no less true that hedge funds have diversified investment strategies. Their convergence rests on the fact that they all:

- Strive for high levels of investment returns, and
- Take the amount of capital under management as a status symbol.

Several experts believe that these two factors, plus high leverage, contribute to a concentration of counterparty risk.

For exposure analysis, the amount of capital under hedge fund management can be divided into cumulative net flows (inflows less redemptions) and cumulative returns on investment positions. Mid-2005 to mid-2006, capital under management grew by almost 30%, of which roughly:

- 10% was due to net flows, and
- 20% to returns on investment positions.

Another concentration takes place within the hedge fund industry itself. The share of capital managed by the largest hedge funds has increased, with the sector bifurcating into two groups: a smaller number of large hedge funds, often backed by important financial groups and managing the bulk of capital; and a much larger number of small hedge funds, each with less financial resources but also with less risk control skills. Moreover, an insufficiently large capital base cannot provide managers with an adequate fee income, and this usually encourages aggressive risk taking.

Several factors determine the viability of a hedge fund. One of the more potent is poor returns, which may trigger redemptions. *Redemption risk* is an important exposure confronting hedge funds, whereby investors demand their money back. This risk plays a key role in determining the volatility of capital bases, but it can affect hedge funds differently because of factors like:

- Redemption restrictions
- Subscription frequencies
- Redemption frequencies, and
- Investor structures.

For funds that do not have sufficient amounts of liquid assets on their balance sheets, unexpected and widespread withdrawals can result in forced liquidations of positions, with an evident effect on markets, including volatility spikes and a drying up of liquidity. Accounting for these facts, in their dealings with hedge funds banks use, among other indicators, two types of net asset value (NAV) decline triggers:

- Total NAV decline, and
- NAV per share decline.

These allow them to terminate transactions with particular hedge fund clients and seize the collateral held. A close watch of counterparty risk is necessary because despite the fact that the massive losses sustained by Amaranth Advisors (a hedge fund in natural gas futures – see Chapter 2) have been absorbed quite well by the financial system, there is still not sufficient evidence that hedge funds' potential for systemic risk is lower than it was in 1998, when LTCM went bust.

Critics say that the September 2006 Amaranth case revealed significant weaknesses in the risk management practices of both the hedge funds themselves and credit institutions, as well as pension funds and other institutional investors that financed them. These included:

- A high concentration of risk
- Miscalculation of relative price movements for different delivery dates, and
- Little regard for market liquidity, which from time to time dries up and makes it difficult to close out positions.

LTCM is by no means the only precedent of a hedge fund that got into deep trouble. Several others have gone bust since that time. More recently, in May 2006, MotherRock, a $400 million fund based in New York, shut down because of bad debts on commodities. 'Hedge funds got hammered and some hedge funds have parked their money in US Treasuries as a place to hide,' said Rich Steinberg, President of Steinberg Global Asset Management in Boca Raton, Florida in October 2006. 'When the trend turns, they'll be back.'[2]

Some experts say that the distribution of single-manager hedge fund returns provides evidence of cases when risk managers of lending banks are confronted with higher counterparty risks towards their hedge fund clients than when they deal with big hedge funds. This, however, does not seem to discourage bank lending to smaller hedge funds because:

- The business is lucrative, and
- Stimulates banks to innovate by providing their hedge fund clients with increasingly sophisticated instruments.

An example is multi-asset trading platforms, which enable fund clients to deal across a wider spectrum of global financial assets. Additionally, VAR-based cross-product margining can provide marginal savings for hedge funds if all trades are implemented with one prime investment bank.

From the perspective of regulators, however, there is concern that persistently low levels of financial market volatility may artificially reduce VAR, thereby making much higher leverage levels possible. This may come at an inopportune moment in conjunction with other major exposures and/or an increase in volatility. Its likelihood also demonstrates that VAR is no longer able to capture exposures associated with the trading of newly developed financial instruments.

4. Credit policy

Policy is the means for avoiding repetitive decisions on the same or similar issues. *Credit policy* consists of a number of policy decisions, rules, procedures and controls put together to govern the hand of loans officers. Credit policy also deals with credit-oriented exceptions to these rules, specifying *if* and *when* these are permitted, under which conditions and under whose responsibility. Still another important part of credit policy is *diversification* of exposure. This theme will be treated in Chapter 8 in conjunction with position risk.

A credit policy consistently found among commercial banks is the evaluation of the counterparty's creditworthiness through credit rating (section 1). Practically all major financial institutions conduct their own credit analysis on the basis of information requested from and provided by the client, and on the basis of their own research. In deciding on credit lines, banks also take into account:

- The nature of their relationship with the counterparty, and
- Competitive pressures in conjunction with the credit market's performance.

Major clients of good credit standing receive more favourable treatment, including lower interest rates for their loans. But they are also continuously monitored and evaluated by the bank's credit office and credit committee. Additionally, globalization and credit market developments see to it that banks use credit ratings by independent agencies.

Among well-managed commercial banks, the value of a banking relationship depends on the counterparty meeting its obligations, as senior executives are greatly concerned with counterparty default risk. In the aftermath of downgrading of obligors' credit, institutions typically respond by:

- Reducing credit lines
- Cutting back on the number of downgraded clients, and
- Shortening the average maturity of business they are willing to take on.

To a significant extent, bank management conceives an increase in credit risk as a result of four developments that are interrelated. First, a general trend towards deterioration of credit standing. Second, a greater awareness about credit exposure, following the 1988 Capital Accord by the Basel Committee. Third, some well-publicized defaults in the corporate sector that affect the lenders' level of confidence.

The fourth reason is that an after-effect of globalization has been greater difficulties in assessing the credit standing of counterparties, as well as their previous credit exposures. As the preceding section brought to the reader's attention, major counterparties like hedge funds are not transparent and this results in deficiencies in information gathering. A similar statement is valid about off-balance sheet exposure through derivative instruments traded OTC.

Before credit rating systems acquired their present-day popularity, many senior bankers had the policy of personally knowing the CEOs of major borrowers. To them, the character of the counterparty was a major determinant of credit risk that could not be expressed in quantitative terms. As advice, this is no different from what J.P. Morgan said in his time when he underlined that *the basis of credit is character*.[3] 'Is not commercial credit based primarily upon money or property?' asked the chairman of the US Congress Committee. 'No sir. The first thing is character,' Morgan replied, 'because a man I do not trust could not get money from me on all the bonds of Christendom.'

In the same vein, Chapter 1 made reference to the Safras. The only thing that mattered to him, Edmond Safra said in an interview, was his reputation for honesty and thrift:

> 'A man's honour [is] the only thing that outlives him. My father used to tell me there are three things you need to succeed in banking: honesty, reputation and hard work.'[4]

Bankers like J.P. Morgan, the Safras, Amadeo Giannini, Andrew Mellon and several others were renowned for their ability to know each major client personally, judging first-hand character and performance. This can only be done with great difficulty in the present world of globalization, networks and electronic banking.[5] Hence the wisdom of developing quality databases and using formal credit rating systems as a proxy – albeit inferior – for personal contact.

As we saw in section 1, a credit rating scale should be detailed enough to present acceptable sensitivity to credit status. Moreover, credit rating must be thoroughly documented, and exhibit both accuracy and precision. This requires that credit evaluation is not one-track. Rather, it should be characterized by both a quantitative and a qualitative approach, as shown in Figure 5.3.

Given that lenders' acquisition of information about borrowers' credit quality is much more problematic for small firms than for large ones, it is not surprising that the ways in which these respective groups obtain credit finance differ significantly. Banks employ a variety of mechanisms to address the information-related problems associated with lending to small borrowers who are not rated by independent agencies, including:

- Tailored loan contracts, and
- Intensive borrower monitoring.

The bank loan market for small businesses also differs from the corporate bond market in its emphasis on the lender–borrower relationship. Through the counterparty relationship, banks may acquire private information over time and use this information to refine the contract terms offered to the borrower.

As the relationship progresses, Tier-1 financial institutions employ data on loan rates and collateral requirements on the lines of credit issued to businesses, to test their dependability. Based on their findings, they may adjust the contract terms – a credit policy that permits them to forge longer-term relationships with the borrower.

For their part, companies that establish a good dependability record with their lender tend to pay lower interest rates. Some research projects estimate this differential at about 60 basis points over a ten-year relationship. Based on quality findings, the hypothesis of *relationship lending* suggests that small businesses with longer-term banking relationships are less likely to pledge collateral.

Moreover, several central banks, commercial banks, investment banks and rating agencies use signals from the stockmarket as a guide to the riskiness of a company's debt. The *implied volatility* of options on a company's shares, for instance, can be viewed as the cost of insurance against the worsening of a firm's prospects, measured by its capitalization:

- When equity prices are falling and the cost of that insurance is high, yield spreads of debt instruments widen
- By contrast, as equities climb and implied volatility falls, prices of corporate bonds and other risky assets rise.

Credit default swaps have been used increasingly as a way to run credit policy, because they are viewed as an indicator of an entity's credit standing. The company's capitalization is taken as the proxy of its *assets* (A). The ratio:

$$\frac{A}{L} \tag{5.1}$$

provides a metric of the company's distance from default point (DP). In this ratio, *liabilities* (L) are taken at book value. If the company is not quoted, then assets must

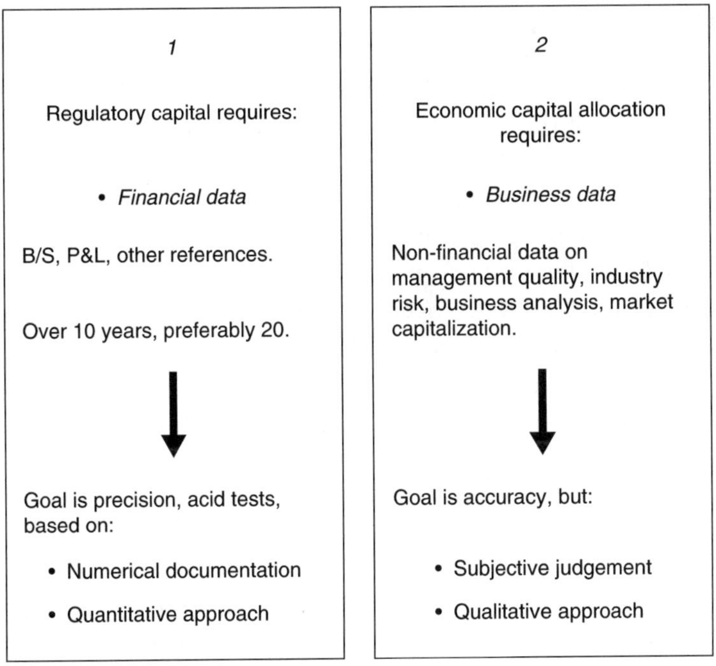

1	2
Regulatory capital requires:	Economic capital allocation requires:
• *Financial data*	• *Business data*
B/S, P&L, other references.	Non-financial data on management quality, industry risk, business analysis, market capitalization.
Over 10 years, preferably 20.	
↓	↓
Goal is precision, acid tests, based on:	Goal is accuracy, but:
• Numerical documentation	• Subjective judgement
• Quantitative approach	• Qualitative approach

Figure 5.3   Evaluation along two channels for credit rating

be estimated through balance sheet analysis and equity value of similar quoted companies.[6]

In conclusion, stock market prices are an indicator used by the main players in the credit market, and in the economy, to value the assets of entities and to tune their own credit policies. The importance of equity prices is shown, in dramatic fashion, in cases of market crashes and panics. In early 1873, the US railroad-related financial panic led to America's first great depression, which lasted six years. Money became tight and banks cut off credit. Serious bankers like J. Pierpont Morgan:

- Increased cash reserves, and
- Steered clear of any speculative investments.

The crisis was exported in no time. In May 1873, the Vienna stockmarket collapsed, creating a domino effect that hit Berlin, Paris and London. This outcome, which was a forerunner of the crash of telecoms in 2000–01, demonstrated that the global economy was highly sensitive to the valuation of equities. The economy contracted. In 1872, the railroads had built 7500 miles of track. Three years later, in 1875, cash-starved railroads would only build 1600 miles.

5. Corporate lending and collateral

William McDonough, the former President of the Federal Reserve Bank of New York and Chairman of the Basel Committee on Banking Supervision, expressed on several occasions the opinion that the financial industry should devote more thought to the appropriate valuation of positions during periods of market stress and illiquidity. McDonough also added that this attention is particularly relevant to the use of *collateral* to protect against credit risk.[7]

McDonough headed the New York Fed at the time of the September 1998 LTCM crisis, and he was the chief architect of the solution to put the hedge fund's main banks to work, rather than taxpayer money, to save the superleveraged fund from bankruptcy. Based on that experience he is said to have commented that:

- Risk control of collateral
- The valuation principles of existing positions (Chapter 8), and
- Credit risk assessment of collateral

are closely related to each other and the bank's creditability. The value of collateral changes as the market moves. Therefore, an adequate level of collateral (commensurate to assumed risk) calls for an evaluation of parameters such as current and potential price developments and related price volatilities, in line with best market practices.

Most credit institutions today use VAR measures (Chapter 7) to estimate the *valuation haircuts* needed to reflect the maximum loss of market value that, assuming historical conditions, could be generated by the collateral with a 99% level of confidence over a given period of time. Additional measures used to calibrate valuation haircuts include fuzzy engineering, back testing and stress testing (section 7).

A sound way to apply valuation haircuts is to focus by asset type, residual maturity and coupon structure. Such haircuts are applied by deducting a certain percentage from the market value of the asset, with initial margins applied to the credit amount. Symmetric margin calls, or variation margins, are made whenever existing collateral no longer matches collateral value requirements. Margin calls can be met:

- By supplying additional assets, or
- By means of cash payments.

For assets corresponding to Tier-1 regulatory requirements (Chapter 10), three haircut groups are often used: fixed rate, floating rate and inverse floating rate instruments. A sound credit risk policy requires that assets using a collateral must always be subject to daily valuation; for volatile and large position valuation this should be done even more often.

The valuation haircuts applied to Tier-2 assets reflect the specific risks associated with them and are usually more stringent than haircuts applied to Tier-1 assets. Four different haircut groups exist for Tier-2 assets, reflecting differences in their intrinsic characteristics and liquidity.

For marketable Tier-1 and Tier-2 assets, a single reference market is often selected as price source. This defines the most representative price on the reference market. It needs no explaining that a dependable reference price source should be used to value the collateral by marking to market. If more than one price is quoted, the lowest of these prices must be employed.

The answer for non-marketable Tier-2 assets, or for those marketable assets that are not normally traded and therefore marking to market is not possible, the answer is marking to model through present-value discounting of future cash flows. Discounting is usually based on an appropriate zero coupon curve. Differences in credit risk between issuers must be taken into account through credit spreads.

Central banks and regulatory authorities are taking a very serious look at collateral requirements, and they are watching the compliance to these requirements by commercial banks. The Statute of the European System of Central Banks (ESCB) explicitly requires that credit operations in all member countries are covered by adequate collateral. This *Eurosystem* collateral framework is designed to protect it against incurring losses in its:

- Monetary policy, and
- Payments operations.

The goal is to assure equal treatment of counterparties and enhance operational efficiency. Common eligibility criteria are applied for collateral accepted for credit operations conducted by the Eurosystem. Moreover, due regard is given to differences in central bank practices and financial structures across euroland, including the need to guarantee sufficient availability of adequate collateral for Eurosystem credit operations.

Indeed, Article 102 of the European Common Market Treaty establishing the European Economic Community prohibits privileged access to credit institutions by public authorities and agencies. This means there can be no discrimination within the collateral framework on the grounds of public or private sector status of issuers.[8]

An intriguing aspect of corporate loans, and of collateral requirements associated with them, is that many companies prefer to use loaned funds – hence leverage – rather than equity.[9] Theoretically, there are different features favouring debt over equity financing. The most commonly stated is tax treatment, but in practice there are several limitations in trying to profit from it.

More pragmatic, and more credible, is the fact that gearing raises return on equity mainly because markets are inefficient and they do not fully factor-in the increased riskiness. According to a recent study, however, accelerating debt and equity return requirements driven by financial risk outpace cost savings of additional substitution of equity by debt.

Part of an equity versus debt, and vice versa, decision is the fact that costs of financial distress or of bankruptcy favour the use of equity over debt. This implies that it is not necessarily a case of debt being a better or worse means of financing than equity, but rather a matter of using them in proportions that fulfil an objective without undue risk – because in the final analysis *risk is a cost*, and a major one for that matter (Chapter 1).

Contrary to banks, manufacturing and merchandising companies don't have the freedom of protecting through collateral the line of credit they extend to their customers. The primary means of distribution of most personal computer vendors, for example, are third-party resellers. Manufacturers need to continually monitor and manage the credit extended to resellers, and they attempt to limit credit risk by:

- Broadening distribution channels
- Obtaining security interest, and
- Utilizing risk transfer instruments (Chapter 6).

Still, any manufacturer's business could be adversely affected in the event that the financial condition of third-party resellers worsens. Upon the financial failure of a major reseller, the computer manufacturer could experience disruptions in distribution as well as the loss of the unsecured portion of any outstanding accounts receivable.

Other credit risks covered only thinly or not at all by collateral are those associated with geographic expansion. In particular, exposures due to expansion and sales manufacturing operations in emerging countries, which are economically and politically volatile, as well as subject to:

- Currency devaluation
- Expropriation, and
- Financial instability.

Different computer manufacturers note that they have generally experienced longer accounts receivable cycles in emerging markets, when compared to US and

European markets. In the event that accounts receivable cycles in these markets lengthen further, or larger resellers in these regions fail, the manufacturer is adversely affected. Hence the wisdom of credit limits.

6. Credit and other limits

In the post-World War II years, and most particularly during the last couple of decades, credit practices have evolved very rapidly, bringing the banking industry a long way from the traditional definition of credit risk, which finds its origin in the reign of Hammurabi (*circa* 1700 BC). The more generally accepted notion of the Hammurabi Code was elaborated in the Renaissance by banks that acted as exchanges and clearing houses all-in-one.

During the Renaissance, Italian banks created a mechanism to handle counterparty exposure in a way other than face to face, by bringing to life the practice of using a structural hub that acted as an intermediary. The concept of *limits to exposure*, however, rested in the banker's good sense rather than on formal structure. As a result, many banks went into bankruptcy because of:

- Lack of diversification in credit exposure, and
- Absence of properly thought-out quantitative risk limits.

This and other experiences emphasized the point that counterparty credit limits are very important for damage control. They should be linked with the probability of default, because of the certainty that default by counterparties might happen even if a bank adheres to a policy of entering into transactions only with investment grade counterparties.

Several credit institutions employ a policy under which the overall borrower's risk limit is established annually. But under current business conditions this is inadequate, because it is too static for comfort. Others establish counterparty limits semi-annually, or on the basis of requirements of their operating units and of the market situation. Factors taken into account during this exercise are:

- Risk level profile and distribution of credits by risk grade
- Customer mix in the credit portfolio, as well as prevailing portfolio mix
- Changes of amounts and instruments by customers from one period to another, and
- Trends in risk rating, percentage mix, critical ratios, amounts outstanding, type and number of customers, as well as competition.

The board, CEO and senior management are responsible for determining the appropriate credit limit structure. Some financial analysts suggest that the best way to proceed is to first establish the *risk appetite* of the firm, then follow with the overall framework within which the system of counterparty risk limit operates.

Whether this or a different approach is adopted, it is important to remember that setting limits is a dynamic, ongoing process that relies for its effectiveness on input from many areas of operations. The imposition of institution-wide credit risk (and market risk) limits is a strategic decision affecting business units, loans offices, desks and traders across the organization.

Both for loans and for trading, a framework of institution-wide limits gives senior management a clear goal for the amount of credit exposure as a whole. Unbundling that risk along divisional and departmental lines provides their managers with a measure of the risks that can be assumed. Another interesting unbundling is according to product lines and geographic operations area. The best way to proceed is by means of an interactive limit management procedure, which includes simulation and experimentation. Among important decision elements for a portfolio of debt instruments are:

- Weighted average risk rating
- Variances from limits
- Target exposures experienced in the short, medium and long term, and
- Special considerations to be given to factors such as country risk.

A sound practice requires that the counterparty risk premium is separated from product-related income, so that it can be addressed on a default-oriented basis, even if further down the line credit risks and market risks are combined. Risk premiums connected to counterparty exposure must cover the default probability of the debtor and a contribution to a possible increase in market uncertainty because of default.

Credit lines must not only be set up, but also monitored. They need to be specified for each counterparty–product combination whose credit limits must be classified by tenor, and set up in all currencies used in transactions. All transactions should be tracked in real time against these credit lines.

Hierarchies of lines and sublines must also be established, with separate credit limits for each. As section 5 underlined, the collateral for limits being awarded must be steadily monitored. Clauses conditioning credit availability can be of two types depending on the characteristics of the line:

- With *revolving lines*, a repayment increases the availability of funds against the line

- With *non-revolving lines* (special transaction lines), a repayment does not alter line availability.

In either case, liabilities must be tracked against the customer's individual credit lines, as well as together with the counterparty's parent company's set of credit lines (if any). This is important in as much as credit facilities awarded to a parent company can be utilized by its subsidiaries and branches. If the transaction creates an overdraft situation, an override should be required with full identification of the authorizer.

Banks operating in the global market have the intention of providing themselves with automatic currency conversion facilities. If the currency of the booking differs from that of the line, the system should convert the amount from the booking currency to the line currency, before checking for availability of funds.

Additionally, an interest and charges function should handle the interest-related input and processing requirements for balance-type accounts, providing flexibility in defining all necessary aspects involved in calculating debit interest, credit interest, charges and credit allowances. This function should be fully parameterized with the system, creating a whole range of exception reports brought to management's attention.

Feedback control is recommended because commercial credits are rapidly growing and this increases the need for a more accurate and up-to-date limit disposition and monitoring system. The adopted solution should target *position risk calculation* (Chapter 8), and include risk premium computing, a steady watch over risk premium limits, country risk assessment and counterparty default risk. The method to be chosen should satisfy two objectives:

- Quantifying counterparty exposure, and
- Assisting in evaluation of the current capital at risk.

An example is the computation of present value of a financial transaction. Present value (PV) represents the present cost of replacing this transaction in the event of default. Net present value (NPV) is calculated as the sum of present value plus add-ons or, in the case of forward contracts, of future cash flows.

While the choice of method is in itself a challenge, institutions must also pay enough attention to other challenges, such as timeliness and effective visualization, to improve end-user perception of computational results. Not only should reporting be online, interactive and in 3-D colour graphics, but it must also visualize the output in a way that leads to efficient management decisions.

Last but not least, good management practice must see to it that the chief credit officer responsible for counterparty risk is also responsible for analysis, evaluation and reporting on prudent limits. While in centralized counterparty risk management the final decision regarding the allocation of credit limits will be taken at headquarters, a well-run credit division will always appreciate critical input from the field.

7. Stress tests for credit risk

Credit risk measurement and management are key to both financial and non-financial institutions. Their function is always important, and they become even more vital when default rates rise. Effective credit risk management is a structured process aiming to assess, quantify, qualify, price, monitor and manage counterparty risk on a consistent and factual basis. This requires:

- Careful consideration of proposed extensions of credit
- The setting of specific limits (section 6)
- Diligent ongoing monitoring during the life of exposure
- Active use of credit mitigation tools (Chapter 6), and
- A disciplined approach to recognizing credit impairment, followed by immediate action.

A financial institution's credit risk management framework must be regularly refined and it should cover all banking business exposed to the risk of default, including trading activities. Key components of a rigorous approach will be: an individual counterparty rating system; a transaction rating system; active credit portfolio management; counterparty credit limits; counterparty, industry, country and regional concentration limits (Chapter 8); and a risk-based pricing methodology (Chapter 11).

In its November 2006 report, the Basel Committee's Research Task Force notes that stress testing of credit risk is not yet as mature as other disciplines in credit risk control, and banks' development of stress testing techniques is still ongoing.[10] The same report also underlines that it is important to differentiate at the outset between two types of stress tests:

- Regular, in which stress is incorporated into the model without changing its structure, and
- More sophisticated approaches with the aim to analyse 'model stress' and gain a better insight.

The Research Task Force also points out that, to avoid pitfalls in the design of an advanced analytical approach, stress test parameters should be *plausible* and *consistent* with the bank's existing credit risk control framework. They should also be adapted to the portfolio under investigation and their output designed so that it integrates seamlessly with existing internal reporting approaches.

Experimentation on stress tests for credit risk can be achieved by identifying a small set of risk factors that have relatively high explanatory power, distinguishing between *core* factors that will be stressed and *peripheral* factors that are affected by the stress event in a manner conditional to the core factors' reaction. To provide management with insight, stress tests of concentration risk (Chapter 8) should focus on:

- Sectors with relatively high credit risk exposures, and
- Sectors that are correlated with other credit risk sectors.

Basel's Research Task Force also makes the point that as long as the bank does not want to fundamentally question its risk control model, it is advisable to choose stress scenarios that are consistent with the existing policies and practices for testing the credit portfolio. Otherwise, stress testing results may have little relevance for credit risk control reasons.

A different way of expressing this is that stress scenarios will have much more of an impact on the bank's risk management if they are consistent, believable, provide continuity of current practices and have a certain probability of actually occurring. Just as important is to have an accounting framework that:

- Captures and aggregates relevant credit risks, and
- Serves as the basis for an effective credit risk control aggregate, including hedging and exposure management.

Provided that the appropriate conditions are fulfilled, stress tests provide added value to senior management. Compared to classical credit risk tests, they give a better focused picture of how a credit portfolio may perform in a crisis.

Beyond this, a stress testing policy for credit risk should be seen as an opportunity to merge new information, such as risk management insights and economic predictions, which are qualitative and therefore able to supplement the credit portfolio model that the financial institution has followed so far. Stress probability of default, stress loss-given default and stress exposure at default fulfil these conditions.

8. SPD, SLGD, SEAD

The board of a credit institution should be keen to establish a holistic policy that covers a whole range of requirements: from regulatory capital (Chapter 10) to economic capital.[11] Equally critical is the seamless integration of a stress testing system that, as of 2007, has become a cornerstone of Pillar 2 of Basel II. (Pillar 2 is the steady review of capital adequacy, along with other criteria of prudential bank supervision exercised by national regulatory authorities.)

Since the time of Basel I (1988), regulatory capital has been associated with expected losses. Originally, under Basel II, the computation of *expected losses* (EL) under the internal ratings-based (IRB) method (with two alternatives: F-IRB and A-IRB) was provided in a comprehensive manner expressed through the algorithm:

$$EL = PD \times LGD \times EAD \tag{5.2}$$

where:
  PD = probability of default
  LGD = loss-given default (also a probability)
  EAD = exposure at default (the amount of money involved in the exposure).

In a credit risk distribution, this area of expected losses lies on the left side, as shown in Figure 5.4. By contrast, *unexpected losses* (UL) are found at the long leg (right side) of the credit risk distribution. The algorithm is:

$$UL = SPD \times SLGD \times SEAD \tag{5.3}$$

where:
  SPD = stress probability of default
  SLGD = stress loss-given default (also a probability)
  SEAD = stress exposure at default (expressed in money).

Banks evaluate credit risk of the non-stress type through a credit request and approval process, ongoing credit and counterparty monitoring, and a credit quality review process. Common practice demands that experienced credit officers prepare credit requests and assign internal ratings based on their analysis and evaluation of the clients' creditworthiness and type of credit transaction.

As the careful reader will recall from section 1, among well-managed banks this analysis emphasizes a forward-looking approach, concentrating on economic trends and financial fundamentals. Credit risk examiners also make use of peer analysis, industry comparisons and other quantitative tools, while the final

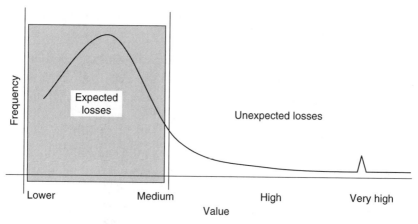

Figure 5.4 Expected losses and unexpected losses from one risk distribution – not two

rating also requires the consideration of qualitative factors relating to the counterparty, its industry, country and management.

In contrast to this approach, stress tests represent a risk-adjusted performance measurement. Typically, stress testing goes beyond the statistical limits confining a normal distribution (the mean plus or minus three standard deviations, $\bar{x} \pm 3s$), aiming to foretell exposure that may materialize in connection to extreme events. The latter might take place at:

- $\bar{x} + 5s$
- $\bar{x} + 10s$
- $\bar{x} + 15s$.

The basic objective of developing stress credit risk measurements is to facilitate prudential management of exposure by prognosticating likelihood and impact of outliers, as well as by identifying sources that give rise to risk concentrations. Even if such events do not happen frequently, they are plausible.

This contrasts with normal risk testing because most often normal tests are made under simplifying assumptions regarding the probability of counterparty default over a specified time interval. By contrast, a more sophisticated estimate of the counterparty's exposure requires:

- *Probability of default* (PD, a percentage)
- *Loss-given default* (LGD, a percentage)
- *Volatility* of LGD estimates
- *Exposure at default* (EAD, expressed in money)

- *Effective maturity* (M, at the discretion of national supervisors), and
- The stress metrics – SPD, SLGD, SEAD.

The computation of SPD may be based either on a historical scenario by examining, for instance, stress default conditions over the last 100 years (which will include the Great Depression), or through hypothetical scenarios of unlikely but plausible PD (criteria for stress tests are discussed in Chapter 7).

As Figure 5.5 shows, macroeconomic variables may significantly affect PD. Notice the significant difference in the behaviour of PD and SPD during expansion, while the two curves tend to approach one another during recession. This is reasonable, since recession is a stress economic condition.

Plenty of factors, including collateral, enter into LGD volatility. A dependable approach to stress loss-given default (SLGD) should capitalize on the effect of different levels of volatility. Ongoing research on LGD presents some interesting statistics on LGD volatility connected to bonds, and could be used as proxy for loans.

Just like the PD, LGD must be stress tested under hypotheses of both external and internal developments unfavourable to the firm, therefore affecting its creditworthiness. A similar statement is valid in connection to stress exposure at default (SEAD). It is appropriate to notice that credit institutions continue it find it difficult to aggregate risk across sectors, as they are confronted by some of the challenges faced in any aggregation, such as:

- Intra-group exposures, and
- Heterogeneous risk types.

One problem is that common definitions, let alone metrics, for risk concentrations across risk types are not currently available. Neither is there a generally accepted definition of risk concentration *per se*. Moreover, the amplitude and scope of the concentrations, and of the domain of exposure defined by them, have widened in recent years to include large commitments to one obligor, product, region or industry – as well as multiple exposures of different member firms of the same conglomerate.

Even more challenges than those presented with PD and LGD confront stress testing EAD. This practice focuses on how the relationship between lender and borrower evolves under adverse business conditions. To a substantial extent, EAD is influenced by decisions and commitments made by the credit institution before default. These are taken as basically depending on:

- Type of loan, and
- Type of borrower.

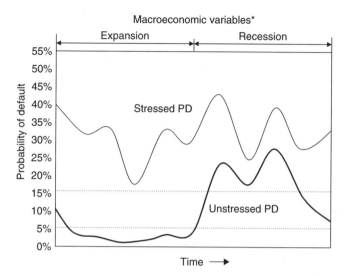

Figure 5.5   Unstressed and stressed probability of default, over time. * GDP growth, or downturn, exchange rates, market psychology, etc. (Based on a study by Basel Committee on Banking Supervision, Working Paper 14, 'Studies on the Validation of Internal Rating Systems'. BIS, Basel, February 2005)

This fairly widespread approach is technically correct but incomplete, because it does not account for the impact of novel instruments, from securitization to other derivatives that alter the classical way of treating loans (Chapter 6), and tends to stray from the typical notion of a borrower.

Because all loan transactions have associated with them a number of characteristics qualifying the credit given to a client, there exist several variables affecting EAD. Apart from type of loan and type of borrower, these include obligor-specific references, current use of loan commitments, covenants attached to the loan, time to maturity, fixed versus floating interest rate, revolving versus non-revolving credit, conditions in the case of restructuring, and the obligor's alternative ways and means of financing.

Notes

1   D.N. Chorafas, *Management Risk: The Bottleneck is at the Top of the Bottle.* Macmillan/Palgrave, London, 2004.

2   http://www.bloomberg.com/apps/news (accessed 10 February 2006).

3   During the 1912 investigation of the Money Trust by the House Banking and Currency Committee, whose special legal counsel was Untermyer.

4   Bryan Burrough, *Vendetta: American Express and the Smearing of Edmond Safra.* Harper Collins, New York, 1992.

5   Even when he was President of Chase Manhattan, David Rockefeller was spending two-thirds of his time around the world meeting clients, and he had in his New York office a database with 10 000 of the most important names – other senior bankers, large clients, heads of state, prime ministers and ministers of finance.

6   D.N. Chorafas, *Modelling the Survival of Financial and Industrial Enterprises: Advantages, Challenges, and Problems with the Internal Rating-Based (IRB) Method.* Palgrave/Macmillan, London, 2002.

7   *Financial Products,* Issue 109, 11 March 1999.

8   European Central Bank, Annual Report 2002.

9   D.N. Chorafas, *The Management of Bond Investments and Trading of Debt.* Butterworth-Heinemann, London, 2005.

10   Findings of the Research Task Force, Basel Committee on Banking Supervision, Working Paper No. 15, 'Studies on Credit Risk Concentration'. BIS, Basel, November 2006.

11   D.N. Chorafas, *Economic Capital Allocation with Basel II: Cost and Benefit Analysis.* Butterworth-Heinemann, London, 2004.

Credit Risk Mitigation

1. Concepts underpinning credit risk transfer

New financial instruments collectively known as *credit risk transfer* (CRT) treat credit risk as a commodity and allow it to be traded in the market. This blurs the dichotomy between banking book and trading book. It also affects traditional credit policies and business models of credit institutions, starting with the way banks look at the debt of large corporate customers.

Because the whole domain of credit risk mitigation policies, instruments and methods is still in its infancy, the changes in strategies, business models and counterparty handholding have not yet been so dramatic. Senior banking executives, however, foresee important developments in the coming years, such as:

- The process of granting and holding loans will likely shift towards a strategy of attracting loans, including lower grade, and
- Creditworthy and less creditworthy debt instruments will be securitized and shifted to parties most willing to bear credit risk.

The CRT market is constituted by banks, insurance companies, pension funds and other institutional investors with an appetite for credit risk. Issuing banks will concentrate on the development of model-based, computer-assisted credit risk assessment, including risk-based pricing (Chapter 11). Not only national but also transborder banking competition for issuance and securitization of loans is expected to intensify, based on:

- Brand name
- Other comparative advantages, and
- Greater consolidation of the banking industry.

No doubt, this will have serious regulatory policy implications. New compliance requirements will arise from the use of credit risk transfer, including greater emphasis on prudential oversight in line with Pillar 2 of Basel II (Chapter 10).[1] In parallel to this, there will be a rather rapid development of new tools and techniques designed to support credit risk transfer in areas of securitization, syndication and loan guarantees.

While some techniques connected to counterparty risk are almost second nature because they have existed for a long time and have become a regular part of banking activity, these are no longer sufficient for the handling of CRT instruments, which are generally complex and opaque. Neither are old credit risk control tools appropriate in a market featuring:

- Many new players, and
- A high growth rate.

Some of the concepts that have so far prevailed with securitizations will be up for re-examination. For instance, today the actual net risk transfer is reduced when banks retain the first-loss positions (tranches) in structured products. This also helps to mitigate concerns that banks cease to monitor the asset quality of their customers, thereby creating moral hazard.

However, some experts suggest that *if* there is a massive rise in the CRT market, *then* such methods are insufficient and ineffectual. They do not respond to *potential risks*, which are sure to exist; their presence requires not only factual pricing, but also rigorous ongoing monitoring of structural issues and their underliers. The European Central Bank had this to say on the pricing issue:

> 'To the extent that long-term rates and risk premia have been driven too low in some financial markets, valuations could prove vulnerable to several potential adverse disturbances, which could leave banks exposed to greater than normal risks ...
>
> There has also been growing unease about the extent of CRT outside the banking system, especially concerning the extent to which hedge funds may have taken on greater credit risk exposure ... [Furthermore] very little is known about how CRT markets would function under stressed conditions.'[2]

With regard to the management of CRT exposure, the Basel Committee requires that if a bank has multiple credit risk transfer techniques covering a single exposure, the credit institution will be required to subdivide the exposure into portions covered by each type of CRT technique.[3] The risk-weighted assets of each portion must be calculated separately. Also, when credit protection provided by a single protection has differing maturities, they must be subdivided into separate products.

Prudence is highly advisable because there is already accumulating evidence that several big banks, and some smaller ones, as well as insurance companies, have become significant risk takers in CRT markets, as *protection sellers* (more on this later). Since a positive outcome relies not only on the transactions being well conducted, but also on their being followed up in terms of credit, market and operational risk, exposure management must be first class, including:

- Correlation analysis
- Repricing of instruments
- Real-time data capture

- Online database mining
- A methodology with solid analytical tools
- Interactive visualization procedures, and
- Integrative solutions, including all banking operations.

Real-time interactive solutions, and the methodology supporting them, must appropriately incorporate into their models every characteristic of the different CRT instruments, as well as the ways they vary in their *funding*: for instance, whether funds are transferred to the protection buyer when the credit risk transfer occurs, hence CRT is a funded product; or credit risk transfer takes place without funds being transferred to the protection buyer, hence CRT is an unfunded instrument.

- Cash, asset-backed securities (ABSs), collateralized debt obligations (CDOs, section 4) and loans traded in the secondary market are funded instruments.
- Synthetic collateralized debt obligations,[4] credit default swaps (CDSs, section 5), guarantees and insurance contracts are examples of unfunded credit risk transfers.

Another important characteristic by which CRT instruments differ is whether risk transfer from protection buyer to protection seller is *direct* or *indirect*. Credit default swaps, basket default swaps and total return swaps are examples of CRT instruments that transfer risks *directly* from protection buyer to protection seller. Credit risk, however, may also be transferred *indirectly* from seller to buyer through special purpose vehicles (SPVs).

An equally important characteristic by which credit derivatives and other CRT instruments differ among themselves is the *timing of payment*. With several credit risk transfer products, when credit events occur the seller does not issue payment until loss verification and compliance checks have been carried out. By contrast, with other credit derivatives, like credit default swaps, protection payments are more or less immediate.

Theoretically, all this seems straightforward. In practice, it is not that way at all, because CRTs are opaque and complex. Regulators worry that credit risk transfer reduces their ability to know where credit risk really accumulates. In the background of current worries about latent credit mega-risk transferred from big banks to other parties is that:

- Today many credit losses are buried,
- But most likely they will show up in new places later on.

Cognizant people in the CRT industry, as well as among regulators, believe that the size of credit mega-risks can cause unpredictable damage to national economies and the world economy as a whole. For instance, loans of about $34 billion were wiped off in the bankruptcies of Enron and WorldCom. However, millions rather than billions of losses showed up in financial statements of big banks.

- The crucial question is: where have these losses gone?
- The most probable answer is that they went to insurance firms, pension funds, hedge funds and smaller banks.

On 18 May 2005, speaking at an international conference of financial regulators in Turkey, Andrew Large, Deputy Governor of the Bank of England, issued a strong warning on credit derivatives, emphasizing the point that credit risk transfer has introduced new holders of credit risk, and this has happened at a time when market depth is untested and the new holders' financial staying power is not exactly known. 'Large risks of instability [are] arising through leverage, volatility and opacity,' Large said.[5]

2. For and against credit derivatives

As the 20th century came to a close, credit derivatives were a novelty and they were hardly traded. Five years later, in late September 2005, the annual report of the International Swaps and Derivatives Association (ISDA) indicated a most significant increase in the volume of outstanding credit derivatives from one period to the next – and this continues unabated.

For example, from almost nothing in 2000, by mid-2006 trading in credit default swaps has ballooned to a notional value of $17 trillion. That still left plenty of room for growth if one considers that interest rate swaps (Chapter 7) are a $160 trillion market, and the market for over-the-counter derivatives (which is unregulated because it involves trades between private parties) stands at $220 trillion.

The market penetration of credit derivatives varies widely by jurisdiction. According to statistics published by the European Central Bank, credit derivatives have a stronger foothold in Germany than in other euroland countries. At the same time, however, though the European credit derivatives markets are still trailing their US counterpart, they have experienced rapid growth in the past few years. Experts say that this is accompanied by an increased potential for instability should conditions take a turn for the worse.

What is scary with this rapid increase in CRT exposure is that with credit derivatives protection sellers are institutional investors who are not particularly sharp in credit risk control, and the credit outlook is deteriorating. Worldwide Standard & Poor's list of 623 large enterprises features many with a negative outlook or credit watch. Sectors that show the greatest vulnerability are telecommunications, consumer products and automobiles.

Government agencies like Fannie Mae and Freddie Mae, the giant mortgage associations, are not in much better shape. In early September 2005, Dr Alan Greenspan, then Fed chairman, wrote to Senator Robert Bennett, a member of the Senate Banking Committee, that one must very quickly do something to reduce the risk portfolio of the two mortgage financing agencies.[6]

Almost a year later, Greenspan startled bond traders at a dinner in New York with two statements. First he said credit derivatives were becoming the most important instruments 'I've seen in decades'. But then he added that he was appalled at the '19th century technology' used to trade credit default swaps, with deals done over the phone and on scraps of paper.[7]

In September 2006, Fitch Ratings published its fourth annual global credit derivatives survey on main market developments between the end of 2004 and the end of 2005. The 75 financial institutions covered in this survey represent major players in the market. The notional principal amount of outstanding credit derivatives contracts had significantly risen, this survey says. The increase of 122% conforms with the trends recorded in surveys conducted by other institutions and industry associations.

Fitch stresses the growing importance of indices and index-related products, which grew tenfold during 2005 and comprise almost one-third of gross positions. Single-name CDSs still constitute about half of the whole market, but their growth has slowed down (more on this later). While the banking sector's overall position remains that of long protection, the survey points out that, particularly in Europe, there were banks whose net position turned to neutral or even became net protection sellers.

By contrast, entities in the insurance, reinsurance and financial guarantor industries continued to act as net protection sellers. Other interesting findings include further confirmation of increasing market concentration, with the top 15 banks and dealers responsible for 83% of gross protection sold on speculative grade and unrated entities. The latter have grown to 31% of the total, reflecting the continuing search for yield.

Interestingly enough, the Fitch survey also found that market making has become the prime motivation for banks' involvement in the credit derivatives market. Additionally, Fitch points out that dependable data on net credit exposures and on concentration of positions would considerably benefit:

- Market participants, and
- Supervisory authorities.

This concern is substantiated by the fact that problems connected to creditworthiness of obligors have wider market effects. For instance, when in May 2005 the credit ratings of GM and Ford were downgraded by all three major credit rating agencies, this led to a very sharp (albeit temporary) widening of yield spreads in the credit markets.

The sharp spread widening in the cash market was reversed relatively quickly and, by June 2005, spreads had already retracted part of this widening and had returned to their April levels. Analysts have been studying the reasons for this reversal. According to several opinions, the low concentration of single names in the underlying portfolios, an aftermath of lessons from previous events like Parmalat, saw to it that the vast majority of the CDO tranches that included the two car makers remained unaffected by the rating changes.

According to other opinions, the main lesson to be drawn, from a financial stability point of view, from the GM/Ford and similar events is that the evolution of credit derivatives has allowed a smoother handling of price adjustments in the underlying cash market. It has also helped to diminish the market impact of mechanical bond index changes. But at the same time:

- It has very significantly increased credit risk exposure, and
- It has kept information about the distribution of credit risk mostly opaque.

The pros say that credit derivatives have given investors the ability to sample the debt markets and get exposure to the precise risks they want. Contrary to classical loans, the pros say, debt is no longer just plain vanilla, it is being designed into products investors find attractive.

Critics answer that, with the popularization of credit derivatives, global financial imbalance is widening and it is not expected to narrow significantly in the future. They also point to the fact that accumulation of credit risk by protection sellers has been a source of unease among central bankers and supervisory authorities.

The pros respond that, on the contrary, the financial system is more secure than ever before, because banks are not as vulnerable to the threat of corporate failures. Critics, however, have exactly the opposite opinion and they say that for those whose job is to dwell on financial worries, the corporate debt market is the place to be.

3.   Exposure associated with credit risk transfer

As credit risk transfer mechanisms, securitization and credit derivatives help to separate credit risks from the original transactions. They also render these transactions tradable in the wider market as self-standing financial instruments. That's the good news. The bad news is a growing credit risk accumulation in balance sheets of companies that have little or no experience in managing credit exposure:

- On the one hand, there is enough evidence that credit risk transfers can make a valuable contribution to the resilience of the banking system
- On the other hand, however, this credit risk is assumed by other market players, usually institutional investors, and it alters the balance in their books.

Moreover, available statistics indicate that the intermediary functions in risk transfer are typically concentrated on only a small number of bankers, who theoretically should have first-class risk management systems. In practice, however, this is far from certain, at least in many cases. Credit derivatives can trigger payment obligations equal to the entire nominal amount. Therefore, special care must be taken with appraisal of the risk involved in assuming a position.

As experience with credit risk control demonstrates, it is not enough to rely completely on ratings, because ratings are one-dimensional. Chapter 5 brought to the reader's attention a long list of other factors – which become even more important than in granting loans because, potentially, major credit exposures may remain opaque for a number of years. Some supervisors think that because of this the risk to the banking system may be significant, as more than 80% of credit derivatives trade is in the interbank market. The remainder is shared between insurance companies, hedge funds and some other entities.

From a broader market perspective, the aforementioned statistics mean that, contrary to the generally accepted notion, there is *no* broadly based transfer of credit risk out of the banking system or the market as a whole. As this information becomes available, some experts suggest that, in fact, it might be that exactly the opposite is taking place because credit derivatives:

- Make it easier to enter into short positions, and
- Speculate on deterioration of an entity's credit quality.

At the same time, a short position, however, requires that securities be borrowed in the spot market through repo transactions. Therefore, speculative transactions aiming to benefit from a company being downgraded by rating agencies are likely to operate through the market for credit derivatives.

Some experts also point out that extensive use of such instruments can accentuate the downside, and underline the greater volatility of the credit derivatives market as contrasted with the more traditional bond market. The upside is that, within the banking industry, securitization and credit derivatives allow the creditor to hedge against the default by the borrower. As such, they can be seen as a novel form of an insurance contract that:

- Separates credit risk from the original financing operation, and
- Transfers this credit risk to a third party, the *risk taker*.

Because a similar statement can be made with most securitized instruments, Basel II prescribes that banks must apply the securitization framework for determining regulatory capital requirements for exposures arising from traditional and synthetic securitizations or similar structures that contain features common to both. This is valid for a wide range of securitized instruments, including:

- Asset-backed securities
- Mortgage-backed securities
- Reserve accounts, such as cash collateral accounts
- Credit enhancements
- Interest rate or currency swaps
- Refundable price discounts
- Tranched cover and liquidity facilities, and more.

With the exception of securitization of exposures, for which no internal ratings-based (IRB) treatment of pool assets has been specified, and under the standardized approach for exposures with a non-investment grade rating of BB+, BB or BB−, no distinction is made between securitization exposures held by originators and those held by the risk takers.[8]

Within this overall perspective of securitization's risks and opportunities, the credit derivatives' goal is to make the separate credit risk marketable. Notice that this can also be done through existing insurance-type products, such as guarantees. One of the reasons credit derivatives are taking the upper ground is that mathematical analysis and information technology make it possible to:

- Try to isolate risks, and
- Combine them in different ways than those used traditionally.

One of the more important is lack of expertise in doing just that, because these derivative products must be marketable. Marketability requires a high degree of standardization, partly provided through the use of master agreements advanced by the International Swaps and Derivatives Association (ISDA) and partly by market response.

The prevailing opinion is that, as standardized and tradable financial instruments, credit derivatives expand their horizon of applications. Standardization relieves the need for individual verification, and tradability sees to it that risk vendors may not even have to own the obligation that they sell to risk takers; they may be acting purely as intermediary.

For seller, buyer and intermediary, risk management should be seen as an integral part of the cost of transferring credit exposure to third parties. For marketability and credit risk management purposes, the originator bank may initially transfer the credit risk arising from the underlying portfolio to an independent special purpose vehicle (SPV), thereby separating the credit risk on the securitized portfolio from other exposures that are its own.

In other cases, the reference obligations are not sold directly to the special purpose vehicle. Instead, they remain on the originator bank's balance sheet, along with the credit risk that they represent. Some practitioners believe that this is a negative, as far as diversification of credit exposure is concerned.

For the economy as a whole, high concentration of credit risk, which is generally characteristic of derivatives markets, is worrisome from a systemic risk viewpoint. In the opinion of some experts, the rapidly growing derivatives trades add to global financial imbalances, which, from a financial stability perspective, represent an important vulnerability for the global financial system – with disturbances leading to changes sparking large trade and price adjustments.

Central bankers also think that a potential withdrawal from the market by one or two of the major intermediary banks in derivatives is sure to result in a serious short-term liquidity risk. In many cases it is very difficult to distinguish a severe short-term illiquidity from a credit institution's insolvency, and the former might precipitate the latter.

4. Collateralized debt obligations

Collateralized debt obligations (CDOs) are issued by a special purpose vehicle (SPV) backed by pools of corporate loans, bonds and other debt titles from hundreds of different entities. These are bundled and sold to investors in much the same way as mortgages are turned into mortgage-backed securities (MBSs). They are structured financial products whose defining feature is that claims on the payment flow from the aforementioned pool of assets, which is:

- Split into various tranches with different risk and return profiles, and
- Designed in a way that each tranche is geared towards individual investor preferences in terms of risk and yield.

Unlike asset-backed securities (ABSs), CDOs are not backed by a large, rather homogeneous and granular pool of assets. Rather, what underpins them is a heterogeneous asset pool. Based on credit default swaps (CDSs, see section 5), synthetically created CDOs have become a popular vehicle for transferring corporate-related credit risk from the banking sector to other financial players.

The fact that several *tranches* of securities with different degrees of seniority in the event of bankruptcy are issued to investors allows re-engineering of the risk and return profile of the underlying collateral pool into different levels of exposure. The European Central Bank says that three elements are required to evaluate CDO tranches:[9]

- *Probability of default* (PD), within a given horizon such as one year
- *Loss-given default* (LGD), usually assumed to equal a constant percentage, i.e. 40%
- *Correlation*, the simultaneous link between the defaults of several entities included in the pool (Chapter 4).

In terms of mechanics, the first-loss tranche, known as *equity*, absorbs the risk of payment defaults, or delays. *Mezzanine*, the next highest tranche, will incur losses if the equity tranche is exhausted. Through this credit-enhancing technique, the *senior* tranche, which lies above the mezzanine, could achieve AAA rating even if the other tranches have a much lower one.

This layered structure sees to it that, as far as credit risk assumed by investors is concerned, defaults of assets from the collateral pool are initially incurred by the first-loss (lowest) tranche, which also features a higher interest rate. But after this tranche had been exhausted, the next tranche(s) will be called upon.

The pros say that CDOs are fairly secure instruments because losses in senior tranches occur only in the case of significant deterioration of credit quality of the asset pool. This means that senior tranches usually have a higher rating than the average rating of the securitized assets, but at the same time pay less interest than the more risky tranches. Sceptics answer that investors:

- Have no information other than the rating about the creditworthiness of entities in the pool, and
- Specifically absent is the *correlation* of default probability characterizing the underlying reference pool (more on this later).

A key task, therefore, is to establish the likelihood of an individual firm being unable to repay its debt – as determined by the distance between the value of its assets and the nominal value of its debt (Chapter 5) – followed by the correlation. The value of assets, which represents a measure of a firm's ability to repay its liabilities:

- Is modelled as a stochastic process, and
- Default is assumed to occur when a firm's assets are insufficient to cover its debt.

In exchange for good fees, many hedge funds are selling insurance against corporate defaults. If there is no default during the life of the contract, the seller pockets the fee. But in the event of a default, the seller must pay out the face value of the contract. To raise that money, the hedge fund must often sell its most liquid assets, sometimes in a falling market.

Distress selling by several hedge funds was, for instance, observed on 10 May 2005 and subsequent days. At the time, experts suggested that member states of euroland and their companies were extremely vulnerable to CDO crisis and panics in the general credit derivatives market, as 50% of all CDOs are euro denominated (and they continue to be so).

The June 2005 'Financial Stability Review' by the European Central Bank (ECB) had this to say on the May 2005 events:

'... The volatility implied in options prices remained at very low levels across several asset classes, possibly induced, in part, through an arbitrage process with credit spreads via collateralized debt obligation markets ... Moreover, the interplay between equity market volatility and credit spreads may have served to underpin a trend of rising leveraged credit investment – where *CDOs of CDOs* gained in popularity. This may have left credit derivatives markets vulnerable to adverse disturbances.'

The prevailing opinion is that CDOs contribute to the financial markets, but they also present new risks. However, there is a downside. From a financial stability viewpoint, regulators have expressed concerns about mispricing and inadequacies in risk management. Most importantly, supervisory authorities face challenges in tracking credit risk around the financial system.

On the positive side, CDOs can assist in mitigating asymmetric information problems that are present in single-name credit risk transfer markets. This represents a diversification of credit risk in a portfolio, making risk and return profiles less sensitive to the performance of individual obligors.

In the general case, the CDO tranche risk depends on the *correlation* of probability of default of the underlying reference pool:

- *If* there is a low default correlation,
- *Then* reference assets evolve relatively independently of each other in terms of credit quality.

This means that the probability distribution is centred on the expected portfolio loss. As we already saw, depending on their degree of subordination, individual CDO tranches react differently to correlation changes. Figure 6.1 provides the reader with a framework that includes all key factors with an impact on the performance of a CDO.

A risk-conscious investor should appreciate that subordinated CDO tranches are financial instruments with leverage, which need to be appropriately stress

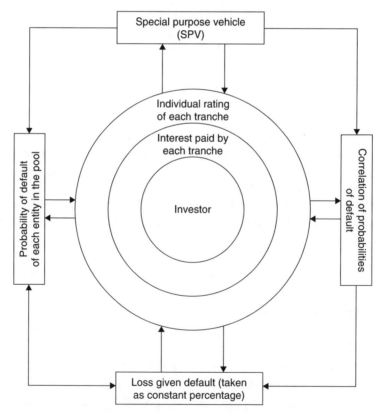

Figure 6.1   Framework chacterizing risk and return with collateralized debt obligation

tested for their risk and return characteristics prior to commitment. Depending on the volume of the tranche and position in the loss distribution:

- Decreases in value of the reference pool have a magnified impact on exposure, and
- This can quickly lead to considerable loss of the nominal amount of the tranche.

While the investor remains exposed to the deterioration of a leveraged instrument, the originator bank usually protects itself against downgrading in credit quality by selling *credit protection* in the credit derivatives market, for assets contained in the reference pool. As already mentioned, hedge funds are active in this market. Insurance companies are also protection sellers.

5. Credit default swaps

Credit default swaps (CDSs) are the most commonly traded credit derivatives. They function like a traded insurance contract against losses arising from a firm's bankruptcy, transferring the risk that a certain individual entity could default from the *protection buyer* to the *protection seller* in exchange for the payment of a premium.

The development of credit default swaps has increased the sophistication with which credit risk transfer can be approached. CDSs allow credit risk to be unbundled from other exposures embedded in a financial instrument and traded separately. In a CDS transaction, the buyer of credit protection pays to the seller a periodic fee, which generally reflects the spread between the:

- Yield on a defaultable security, and
- Risk-free interest rate of a G-10 government bond.

In a CDS transaction, this premium is expressed as an annualized percentage of the transaction's notional value, and constitutes the market quote for the CDS. In this sense, the CDS is an insurance contract protecting against losses arising from a default. Therefore:

- It is not surprising that insurance companies are quite active in the CDS market
- What is surprising is that they do so without necessarily appreciating the full amount of assumed credit risk.

In the event that the reference entity defaults, the buyer delivers to the seller debt owed by the defaulted entity, in return for a lump sum equal to the face value of the debt. Until credit risk transfer mechanisms have been developed, this kind of exposure was the domain and competence of commercial banks. Three basic types of recovery product are presently available on the market:

- *Ordinary CDS contracts.* With this instrument the value of protection is not known in advance. However, ordinary CDS contracts allow investors to separate recovery and default risk.
- *Fixed recovery CDSs*, also known as digital default swaps. Their characteristic is that the counterparties agree upon a recovery rate they will use after a credit event. A fixed recovery CDS buyer makes periodic payments to the seller, who provides protection to the buyer in case a credit event occurs.
- *Recovery locks*, or simple recovery swaps, where no cash flows are exchanged prior to a credit event. In the case of recovery locks, if a credit event occurs the seller delivers a defaulted obligation to the buyer in exchange for a pre-agreed fixed payment (specified in the contract), which represents the recovery value. Recovery swaps are quoted in terms of percentages of the notional principal amount and express the fixed recovery value that is exchanged after a credit event. Fixed recovery swaps and recovery swaps are closely linked.

Some people consider the more traditional credit default swaps as the 'plain vanilla' version of credit derivative instruments, probably because they are characterized by a simple algorithm, expressed in If … Then terms: *if* a given event takes place, *then* the protection seller must pay the agreed compensation to the protection buyer.

The pros answer that the concept of a swap is that simple, and by transferring credit risk from the protection buyer to the protection seller, ordinary credit default swaps have opened new business opportunities. Prior to them, it was not possible to short a loan; and moreover CDSs, which involve their own credit risk, help in price discovery:

- Price discovery is very important at a time when the market is in need of information about credit exposure, and
- The pricing of default swaps helps to reveal a great deal of market information about expected credit risk.

Theoretically, the price of a credit default swap is based on the financial service it provides – namely, insurance against companies defaulting on their financial obligations. In practice, this price is a market variable linked to investors' credit risk appetite and other characteristics of the market's behaviour.

Theoretically, recovery rates should be an important factor in determining the price of credit risk. When interest rates are rising and there is an increasing likelihood of general credit conditions worsening, a great deal of attention should be paid to recovery rates. Experts suggest that a CDS premium, which is an expression of views by market participants about the price of credit risk, should reflect both:

- Probability of default of the reference entity, and
- Expected recovery value, should a credit event occur.

Protection buyers, however, do not know in advance the amount they would receive following a credit event, leaving them exposed to uncertainty about the ultimate recovery rate. This tends to be less important for investment-grade CDSs, because variations in their expected recovery rates tend to be low, the standard recovery values also tend to be low and the standard recovery rate used by the industry in pricing is 40%.

The other side of the equation is that recovery rates tend to be cyclical, declining as economic conditions deteriorate. Changes in expected recovery values tend to be more relevant for lower credit quality names closer to default, because the actual recovery value of a defaulted security plays a crucial role in determining the actual returns earned by affected investors.

Additionally, risk management connected to credit default swaps should pay attention to *mismatches*. In order to be able to benefit from purchased protection, when a credit event occurs, the buyer of protection needs to deliver the appropriate amount of the defaulted reference entity's obligation to the original protection seller. Mismatches happen between:

- The amount of protection bought, and
- The volumes outstanding of the underlying debt instruments that could potentially be delivered.

An example is the case of Delphi, the car parts maker and former division of General Motors, which defaulted on its debts in 2005. As the company held an investment-grade rating until the end of 2004, it was referenced in a large number of CDS indices and CDO transactions. It was also among the most frequently traded names in the CDS market. The challenge was created by the fact that:

- The amount of protection bought was estimated at more than $25 billion
- But the volume of outstanding Delphi obligations, including loans and bonds, amounted to less than $5 billion.

Situations may arise whereby the prices of defaulted debt can soar to levels well above any reasonable recovery rate. When this happens, it can have broader negative implications, as they may distort the fundamental valuations of defaulted assets, create problems with the physical settlement of derivatives contracts, and dent the confidence market players have in the instrument.

6. The market for credit derivatives and its liquidity

In March 2005, the Bank for International Settlements (BIS) published its regular Triennial Central Bank Survey of Foreign Exchange and Derivatives Market Activity. One of the main findings of this survey was that, in comparison with the last survey conducted in 2001, both turnover and outstanding volumes had grown to new highs.

In the case of OTC derivatives, for example, outstanding notional amounts increased by 120% between June 2001 and June 2004, reaching $220 trillion in June 2004. This represents an increase of approximately 80%, after adjusting for currency movements.

A quite remarkable growth was recorded in the credit derivatives market, where volumes rose more than sixfold, from $700 billion to $4.5 trillion, in the same period. Credit default swaps accounted for most of this increase, largely due to:

- Standardization of contractual terms, and
- Establishment of CDS indices and trading platforms.

Since 2000, the market for CDOs and CDS took off rapidly in Europe, too, both in number of deals and in money terms. Experts say that one of the original reasons was regulatory capital arbitrage by loan-originating banks. Then the goal of trading in credit derivatives gradually moved away from balance sheet management to arbitrage CDOs, driven by a desire to exploit arbitrage opportunities between higher yielding assets and lower interest-bearing liabilities. Subsequently, a two-tier business opportunity has evolved:

- Customized market, and
- General, or public, market.

In the customized, bilateral market, portfolios are highly concentrated, which poses challenges for tracking this market's size and for monitoring market developments (see also Chapter 10). Investors in this market tend to be more sophisticated and rating agencies play a less crucial role than in the general market.

By contrast, the public market becomes increasingly standardized and features large granular portfolios. Not only is this market segment continuing to be rated, but also credit ratings are very important. Investors tend to be less sophisticated than in the customized market, and they rely on rating for risk assessment, as well as on pricing.

According to experts, liquidity plays a crucial role in the public market. Therefore, understanding and measuring market liquidity with credit risk transfer instruments is extremely important for all market participants. Not only does the level of liquidity matter, but also its volatility and the pattern of how it evolves as a consequence of:

- Market-driven, and
- Regulatory-driven developments.

Concern about liquidity with CDOs, CDSs and credit derivatives in general may look a little strange because liquidity has been boosted by the use of derivatives (and by carry trade). CRT instruments may still have a negative impact upon liquidity, particularly under conditions of market stress. To appreciate this reference we must distinguish between:

- Search liquidity, and
- Systemic liquidity.

During relatively quiet periods, the liquidity premium is driven by *search costs*. These are the costs incurred by traders and market makers in finding a willing buyer for an asset purchased, while the market maker/dealer is making markets in this asset. This is an asset-specific liquidity.

By contrast, systemic liquidity is linked to the degree of stress, if any, existing in a market. If all investors attempt to take the same positions at the same time, then the homogeneity of their behaviour will soak up liquidity. Disappearing systemic liquidity refers to negative liquidity conditions in the market as a whole.

Some experts suggest that the transfer of credit risk in portfolio form through synthetic CDOs and standardized CDSs can have a positive impact on systemic liquidity. Behind this opinion lies the hypothesis that portfolio instruments increase systemic liquidity by allowing a more general dispersion of credit risk across a diversified investor base. However, other experts disagree, saying that experience with these instruments is still in its infancy, and general statements are unwarranted.

More convergent opinions can be found regarding search liquidity. It seems likely that credit derivatives markets helped in reducing search costs by swamping hedging and funding costs. Until there is proof to the contrary, the prevailing opinion is that credit derivatives have the potential to:

- Boost search liquidity, and
- Strengthen the resilience of the corporate bond market to adverse events.

Support for the latter argument is provided by the use of plain vanilla credit derivatives in the aftermath of the General Motors and Ford credit rating downgrades in May 2005. At that time, in the aftermath of credit downgrades, corporate bond investors effectively unwound their exposures to these issuers.

On 31 May 2005, General Motors' and General Motors Acceptance Corp (GMAC)'s debt was transferred from investment-grade bond indices to junkland. Curiously, however, spreads on Merrill Lynch's high-grade American corporate index tightened, from 111 basis points over Treasuries in mid-May to 95. Spreads on junk bonds have also narrowed, by more.

Adding to the puzzle, GM's benchmark bond due in 2033 was selling for more than it did before the downgrade. 'The market has held up better than we expected,' said Michael Fuhrman, North American head of electronic trading at GFI Group, an interbroker dealer in credit swaps. He added that: 'Despite the turbulence, with moves five or six standard deviations away from what many models predicted, the CDS market enabled investors to transfer risk with no systemic problems.'[10]

This may be so, but it is no less true that a challenge facing regulators, and the market at large, is that the rapid growth in the OTC derivatives markets, of which credit derivatives have become a major segment, is *not* being matched by equivalent growth in investment in infrastructures for:

- Back office
- Risk management
- Clearing and settlement, and
- Servicing of the outstanding transactions until maturity.

The need to address infrastructural issues is made even more urgent from the point of view of their market positioning. Positions are used to offset the unwanted components of the risk with other market makers, but the more sophisticated the financial instruments, the greater the need for analysis and experimentation:

- Sometimes outstanding positions with other market makers often go in opposite directions, effectively cancelling each other out
- Even so, however, they still need to be kept in the dealers' books and serviced.

It is no secret that problems of extensive credit line utilization and of insufficient back-office capacity have been aggravated by credit derivatives. The issues such problems pose have to be addressed from different angles to satisfy the requirements of all market players. Accountants can play a key role in the process of enabling senior management to be in charge, and a similar statement is valid about the role of technologists.

Notes

1 D.N. Chorafas, *Economic Capital Allocation with Basel II: Cost and Benefit Analysis*. Butterworth-Heinemann, London, 2004.
2 European Central Bank, Financial Stability Review, Frankfurt, December 2006.
3 The term used by the Basel Committee is 'credit risk mitigation' (CRM).
4 Which consist of large pools of CDSs.
5 *EIR*, 27 May 2005.
6 *EIR*, 14 October 2005.
7 *The Economist*, 1 July 2006.
8 Basel Committee, 'Instructions for QIS5'. BIS, Basel, July 2005.
9 European Central Bank, Financial Stability Review, Frankfurt, December 2006.
10 *The Economist*, 18 June 2005.

7

Market Risk

1. Market risk defined

Market risk refers to the risk of potential loss arising from adverse effects due to changes in interest rates, currency exchange rates, equity prices and other relevant market variables, like commodity prices. In the background of such price changes is volatility, but a transaction or position (Chapter 8) may also be exposed to a number of other risks that impact upon the fair value of financial instruments – for instance, liquidity, economic conditions, inflation, political and social upheaval, war and so on.

Since the 1970s, companies have selectively managed these exposures through the use of derivative instruments. As regards foreign exchange risk, for example, the objective is to protect their cash flows related to sales or purchases of goods or services from market fluctuations in currency rates. However, the derivative instruments themselves include market risk, and much depends on:

* The type of instrument used for hedging
* Its time horizon
* Its market cycles, and
* The fact that the hedging may be asymmetrical.

Several crucial questions must be answered prior to deciding on how to hedge market risk. For instance: Do we use a correct measure of risk? Are we appropriately tracking our market risk exposure? How can we improve our prognostication of market shifts? Which specific instruments may help us in hedging their after-effect?

Market risk is incurred through trading activities and inventoried positions. In the banking industry, it arises primarily from market making, client facilitation, proprietary positions in equities, fixed income products, foreign exchange products and other commodities.

Expected losses from market risk are reflected in the valuation of the institution's portfolio, which is the theme of Chapter 8. Adjustments to fair value are the result of market volatility, price uncertainties, lack of liquidity, absence of investor interest, inventoried positions and other factors.

Since the 1996 Market Risk Amendment, *statistical loss* is measured using value at risk (VAR), which expresses potential loss on the current portfolio assuming a specified time horizon. Value at risk is measured at the 99% level of confidence (Chapter 4), on one-day and ten-day holding periods.[1]

VAR estimates are based on either a parametric approach or historical simulation. The goal is that of assessing the impact of market movements on the current portfolio, based on at least five years of historical data. Theoretically, one-day VAR exposure expresses the maximum daily mark-to-market loss the institution is likely to incur at the 99% confidence level on the current portfolio:

- Under normal market conditions, with
- A larger loss being statistically likely only once in 100 business days.

This 'maximum daily loss' is an overstatement. It is wrong because the 99% level of confidence VAR leaves out 1% of expected losses, usually at the long leg of the risk distribution. As it also includes unexpected losses, this 1% may have an awfully large impact. VAR is anyway a weak model for market risk, originally developed (in the early 1990s) at the request of the Morgan Bank's CEO, who at 4.15 p.m. every afternoon wanted to have a snapshot of his bank's market risk exposure.

Stress testing (section 6) is a superior tool because it permits assessment of extreme events against a set of scenarios. Values reflecting stress moves in market variables may be derived from severe historical events, or be based on prospective crisis scenarios developed from the current economic situation and perceived macroeconomic trends.

Therefore, it is not surprising that well-governed institutions keep stress factors under continuous review, enhanced when necessary to reflect changing market and economic conditions. Regulators promote stress tests because they know that stress loss scenarios contribute to better management by:

- Helping to prevent undue concentrations (see also stress tests for credit risk in Chapter 5)
- Assisting in establishing limits in exposure to individual market risk variables, and
- Making possible experimentation on price volatility, as well as on market depth and liquidity.

The rub is that to develop and use advanced market risk models, a bank must have both rocket scientists and the appropriate internal culture. This is starting to happen. Five years ago, such a bank would have been a rare bird – but not today. The circle of credit institutions that can benefit from eigenmodels increases, even if only the bigger banks have so far been advocates of advanced market risk control methods.

Experience shows the wisdom of making market risk tests an integral part of the market risk definition. Based on both VAR output and stress tests, scenario analysis permits estimation of the potential immediate loss after normal and

extreme changes in market parameters. Hypothetical scenarios provide an opportunity for:

- Exploring a range of likely market behaviour
- Integrating the results of, say, interest rate sensitivities with default risk
  and economic conditions.

A testing methodology for market risk more advanced than VAR is always important, but it is a 'must' with derivative financial instruments, as it can be instrumental in their correct pricing. 'I believe some intermediaries are writing 30-year
options,' said a central banker at a risk management symposium. 'Quite how confident anyone can be that the premium received for such options is an adequate
reward for the risks taken is a subject which falls into my personal knowledge gap.'

People with a significant background in pricing derivative financial instruments
suggest that many pricing hypotheses prove to be wrong and, therefore, all of
them should be carefully tested. Moreover, the longer the maturity:

- The greater the risk factor that should be applied, and
- The higher the level of confidence that must be chosen.

At longer maturities, for instance 10 years, at the 99% confidence level market
risk tends to be an asymptote to 100% of a given risk factor – whichever may be
its value. Not many financial institutions account for this fact, whether or not it
is present in their transactions, their trading book and their investment portfolio
(Chapter 8).

In conclusion, even if the approach a bank has taken in estimating its market
risk exposure provides a workable framework, there is little doubt that this can
be improved in terms of accuracy through more powerful tests, greater skills and
high technology, as well as senior management's insistence that methods, tools
and organizational structures for risk control are steadily reviewed and improved.

2. Trading book risk

Market risk affects both the trading book and investment portfolio positions. This
is true of all traded assets and liabilities, including debt and equity securities,
derivative instruments, loans, commodities, and other newer types of assets like
credit for carbon emissions. These assets and liabilities are classified into two
major groups: *hedges* and those held for *trading purposes*. The difference is based
on management's intent for each individual item.

In the past, prior to accounting standards like GAAP and IFRS, conservative banks accounted for their inventoried instruments on the basis of the lower of original cost or current price (the latter being rather liberally defined). For inventoried wares, the accounting rule offered three options:

- First in, first out (FIFO)
- Last in, first out (LIFO), or
- Weighted average of prices.

Today, for security transactions recorded on a trade date basis and mapped into the accounting book, the options are: original value (cost) or fair value. *Fair value* is defined as the price agreed by knowledgeable willing parties in an arm's length transaction, under conditions other than an involuntary liquidation or distressed sale. The difference is in management intent:

- A hedge that management intends to keep to maturity is carried in the books at original value
- A transaction resulting in an asset or liability held for trading must be accounted for in fair value.

Quoted market prices are used when available to measure the instrument's fair value. This is known as *marking to market*. If quoted market prices are not available, fair value is estimated using valuation models that consider prices for similar assets or similar liabilities, or alternatively by simulating the commodity's value. This is known as *marking to model*:

- Marking to model always considers a functioning market, not the case of panics
- Yet, it is in the case of a panic that a given portfolio may become nearly worthless overnight.

Marking to model is necessary because many instruments, like over-the-counter (OTC) derivatives, have no quoted market price. If marked to model, their market risk is expressed as a change in the price of the *underlier* plus some other factors, such as time and price. For instance, a forward obliges one party to buy and the other party to sell the underlying instrument at a specified time and price. However, it is sensible to keep in mind that the market price can be quite different at exercise time.

Changes in the value of derivatives held for trading have to be proportionate to changes in the price of the underlier, but not necessarily in a linear fashion. Also, market risk of an option-based derivative can be much more complex to model, because it depends on factors affecting option valuation, such as:

- The option's exercise price
- Time remaining to expiration
- Volatility of the underlier, and so on.

Securities borrowed and securities loaned that are cash collateralized are included in the balance sheet at amounts equal to the cash advanced or received. If securities received in a transaction as collateral are sold or re-pledged, they are recorded as securities received as collateral, and a corresponding liability to return the security is also recorded. Fees and interest received or paid are recorded in 'Interest and dividend income' and 'Interest expense' respectively, on an accrual basis.

Purchases of securities under resale agreements (reverse repurchase agreements) and securities sold under agreements to repurchase substantially identical securities (repurchase agreements) are treated as collateralized financing transactions, and carried at the amount of cash disbursed or received respectively:

- Reverse repurchase agreements are recorded as collateralized assets
- Repurchase agreements are recorded as liabilities, with the underlying securities sold continuing to be recognized in 'Trading assets' or 'Investment securities'.

Assets and liabilities recorded under the above-mentioned agreements are accounted for on an accrual basis, with interest earned on reverse repurchase agreements and interest incurred on repurchase agreements reported in 'Interest and dividend income' and 'Interest expense' respectively. Reverse repurchase and repurchase agreements are netted *if*:

- They are with the same counterparty
- They have the same maturity date
- They settle through the same clearing institution, and
- They are subject to the same master netting agreement.

A bank's accounting rules and regulations must comply to both Basel II and IFRS. Accounting entries necessarily reflect changes associated with risk estimates and capital requirements, with reference to the trading book, as these aim to clarify the types of exposures qualifying for capital charge, as well as providing guidance on prudent valuation.

Changes effected by new regulations for the trading book include the exclusion of a limited number of positions from a trading book capital charge, because they are subject to capital requirements under credit risk or securitization frameworks of the new capital adequacy requirements. At the same time, such changes have brought explicit requirements for prudent valuation methods for trading book positions.

Changes under Basel II's Pillar 1 (capital adequacy clauses) also include the updating of standardized specific risk charges for sub-investment-grade government debt positions and non-qualifying debt positions. They also incorporate revisions to qualifications and treatment for modelling of:

- Specific risk
- Default likelihood, and
- Event risk.

There is also a Pillar 1 requirement that banks using internal models incorporate stress testing in their Pillar 2 (national supervisory requirements) internal capital assessment. Capital requirements, connected to trading book positions, target instruments held with trading intent for short-term resale, and/or with the intent of benefiting from actual or expected short-term price movements, or to lock in arbitrage profits.

This definition prevents any positions that are not financial instruments from being booked in the trading book. It also specifies that an instrument having the nature of an exposure that is other than short term, or that constitutes a hedge for regulatory capital purposes of a banking book credit risk exposure, should not be included in the trading book. Correspondingly, Pillar 2 clauses seek to strengthen banks' assessment of their internal capital adequacy for market risk, taking into account the output of their:

- VAR model
- Stress tests, and
- Valuation adjustments.

Basel II Pillar 2 standards require that banks demonstrate that they hold enough internal capital to withstand a range of severe but plausible market shocks. Internal capital assessments include an evaluation of market concentration and liquidity risks under stressed conditions, as well as market risks that are not adequately captured in a VAR model. For example:

- Gapping of price
- One-way markets
- Jumps to defaults
- Non-linear/deep out-of-the-money products
- Significant shifts in correlations (Chapter 4), and so on.

In order to keep trade book risk under control, new Pillar 2 rules require that banks demonstrate to their supervisor that they combine their different risk measurement techniques in an appropriate system; also that their way of arriving at overall internal capital assessment for their market exposure is sound.

Rules concerning Basel II's Pillar 3 (market discipline) seek to improve the robustness of trading book disclosures, requiring that banks inform about their internal capital allocation for the trading portfolio, disclose qualitative information on trading book valuation techniques, and demonstrate the soundness of standards used for modelling purposes – as well as make transparent the methodologies they used to achieve a rigorous internal capital adequacy assessment.

'In politics you judge the value of a service by the amount you put in. In business you judge it by the amount you get out,' suggests Margaret Thatcher.[2] The new rules for trading book risk aim to improve the amount banks get out of trading but make their risk management system more rigorous. This benefits all of the bank's stakeholders.

3.   Challenges to valuation of the trading book

Since the 1996 Market Risk Amendment, to capture the market risk arising from their trading book, banks use either an advanced eigenmodel approach or value at risk, which remains a regulatory reporting requirement. Experience based on years of implementation has, however, demonstrated that VAR cannot fully capture all trading book risks, particularly those characterized by:

- Changes in correlations and volatilities
- Intra-day trading activities
- Exposures arising from exceptional market cases
- Exposures at the long tail of a risk distribution, and
- Specific risk associated with the credit quality of securities issuers.

Moreover, the recognition that there also exists *model risk*, associated with all mathematical artefacts, has led the Basel Committee to require that banks multiply VAR results by a factor of 3 to arrive at a more appropriate capital charge, or more than that if results of back testing don't meet regulatory standards. Also, to increase this VAR multiplier to 4 for specific risk, if they cannot appropriately capture:

- Event risk (Chapter 9), and
- Default risk (Chapter 5).

Critics say that the 4× multiplier has created a disincentive for banks to improve their own risk models in order to capture better default and event risks, because this would generally result in higher capital charges. Another shortcoming of VAR is its limitations in addressing concentrations of market risk, which:

- Diminishes banks' ability to diversify market risk factors
- Renders opaque the contribution of industry sectors, and
- Opens the gates of contagion to an institution's market risk exposure.

The pros say that concentrations are captured in some VAR applications by adjusting correlation coefficient factors for the same issuer, across products. This argument forgets that banks are not very strong in computing correlations (Chapter 4) and therefore an added value tool would be welcome. The use of a liquidity-adjusted VAR for long-term equity holdings has apparently given commendable results.

Moreover, as we saw in Chapter 5, well-managed banks are sensitive to exposures to both single names and industry sectors. Therefore, they see to it that such exposures are captured at trading desk level across products. Aggregating single-name and industry sector trading exposures is, however, a challenging job, particularly so when:

- Combining cash and derivative positions
- Integrating equity and credit instruments
- Unbundling baskets of assets, and
- Decomposing risk components of an asset, such as interest rate, forex rate, credit spread and so on.

To make matters more complex, since 1996 plenty of credit risk-related products have been booked in the trading book. Examples are credit default swaps (CDSs) and tranches of collateralized debt obligations. As explained in Chapter 6, such instruments may lead to a concomitant rise in default and jump-to-default risk. Both have proved difficult to capture adequately with VAR.

Additionally, a growing number of inventoried instruments held in the trading book are generally not liquid, giving rise to risks that are very difficult to track, monitor and measure with VAR. In fact, not only VAR as a model, but also the trading definition itself is challenged by instruments for which liquidity is questionable and/or that are held for medium-term periods. Examples are:

- Credit-related products, such as loans, bonds, CDOs and other credit derivatives, and
- Exotic derivatives like long-term foreign exchange and interest rate swaps, equity swaps, weather derivatives and the like.

The importance of these references is magnified by the fact that while ten years ago such trading transactions were more or less the exception, today their number is fast growing. In the sample of banks participating in a recent study by the Basel Committee, the instruments outlined in the above two bullets represented up to 15% of institutions' trading book contents.

The years of VAR utilization have led regulators to the conclusion that the model answers some of their requirements, while for others it has limitations or is not quite appropriate. Another factor is the lack of standards for modelling specific risk, which has led to wide disparities in the robustness of models required by national supervisors.

In the aftermath of VAR's inability to capture market risk associated with new financial instruments, regulators seem to have concluded that there is a need for better valuation methodologies, including closer interaction with new accounting standards, their interpretation and their practical implementation. One of the basic regulatory requirements, where accounting plays a key role, is that of evaluating the adequacy of capital treatment for less liquid positions currently held in the trading book.

With 'The Application of Basel II to Trading Activities and the Treatment of Double Default Effects',[3] the Basel Committee intends to improve the identification of assumed market risk and of associated capital estimates. This is done by enhancing the risk sensitivity of methods used for assessing risks within the trading book, by specializing them as Pillar 1, Pillar 2 and Pillar 3.

When there is a market for inventoried trading book positions, generally banks mark derivatives to the mid-market price, making adjustments to take into account close-out costs, illiquidity, spread model risk and the like. However, there is no general rule for such adjustments and, hence, they differ across markets, jurisdictions and institutions. Some banks assume a short valuation horizon of about two weeks, while others adopt a longer horizon.

Research by the Basel Committee brought into perspective that most banks face valuation challenges for complex derivatives, or transactions that do not have readily available market inputs.[4] Examples are products with long-term volatility, distressed assets and illiquid instruments like emerging market bonds, which are infrequently traded. Other examples are products with non-linear risks, structured instruments, high yield debt and weather derivatives. For these, most banks infer the value by using:

- Proxies
- Stress tests

- Stress scenarios, and
- Different add-ons.

All these bullets are used to supplement VAR measures. For example, stress tests have become useful sources of information on jump-to-default risk on credit products, as well as in monitoring liquidity risk on exotic interest-rate instruments. In the judgement of banks participating in this 2005 Basel survey, marking to market can be a challenging task for positions where valuation is dependent on unobserved implied correlations or volatilities, as well as where liquidity of the market is an issue.

4. Interest rate risk and organizational risk

Experience shows that many balance sheets are left exposed to interest rate risk, as changes in long-term interest rates translate into a change in *net present value* (NPV) of liabilities inventoried in an entity's portfolio. In order to lessen the impact of interest rate risk, assets backing the liabilities' position should be chosen so that they broadly match the duration and convexity of these liabilities.[5]

The challenge is to execute according to this principle. For instance, in the euro zone there are few bonds available with maturities beyond ten years, making it difficult to eliminate balance sheet interest rate sensitivities, which have proved to be challenging. One way is to turn to equities, with the dual purpose of:

- Longer-term hedging of liabilities, and
- As a means to increase yields on the investment portfolio.

However, when equity markets tumble, as happened in 2000 and 2001, the losses on equity holdings strain the company's solvency and its reserves are eroded. For this reason, some entities react to their growing balance sheet mismatches by seeking higher returns in the credit derivatives market, but their portfolio becomes more risky.

Common sense has it that all inventoried debt instruments are less exposed to market risk, but this is not 100% true, particularly when fixed interest rates are subject to interest rate risk. In the loans book, for instance, apart from credit risk there is interest rate exposure because of fixed interest rate loans. For internal management accounting purposes, but not for regulatory reporting:

- Interest rate risk is sometimes weeded out of the loans book through internal interest rate swaps, and
- It is switched into the trading book, where it is marked to market along with other derivative instruments.

Underpinning dynamic hedging strategies, *interest rate derivatives* are a frequently used tool for hedging and profit making. Interest rate options and interest rate swaps are popular instruments. Two factors have contributed to the growth of *interest rate swaps* (IRS) and *interest rate futures* among credit institutions and investment banks:

- The significant growth of the market for fixed-income obligations, and
- The volatility of interest rates, which over the last 15 years has increased as they are now used for monetary policy reasons.

In the case of an interest rate swap, the counterparties swap interest payments on a given notional principal amount. This mainly involves fixed payments linked to a short-term interest rate. For central government, the advantage of using a swap contract is that it can separate the interest risk associated with issuing a bond from liquidity risk. This enables conversion of a ten-year fixed-rate bond into a debt at money market conditions.[6]

All players trading in interest rate futures and interest rate swaps need to perfectly understand the yield relationship implicit in the term structure of interest rates, which underpins the *yield curve*. A yield curve is plotted against the default-free yield of government securities:

- At a given moment in time
- With different terms to maturity.

The market for *interest rate options* is flourishing, accounting for about 70% of financial options traded worldwide – and it is the largest segment of the entire derivative financial instruments market. (The term 'interest rate options' also covers options on bonds and on bond futures.) Their pricing is a challenging and often dangerous job, because they are based on estimates of *future volatility*, which may be subject to conflicts of interest. Other things being equal:

- The lower the projected future volatility, the lower will be the options price, and
- The lower is their price the better these options will sell, but *if* volatility is misjudged, *then* the options writer may face a torrent of red ink.

In trading jargon, this irrational expectation of lower volatility is known as *volatility smile*. It flourishes when volatility projections are guesswork, based on hope or are outright manipulations. A trading desk can use the volatility smile to distort the value of options, swaps and other instruments. The usual strategy is to convince management that one is documented in expecting that volatility will subside – hence, a cheering up.

Mispricing errors also happen because of organizational failures, such as building up firewalls that isolate different departments, and the opposite, the mixing up of duties. Everybody knows that those who trade should *not* also be responsible for back-office work, as happened with Nick Leeson at Barings, causing the venerable bank to go bankrupt. But few banks really establish *and police* the necessary separation procedures between front desk and back office.

Companies that put deals together might be knowledgeable about current volatility, but realistic estimates regarding future volatility are not always free of bias. To assure that there is a separation between traders and accountants, several central banks have been promoting the creation of a *middle office* endowed with risk management functions. Sometimes, this middle office uses external agents to check pricing; this, however, is not foolproof.

In March 1997, NatWest Markets, the investment banking arm of National Westminster Bank, paid the volatility smile that led it to misprice its options. The bank's controllers first found a £90 million ($170 million) hole in its accounts, which quickly grew to £300 million ($570 million) and beyond. As was stated at the time:

- Risk management in the middle office did not have good enough computer models, and
- The bank had accepted brokers' estimates of volatility, which turned out to be overgenerous.

Eventually, NatWest sold bits and pieces of its investment banking subsidiary and was itself acquired by Royal Bank of Scotland. If financial institutions learned anything from what happened, it is that *volatile instruments* like derivatives produce exposure that may resonate throughout the entire enterprise. Management oversight can be very costly.

Market acceptance of interest rate derivatives documents that interest rate risk is manageable, provided one knows very well what he or she is doing. Additionally, to prognosticate adverse effects on their balance sheet, and therefore be able to act, companies must monitor their exposure to interest rate changes very carefully, including the able use of stress tests.

Credit institutions may also be exposed to valuation risk on their investment and trading portfolio, as well as to the risk of an adverse impact of interest rate changes on the demand for credit. Credit quality and customers' ability to service debt may also be affected by interest rate changes. Other exposures are:

- *Optionality*, such as prepayment of assets in the banking book or off-balance sheet items, and
- *Basis risk*, which arises from imperfect correlation in the adjustment of rates earned and paid on different instruments with otherwise similar repricing characteristics.

Measuring valuation risk in banking books requires detailed information on remaining maturities as well as purchasing prices. It is also necessary to assess valuation risks in fixed income trading portfolios. Both types of information are rather scarce at the present time, because institutions have not taken the necessary steps to restructure their accounting systems.

5. Interest rate risk and foreign exchange risk

Interest rate risk and foreign currency exchange (forex) risk are two of the principal market risks that can hit an industrial firm, bank, insurance company, pension fund or asset management entity. All sorts of organizations have cash flow obligations to meet, and part of the investments they make as a 'war chest' are exposed to volatility of these two (and more) market risk factors:

- In the global marketplace, bonds are subject to interest rate risk and currency risk
- The value of stocks fluctuates as a result of equity price risk, and also of currency risk in the case of international investments, and
- Both debt instruments and equities are exposed to other risk factors like country risk, against which investors must always be able to reposition themselves.

A portfolio of investments, and most particularly a leveraged portfolio, can face trying times by being exposed to several market risks at once – particularly so as in the globalized economy there are many financial instruments: interest rates, currency exchange rates, equities and all sorts of derivatives are popular investment vehicles.

In principle, British investors can hedge against exchange rate risk by converting their future payment amount disbursed on their pound denominated investment into dollars in advance through covered interest parity. The principle underpinning this hedge states that the ratio between the forward and spot rates of the pound/dollar exchange rate must equal that between the interest factors of investments in the two currencies:

- Theoretically, returns on a domestic pound investment and a foreign dollar investment hedged by a forward transaction are equal
- In practice, market anomalies see to it that they are not; hence they are vulnerable to arbitrage exploiting interest rate differentials and/or forex differentials for profit.

Investors tend to favour covered interest rate parity. By contrast, speculators usually choose uncovered interest rate parity, connected to cross-border capital flows. Covered interest parity investments, however, have to be managed. This is done by comparing for each trading day the relationship between forward and spot pound/dollar exchange rates to the interest rate factors for three-month money market funds between America and Britain. (Mathematically, this can be tested by regressing the exchange rate ratio on the interest rate ratio.)

Uncovered interest rate parity implies that expected pound exchange rate depreciation vs. the dollar can be virtually matched by a correspondingly higher rate of interest from an investment in Britain compared to an investment in the USA.

- *If* a speculator does not hedge a transaction on the forward market
- *Then* resulting profit or loss hinges on future changes in spot exchange rate.

The model that addresses simultaneously interest rate and forex rate risk must be sophisticated. A British investor will earn more on a US investment than on a comparable investment in his or her country as long as a US interest rate advantage is not neutralized by a depreciation of the American dollar against the British pound. Under these circumstances:

- *If* one bases investment decisions on this strategy, he or she will weigh the portfolio more heavily in favour of US debt instruments
- On the other hand, *if* a majority of investors follows the approach to preferring US debt, this will result in significant capital export to the USA and will have other consequences.

Based on the late 18th century hypothesis by Thomas Reber Malthus with rats, cats and old maids, an appreciable trend towards dollar-denominated bonds will tend to have two consequences. One is falling interest rates in the USA, reflecting a rise in the price of debt instruments (which has been happening widely, with Chinese and Japanese buying US Treasuries and other dollar-denominated bonds). The other is an appreciation of the dollar, but:

- *If* the fundamentals remain unchanged
- *Then* this will lead to expectations that the US dollar will depreciate.

According to Malthusian theory, uncovered interest parity theory claims that in the medium term a state of equilibrium will be reached. In this, the expected returns on an unhedged investment in foreign currency should match those of a comparable investment in domestic currency. Will it?

In practical terms, in the early years of the 21st century the pound/dollar has not necessarily followed this hypothesis, as attested by the mid-August 2005 appreciation of the pound while British interest rates moved south and US interest rates went north. The Malthusian hypothesis is further shattered if one observes that the euro/dollar exchange rate tended to run counter to the interest rate differential.

This does not necessarily mean that Malthus got it wrong; it might have been right in his time, but after more than 200 years many things have changed. When this happens, theories sometimes turn on their head. In this particular case a significant risk premium has to be added to uncovered interest parity. On average, this means that a given interest rate advantage of a foreign investment should exceed the expected rate of appreciation of domestic currency by the amount of the risk premium required at transaction time.

This is, of course, a hypothesis that has to be tested. A fairly common test would be to assess the impact on currency rates of an upturn in long-term interest rates of the magnitude seen in 1994, when yields on US ten-year bonds increased from 5.8% to 8.1%, an impressive 230 basis points within a short period. For global banks another interesting test is that of a matrix of simultaneous interest rate and currency exchange changes in regard to their impact on their assets and liabilities.

With many instruments, *mismatch risk* should be a focal point. Also known as repricing risk, mismatch is the risk that banks' interest expenses will increase by more than interest receivables when interest rates change. Its origin lies in maturity mismatches between assets and liabilities. In foreign exchange, commercial banks face mismatch risk when they transfer money from one country to another for lending and investments, then they want to repatriate this money. That's why management often tries to raise money for loans locally.

6. Stress tests for market risk

Well-governed financial institutions regularly conduct stress tests in order to better evaluate the market risk they have assumed. Several research projects have revealed that there is a great deal of diversity in the way banks apply stress tests for market risk. As the careful reader will recall from previous references, the method I suggest involves simulating the effects of outliers, yet conceivable situations could potentially occur on:

- On-balance sheet, and
- Off-balance sheet positions sensitive to market risk.

The aim of these stress tests would be to provide a basis for judging whether the institution has sufficient capital to withstand the assumed stress situations. Provided they relate to the most significant market risks the bank is facing, in interest rate risk, currency exchange rate risk, equity price risk, commodities risk and derivatives risk, the results may be quite revealing.

Take equity price risk as an example. The bank's investment portfolio has equities accounted for under the cost method, as well as equity investments in publicly held companies that are classified as available for sale. The latter securities are exposed to price fluctuations and are generally (though not always) concentrated in more volatile entities, such as high-technology and communications firms, many of which may be small capitalization stocks.

Many credit institutions do not hedge their equity price risk, while others use equity derivative financial instruments (that are themselves subject to equity price risks) to complement their investment strategies – or simply for hedging reasons. Unhedged equity portfolios must be subjected to regular stress tests, which may be of two kinds:

- Percentage change in equity price, and
- n standard deviations from the mean of the distribution.

The first method examines the consequences of a 10% and 20% adverse change in equity prices, along with the financial loss that would result in fair value of available-for-sale securities and proprietary portfolio. A frequently used, rather simple model assumes a corresponding shift in all equity prices. This may be good for small banks and individual investors.

Because equity prices of individual companies are dispersed across many different industries, which do not always move in the same direction, a more sophisticated stress testing model would vary the percentage change by industry sector.

This approach may be based on historical or hypothetical downside price pressure. A similar approach is applicable with other commodities. (In the first week of January 2007, the price of oil fell by 9% and pulled along the equity price of quoted oil companies.)

Examples of historical events affecting equities are the crash of the NYSE in 1987, Japan in 1990–2004, East Asia and South Korea in 1997, dotcoms and telecoms in 2000, Enron in 2001, Global Crossing and WorldCom in 2002. International references on stock market behaviour are important because large, globally operating banks generally have equity holdings spread over several markets, including emerging countries.

The crash of the New York Stock Exchange in October 1987 provides a good reference for stress tests based on the long leg of the risk distribution, because it was a *14.5* standard deviations event. Other stock market downturns are *10s* events and they occur every few years (for which traditional approaches to market risk estimates, like VAR, are utterly inadequate). Among stress tests, the more sophisticated are incorporating the roles played by:

- Market makers
- Traders, and
- Investors.

Stress testing for interest rate risk concentrates on various types of yield curve shifts, accounting for the fact that institutions hedged against a rise in interest rates act upon the expectation of rising yields by taking short interest rate positions or buying put options. Among larger credit institutions, the importance of short interest rate positions and the use of put options has increased significantly over the last four years.

A different way of looking at this reference is that market risk stress tests should reflect a bank's prevailing conditions, not abstract cases. For instance, long interest rate positions are predominant among smaller and medium-sized banks, and this indicates that they are pursuing a more traditional buy-and-hold strategy.

Exchange traded futures can also benefit from stress tests. Given the likelihood that, with extreme events margins risk being exhausted, in calculating margins for individual futures positions several clearing houses now set them at a level that will provide protection against 99% of one-day price movements. They make an estimate of the appropriate margin level by inspecting the distribution of price movements over recent months. This 99%, however, does not always provide an adequate estimate of the size of future extreme price moves because spikes at the long leg of the distribution are left out.

Table 7.1   A bank's exposure to loans and derivative risks, with standard VAR and stress testing (note the difference)

	Loans	Derivatives	Total
Standard VAR	30	**100**	130
Stress analysis	70	1400	1470

Clearers adjust their formerly empirical estimates with the likelihood that previously observed extreme moves are likely to be repeated, and they also account for the potential impact of possible future events, which is essentially a stress test. The use of Extreme Value Theory (EVT) provides a way of estimating the potential for extreme market moves, and is therefore a useful framework for assessing the adequacy of clearing house resources.

For all types of financial institutions, an important family of stress tests is that which targets a bank's ability to withstand simultaneous shock assumed in equity prices, interest rates and currency exchange rates under different levels of volatility. In addition to this, a methodology is also needed to model:

- Information asymmetries
- Behavioural biases, and
- Uncertainties in price inference.

All three bullets represent crucial considerations in a rigorous testing policy, and can be studied through simulations involving exposure to derivative financial instruments. Because derivatives are leveraged, stress test results magnify the after-effect of adversity. Table 7.1 presents an example of a credit institution's exposure connected to loans and derivatives under standard VAR and stress conditions, though only at $5s$ (derivatives exposure under VAR is taken as equal to 100).

Notes

1   For a detailed discussion on VAR shortcomings, see D.N. Chorafas, *Modelling the Survival of Financial and Industrial Enterprises: Advantages, Challenges, and Problems with the Internal Rating-Based (IRB) Method*. Palgrave/Macmillan, London, 2002.
2   Margaret Thatcher, *The Downing Street Years*. Harper Collins, London, 1993.
3   Basel Committee, *Trading Book Survey: A Summary of Responses*. BIS, Basel, 2005.
4   Basel Committee, *Trading Book Survey: A Summary of Responses*. BIS, Basel, 2005.
5   D.N. Chorafas, *The Management of Bond Investments and Trading of Debt*. Butterworth-Heinemann, London, 2005.
6   Deutsche Bundesbank, Monthly Report, October 2006.

Position Risk

1. Position risk defined

When a bank concludes a transaction, it assumes an obligation whose value will increase or shrink throughout its duration, depending on its particular characteristics, investor appeal and the market behaviour relative to it. Correspondingly, this rise or fall in value reflects itself into recognized but unrealized gains and losses.

- If a long position becomes more valuable, counterparty risk will grow
- If the position's value moves south, counterparty risk decreases but market risk increases.

A position in a bank's or investor's portfolio may be long or short. The term *long* describes a producer, trader or investor who has bought an actual commodity. *Short* reflects the condition of people and entities who have an obligation to deliver the commodity but do not own it. Hence, they will have to borrow it or buy it at a later date.

The careful reader will remember that positions may be taken for *trading* or for longer-term holding (including hedging) reasons. Interest rates, currency exchange rates, derivative products, oil and base metals are examples of positions often residing in the trading book, and typically classified as *available for sale*.

Securities for longer-term investments may be instruments (including derivatives) classified as *held to maturity*. Bonds, equities, precious metals and other commodities are examples for which management has the intent and ability to hold in the portfolio. In IFRS and GAAP general accounting:

- Held-to-maturity positions are classified as such, and carried at amortized cost net of any unamortized premium or discount
- Debt and equity securities, as well as other commodities classified as available for sale, are carried at fair value, by marking to market or model.

Under the rules of regulatory (general) accounting, unrealized gains and losses, which represent the difference between fair value and amortized cost, are properly recorded and usually reported net of income taxes; the exact method of financial report is evidently subject to the accounting laws prevailing in a given jurisdiction. Unrealized losses are a good proxy of position risk.

Depending on the prevailing accounting standards for financial reporting, recognition of an impairment loss on debt securities may be recorded in the statement of income if a decline in fair value below amortized cost is considered other than temporary. Correspondingly, recognition of an impairment loss on equity securities will be recorded in the income statement if a decline in fair value below the cost basis of an investment is considered other than temporary. Recognition of an impairment loss for debt or equity securities establishes a new cost basis.

Unrealized losses are recognized in the income statement when a decision has been taken to sell the security, given that investment positions are held with a longer-term view than trading positions. Unsurprisingly, this may pose difficulties for risk quantification because of prevailing market conditions. For instance:

- Liquidity is limited
- Market quoted prices are not readily available, and
- There might be legal or other constraints on sale of certain commodities.

Therefore, although such positions are subject to fair value accounting, risk measures applied to trading positions may not be quite appropriate to investment positions. But there are elements of credit risk control that can usefully be applied to these positions, such as:

- Debt capacity analysis, and
- Valuation techniques.

As a matter of policy, valuation reviews must be conducted regularly for all material investments. A sound approach starts with a rigorous evaluation of new and old positions, as well as a defined business plan that addresses both financial reporting and management accounting requirements, including:

- Purpose
- Likely timeframe, and
- Expected or targeted returns.

A sound position management practice requires continuous monitoring against the prevailing investment plan, including limits per type of investment and for the total portfolio. Against this background there is always the possibility that, in terms of management accounting, the current risk assessment methodology may undergo a general revision, particularly if real economic prospects are not reflected in the present method.

Changes in management accounting methodology may also be triggered by a revision of strategic investment goals. Several banks commented that senior management wants to have better documentation in case of major market price adjustments in a weaker global economic climate. A self-reinforcing negative momentum can be generated by the interaction between different market-related risks, like:

- Market liquidity, and
- Counterparty exposure.

Because of macroeconomic risks in the globalized economy, events that presume a stronger downturn in the real economic environment merit particular attention. Where financial market prices are based on overly optimistic macroeconomic assumptions, simulation should focus on risk and return outlook associated with reasons underpinning disruptions in financial markets.

For instance, the temporary increase in financial market volatility in the second quarter of 2006 has shown that, even in a fundamentally sound environment, a correction, driven largely by turnaround in risk appetite, can take on considerable dimensions. *If* the economic setting is weak, *then* there is a growing risk that market players' declining appetite for risk and cyclical weakening may become mutually reinforcing.

In this case, position risk should be examined not only on an independent position basis, but also in terms of correlation between positions. Stress periods are often characterized by surprising changes in correlation between individual asset classes. During May to June 2006 and January 2007 this was reflected in a sharp rise in positive correlation between:

- Share prices, and
- Some commodity prices.

Moreover, a rise in the implied volatility in the equity markets and the risk premiums in the bond markets was apparent over the May to June 2006 timeframe. The market was affected by a temporary lessening of risk appetite, which led investors simultaneously to vacate many riskier asset classes.

The after-effects of these events have been felt in many positions. Financial instruments that had previously recorded rapid and sharp price gains were particularly affected. Portfolio shifts associated with a general trend towards lower-risk and more liquid assets can trigger severe short-term price volatility, even in a portfolio of broadly diversified assets.

2. Credit risk concentration

Because many books, scholars, bankers and regulators praise the advantages of diversification, it is a deliberate choice to start this section with the broader concepts of concentration, diversification and their challenges. Then, in section 3, an example of diversification will be taken with debt securities positions.

Every strategic plan confronts the challenge of top management policy torn between diversification and focus on a single product line. The choice a company's board and CEO must make between diversification and concentration is neither an easy one nor are its consequences as clear-cut as they might seem to be. Indeed:

- Recent studies have cast doubt on the widely accepted notion that diversification offers unquestionable benefits, and
- At the same time, the way in which most investors measure diversification through reference to broad industry sectors can be misleading.

Theoretically, concentrations of exposure in credit risk and in investment positions are two different issues. In practice, as we will see in this section and in section 3, the two share many common principles, as well as approaches to the control of exposure. Therefore, up to a point, the method used with one of them could be seen as a proxy for the other.

Also, theoretically, diversification is considered to be desirable because risk is spread over a wider landscape of lending and investment possibilities. In practice, this view ignores the fact that both the initial study and subsequent management of diversification engender their own types of risks – and sometimes these may be serious.

Imperfect diversification is one of these risks. In 2006, a Basel Committee Research Task Force did an excellent study on credit risk concentrations and the way they affect the portfolios of commercial banks. This study pointed out that risks may arise from two types of imperfect diversification:

- *Name* concentration
- *Industry sector* concentrations.

Name concentrations lead to specific risk and they occur because of large exposures to individual obligors. In the background of sector concentrations is imperfect diversification across industry sector. (Both violate basic assumptions of the Asymptotic Single-Risk Factor (ASRF) model, underpinning regulatory capital calculations of the internal ratings-based (IRB) method of Basel II.) Name and sector concentrations may be magnified by a third key exposure factor:

- *Contagion* risk.

Default contagion is the probability of an obligor's default conditional on another counterparty defaulting (in mathematical logic this is known as Bayesian probability, or abduction). Contagion risk can be seen as a halfway situation between name and sector concentration, with default dependency driven by close links between two obligors, which are not captured by the sector structure, leading to wrong-way risk.

Contagion risk is created through exposures to independent obligors that exhibit greater default dependencies than might be expected from their sector affiliations. These may, for instance, arise in the context of supply chain business interconnections or because of not-so-transparent correlations (Chapter 4).

Because concentration risk is very important, one might think that the financial industry has already developed appropriate tools and methods for its measurement and monitoring. The findings by the Basel Committee's Research Task Force, as well as opinions expressed at a workshop it organized in November 2005, which involved supervisory, academic and industry participants, revealed that there is a great deal of diversity in the way banks measure and treat concentration risk:

- Some rely on simple ad hoc indicators of concentration risk and its likelihood
- Others (the more sophisticated) use portfolio credit risk models incorporating interactions between different types of exposures.

The measures banks employ as regards concentration risk vary from one institution to the other. Generally, however, they include: an exposure limit system, economic capital models and tools allowing one to account for concentration risk in pricing new exposure. Some banks also use stress tests that include a concentration risk component.

An interesting finding of the Basel Committee's Research Task Force has been the patterns of asset correlations across and within sectors, which are basic determinants of credit concentration. The effects of name and sector concentrations, however, were found to be asymmetric, with sector concentrations being the more serious case. According to the published report:

- Name concentrations can add between 2% and 8% to credit value at risk
- The impact of sector concentrations is much more severe, and it can increase capital needs by 20–40%.[1]

Additionally, exposure associated with name concentration is better understood than industry sector concentration risk. This understanding is promoted by the fact that a number of analytical measurement tools exist for name concentrations, some of them based on ad hoc measures, while others employ credit risk models.

Another interesting finding by the Research Task Force is that commercial banks and supervisors do not necessarily have the same interpretation of concentrations and their risks. Supervisors interpret concentration risk as a deviation (plus or minus) from Basel II's Pillar 1 minimum capital requirements. By contrast, credit institutions perceive that sector concentration, often referred to as *diversification*, warrants capital relief relative to Pillar 1, the latter being interpreted as the non-diversified benchmark of concentration exposure.

3. Market risk concentration

Historically, the process of diversification in the broader sense of the term has moved in a sinusoidal manner between the states of fashionable and unfashionable. In the 1960s the US stock market was dominated by conglomerates such as General Electric, Litton Industries, ITT, General Motors, RJR Nabisco and others. Then came the poor performance of the US economy through the 1970s, which created pressure for a change in strategy to improve returns.

That meant the break-up of several big companies with multiple product lines, hence theoretically diversified market risk. Evidence also became available that entities with focused strategies were more successful at withstanding the economy's woes, as well as the competitive onslaught from Japan.

This continued into the 1980s. The proportion of American companies listed on the stock exchange that were practically monoliners increased from 38% in 1979 to 58% in 1988 – which evidently does not mean that companies operating in a single industry are de facto the better solution.

One of the drawbacks in expressing a documented opinion about which approach may be the best, conglomerate or monoliner, lies in the fact that definitions are wanting. On many measures IBM would be viewed as focused, since it concentrates on selling information technology products and services to corporate customers, yet its product lines have spanned over everything from semiconductors to software marketing and management consulting, which makes the company nearly a conglomerate.

In many cases, diversification of the way it is classically defined according to industry sector tells us little about how well a company is balancing its product lines against market forces, with the aim of increasing returns. Apart from the fact that the quality of management makes a big difference, it is necessary to drill down much deeper – from accounting books to R&D and beyond – before deciding which strategy makes more sense.

A similar statement is valid about portfolio diversification and the advantages this may present in terms of risks being assumed. One of many things that can go wrong with a diversification project is that a decision made by the board and CEO:

- Is not properly explained to the people supposed to implement it, and
- The feedback management receives from line executives is not really crisp.

The board may decide that the better diversified the portfolio is, 'the lower the economic capital to be allocated'. That may be right theoretically, but the practical challenge is in the detail. 'The devil is in the details,' Mies van der Rohe, the architect, used to say. Consider the following real-life example.

As a way of confronting the challenge of market risk concentration, the president of a bank gave to one of his senior traders the mission: 'Create me a portfolio with 40 single "A" bonds of European banks.'[2] Sounds reasonable? It is not so. A post-mortem study established that this mission, and the way it was executed, had the following defects:

1. *The sample was too small.* For instance, a sample of 100 might have provided a better balance in terms of diversification. The portfolio was concentrated in one industry – financials. Therefore, it was highly dependent on that one industry in terms of both credit risk and market risk concentration.

2. *The originators of the 40 bonds were only 17 banks.* This greatly increased concentration in terms of risks the president of the company wanted to diversify.

3. *The 17 banks were chosen from only two neighbouring countries, which belonged to the same economic community.* The fact of belonging to euroland increased the concentration effect in currency risk, over and above the fact that the two economies move in unison.

4. *The portfolio gave equal weights to the 40 bonds.* The weights should have been unequal, using the attractiveness of each bond expressed by a number of factors: duration, interest rate and other characteristics. The choice of adequate diversification criteria is therefore a key issue. Not only should corporate governance ensure that the goal is clear, but it also should not leave gaps in interpretation that lead to poor diversification results.

Moreover, major price adjustments in individual market segments, as well as a fundamental revaluation in the financial markets owing to a turnaround in expectations and risk tolerance levels, may turn a diversification policy on its head. A key factor in this respect is the possible interplay between market price risk, market liquidity risk and counterparty risk, which can:

- Restrict market liquidity, and
- Amplify asset price adjustments.

Ironically, the more the financial system is market oriented, the greater these exposures become. For instance, a reassessment of risks associated with corporate bonds will probably not only push up their risk premiums, but also cause sellers of credit protection to up their prices – or withdraw from the credit derivatives market, with the result of reducing market liquidity in this segment, causing prices to respond accordingly.

Should this event occur, it would put pressure on market players who, because they believe they are diversified, have poor risk management services. As an after-effect, if they fail in continuous monitoring of liquidity and forego the need to observe risk caps, they could be forced to liquidate risk positions if prices fall. This can happen in spite of attention having been paid to diversification principles.

A strategy more effective than calling for diversification in general and meaningless terms is putting limits on concentration. When this is done in a proactive way, and fully accounts for exposures associated with concentration risk, the institution positions itself in a good way for weathering the coming storm. Economic capital (as distinct from regulatory capital) can serve as an agent. As one of the senior executives of a money centre bank had it:

- 'The total distribution of economic capital is subject to limits to concentration'
- 'We look carefully at, and account for, big names and major exposures', and
- 'We stress test positions with major counterparties, across industry and instrument classes.'

The message conveyed by this decision maker is that because his bank is very sensitive to concentrations, it has been able to keep itself out of Enron, WorldCom, Parmalat and similar trouble. Notice that the same strategy is applied as regards correspondent banking, taking account of the fact that bank credit ratings are dynamic and their distribution constantly changes – not always for the better.

4. Position risk with debt instruments

All investments, bonds and other debt instruments are subject to *market risk*, associated with interest rates and *credit risk* resulting from the issuer's creditworthiness. Theoretically, interest rates are the domain of the central bank's monetary policy. In practice, market factors can also have a significant impact on interest rates.

For instance, the expectation of moderate economic growth coupled with low inflation may characterize a movement of yields on ten-year bonds that is flattening the yield curve. The opposite expectations steepen the field curve. The market also impacts upon term premiums that compensate investors for the increased price risk of longer-term bonds.

Also impacting upon the shape of the yield curve are contradictory interests. For example, while the low level of long-term yields has a certain stabilizing effect on the business environment of financial institutions, the profits these institutions make through maturity transformation are under pressure owing to a flatter yield curve. Critical framework conditions for the bond market also include:

- The dependability of monetary and economic policy, and
- Expectations that in the future intensive global competition will counteract potential price pressures.

Factors such as major capital inflows or a regulatory increase in demand for longer-term securities from insurance firms and pension funds put downward pressure on capital market yields, and contribute to significantly lower capital market interest rates, beyond the impact of the central bank's monetary policy decisions.

According to economists, this action is associated with a decoupling of real long-term yields from both cyclical behaviour and from long-term growth expectations. At the same time, such decoupling includes the risk of an abrupt upward correction of long-term yields, a scenario fraught with risk for the financial system.

Against this background, what should a portfolio manager do to be ahead of the curve? The answer returns us to our discussion in sections 2 and 3 on the concept of limits to concentration. Classically, this takes the form of capital allocation between bonds, equities, other commodities and cash. This allocation is dynamic. Figure 8.1 shows the one-year net accumulation by insurers and pension

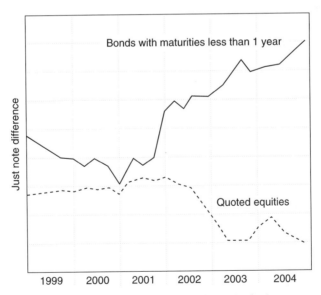

Figure 8.1 Six-year trend in net purchases of bonds and equities by insurers and pension funds in euroland. (Statistics from the European Central Bank)

funds of bonds and equities in euroland in the 1999–2005 timeframe (statistics of the European Central Bank, Monthly Bulletin, April 2005).

Each of these investment classes must itself be analysed with respect to its individual merits as well as in terms of its fitness with other portfolio positions. Experts suggest that the three most widely accepted principles with debt instruments are:

* Creditworthiness
* Generation of stable returns, and
* Optimization of overall portfolio risk.

A senior banker participating in the research that led to this book commented that, based on these three bullets, his institution only considers the highest rated bonds, AAA and AA, when putting together a bond portfolio. Only in exceptional cases will it consider bonds with ratings as low as BBB, and it definitely excludes non-investment rated bonds.

The banker also added that all positions in the bond portfolio are actively managed. The long-term turnaround in bond yields puts them at significant risk in the case of rising yields – which are practically always followed by falling prices. With regard to managed portfolios, while the majority of bonds are in the reference currency of the client (the client may choose from five different currencies), the bank may add some foreign currency bonds depending on the currency outlook of its specialists.

To arrive at a specific duration, the bank uses *slice management*. Duration slices are 1–3, 3–5, 5–7, 7–10 and above 10 years. By assessing the proper weights to these slices, the bank reaches a pre-specified duration of the bond portfolio and an average yield. However, the definition of duration and of currency mix is subject to the weekly meeting of the investment committee, which defines the framework of the investment strategy.

Specific strategy teams (bonds, equities, currencies and alternative instruments) implement the strategy established by the investment committee. They also define the tactical allocation and daily transactions of the portfolio. Duration-wise, positions are kept quite close to the benchmark in almost every country in which these debt instruments originate.

Institutions that include non-investment grade bonds in their portfolio, and those of their clients, appreciate that higher interest rates than those obtained in investment grade bonds are available through *junk bonds* and so-called *leveraged loans*. The latter are speculative-grade loans secured by company assets.

Unlike the original junk bonds of the 1980s, leveraged loans have floating interest rates, a few percentage (basis) points above the London Interbank Offered

Rate, or LIBOR (LIBOR is the cheapest rate banks charge one another for short-term money). But a few basis points don't really compensate for a much lower credit rating.

Leveraged loans were once traded quietly among bank syndicates and a few institutional investors. More recently, however, these loans are attracting plenty of money from hedge funds, pension funds, mutual funds and others. According to Standard & Poor's, investors funded a record $295 billion in leveraged loans in 2005, three times as much as in junk bonds.[3]

5. Position risk with equities

As far as credit institutions are concerned, the International Monetary Fund (IMF) is developing a methodology for compiling pertinent equity indicators in a way that constitutes a comprehensive guide that can function as a general reference. Its main pillars are:

- *Capital adequacy* – regulatory capital to risk-weighted assets, regulatory Tier-1 capital to risk-weighted assets, non-performing loans net of provisions to capital
- *Asset quality* – non-performing loans to total gross loans, industry sector distribution of loans (see section 2) to total loans
- *Earnings and profitability* – return on equity, return on assets, interest margin to gross income
- *Liquidity* – liquid assets to total assets (liquid asset ratio), liquid assets to short-term liabilities
- *Sensitivity to market risk* – net open position in foreign exchange to capital, and other net open positions.

As the reader will appreciate, this list pays only minor attention to credit risk *per se* (second bullet), while it concentrates on factors directly related to market risk.

Other things being equal, equity positions have more market risk and less credit risk than bond positions. Within the overall investment capital allocated to equities, the exposure assumed in every position starts with selection of assets, and may be magnified by the failure to steadily follow risk and return associated with that position, in terms of:

- Yield,
- Upside in price, and
- Company fundamentals.

HealthSouth provides an example on how wrong investment decisions can be, even when made by experts. Reports of mutual fund holdings indicate that as much as 9% of HealthSouth's stock was accumulated through autumn and winter 2003 at around its high price, by funds of the Fidelity family led by Fidelity Advisor Mid Cap.[4] Failure in compliance was the reason for this equity's major slide.

A more frequent reason for position risk with equities is half-baked or outright biased analyses, as happened so often in the late 1990s. In the aftermath of scandals connected to investment advice, which shook up the equities investment industry in the wake of the stock market bubble of 2000, and the ensuing crash of internet companies, many banks have been rethinking the financing of their equity research activities. Unable to share in investment banking revenues, research departments:

- Have shrunk in size, and
- Parted company with their lavishly paid stars.

Some banks, like Deutsche, said that they would combine equity and debt research to provide clients with an integrated approach, and also help in reducing research costs. Other banks, like Citigroup, made investment research a separate entity to be kept at arm's length from investment banking.

Practically nobody said that research is not a useful calling card for all sorts of banking business. The challenge has been associated with what it offers and what it costs. Pressure on research, some experts said at the time, could lessen if trading volume picks up. And more demand for research and analysis would certainly come if stock volatility increases – but up to February 2007 it did not.

These and other statements were made while the after-effects of the bubble were still being felt in the investor community. Banks tried to be convincing in their statements that from now on equity analysis will be objective and the mistakes of the late 1990s will not be repeated. But is this true?

The new challenge in equity research, some experts say, is the stream of one-sided securities analysis. By 2006, many investors had been concerned that 'buy' ratings on shares outnumber recommendations to 'sell' by five to one. This is evidently reflecting bias among analysts. While what the *right ratio* should be is hard to say, the pattern is generally lopsided:

- 40–55% 'buy'
- 42–53% 'hold'
- 4–9% 'sell'.

Notice that in terms of frequency more than 40% of recommendations are to 'hold', which reflects the analyst's uncertainty, and this is valid for nearly every

Table 8.1 Investment rating distribution of a global equity group

Coverage universe	Count	Percentage
Day 1		
Buy	1095	44.05
Neutral	1207	48.55
Sell	184	7.40
Total	**2486**	
Day 2		
Buy	1076	40.21
Neutral	1399	52.28
Sell	201	7.51
Total	**2676**	

equity. Investors are also worried that cyclical momentum, which means herd mentality, inflates asset prices without support by fundamentals – one more reason for the predominance of 'hold' recommendations.

Based on actual buy/hold/sell ratings of a major investment bank, Table 8.1 presents the rating distributions at two consecutive sampling times in September 2005. The statistics show a minor redistribution between 'buy' and 'neutral' (hold), while the percentage of 'sell' remained unchanged. Curiously, what has changed from one day to the next is the number of companies covered, which increased by 7.6%.

Another reason for doubting the depth of the analysis, and the investment recommendations that go with it, is that the large majority of new arrivals fell into the 'hold' category. As can easily be seen in Table 8.1, the 'neutral' position increased from 48% to 52%. 'Neutral' in practice means 'I don't quite know' and on average one in two positions are in this class, which provides no input of any value to investment decisions.

Just as lopsided is the investment analysis of energy companies shown in Table 8.2, from the same timeframe. Table 8.3 reflects investment rating results from two other equity groups: banking and soft drinks. This irrational trend towards highly favourable ratings has been at the heart of the herd mentality that led to the market bubble of the late 1990s.

Critics say that there is often a conflict of interest, because only analysts who look favourably upon a firm's prospects are bringing in investment banking business. Also, the 'good guys' are given the most valuable data on the company, while analysts who pose tough questions get short shrift from the managers of the rated firm.

Table 8.2 Investment rating distribution of an energy equity group

Coverage universe	Count	Percentage
Day 1		
Buy	74	53.62
Neutral	58	42.03
Sell	6	4.35
Total	**138**	
Day 2		
Buy	54	43.20
Neutral	63	50.40
Sell	8	6.40
Total	**125**	

Table 8.3 Investment rating distribution of banks and soft beverages

Coverage universe	Count	Percentage
Banks		
Buy	78	33.91
Neutral	126	54.78
Sell	26	11.30
Total	**230**	
Soft beverages		
Buy	8	61.54
Neutral	4	30.77
Sell	1	7.69
Total	**13**	

Contrary to the statistics shown in the preceding three tables, the objective of rigorous equity analyses should be to obtain and provide an accurate picture of the strengths and weaknesses of companies put under the magnifying glass. This can make it easier for market participants to distinguish between healthy and ailing entities.

A set of ratios allows continuous monitoring of equity exposure. For instance, a frequently used indicator is return on equity (ROE), expressed as the ratio of the pre-tax return (R) to balance sheet equity (E):

$$R/E \qquad (8.1)$$

Another valuation is the ratio of the pre-tax return to the *operating results*, R_{op}:

$$R/R_{op} \tag{8.2}$$

This ratio indicates the impact of risk provisioning, special write-downs and other income/expenditure on overall return.

The use of *operating income*, I_{op}, provides another metric denoting operational efficiency (it corresponds to: $1 - \text{cost-to-income ratio}$):

$$R_{op}/I_{op} \tag{8.3}$$

Still another metric, known as revenue efficiency, indicates the contribution made by the revenue side to ROE:

$$I_{op}/E \tag{8.4}$$

The ratio of operating income to risk-weighted assets (RWA) is a measure of asset productivity. It focuses on income in relation to risk:

$$I_{op}/\text{RWA} \tag{8.5}$$

An entity's risk profile is measured by the ratio of risk-weighted assets to total assets. This is an increasingly popular metric, with proxy for assets A, the stock market capitalization of the firm:

$$\text{RWA}/A \tag{8.6}$$

Leverage of the balance sheet is determined by the ratio of capitalization-based assets to balance sheet equity:

$$A/E \tag{8.7}$$

In essence:

$$\frac{R}{E} = \frac{R}{R_{op}} \cdot \frac{R_{op}}{I_{op}} \cdot \frac{I_{op}}{\text{RWA}} \cdot \frac{\text{RWA}}{A} \cdot \frac{A}{E} \tag{8.8}$$

6. Risk appetite

Limiting concentration is a sound strategy, but its implementation cannot be done in the abstract. It must reflect investor tolerance to position risk connected to reappraisal of prices of the whole array of financial securities and other commodities. Invariably, reassessment leads to questions about whether investors perceive risks as being low and whether they are prepared to accept serious losses.

Apart from the impact on positions themselves, a growing *risk appetite* has after-effects on financial stability. Excessive risk taking pushes asset prices beyond their intrinsic value and, if it persists, could sow the seeds of financial market stress because of:

- Misallocation of capital in the economy, and
- Development of disorderly conditions in financial markets.

Risk appetite and risk aversion are different but complementary concepts that can be used to measure the degree of leveraging in financial markets. *Risk aversion* refers to the reluctance of an investor to accept a position with uncertain risk and return, rather than another position with a more certain exposure but lower expected return.

Several years ago, analysts and rocket scientists tried to create risk appetite models, but it has been gradually found that these are ineffective in forecasting the truly big sell-offs when risk appetite turns to risk aversion. The market downturn and sell-off of mid-May 2006 had little to do with the macroeconomic situation (which enters into these models), even if a sustained bear market can lead to poor economic conditions.

In the opinion of several analysts, a prolonged period of low volatility is a sign of unhealthy risk appetite. Several experts suggest that the mid-May 2006 event had plenty to do with an excessive appetite for risk, which provoked a wave of risk aversion. Many experts now think that:

- The degree of risk appetite prevailing in financial markets can be observed only on an aggregate basis, and
- It contrasts with the degree of *risk aversion*, a concept that explains the behaviour of investors in periods of uncertainty.

Several studies in this domain involve the examination of a set of financial market variables that have historically shown a high level of sensitivity to swings in risk tolerance. Others chose interviews of financial market participants about their opinion on the pricing of different risky assets. Sometimes, however, the polling of experts' opinions features accuracy risk.

For instance, when on 11 January 2007 the price of a barrel of crude hit $52, several analysts and traders suggested that the $75 price it reached in mid-2006 was overdone by at least $15–20, due to geopolitical reasons and speculation. In fact, in mid-January 2007 some traders went short on oil and suffered because of it due to the dual effect of Iranian belligerence and a delayed cold winter. On the other hand, interviews with experts during the market downturn in May 2006 gave a useful warning that volatility was rising (shortly thereafter, volatility again had a low profile).

A good way of assessing risk appetite and risk tolerance is to start with the most basic of all notions: that risk can be best expressed as a *future cost*. The bottom line is that risk creates claims on income in a manner that might be seen as similar to interest expenses and overheads. But because risk claims are prospective and contingent, cash-equivalent costs don't initially appear on the books. Subsequently, they do so when:

- Positions are liquidated, and
- Losses are written into the income statement.

Up to a point, the qualification (and quantification) of risk as a cost is possible if we have refined information elements going beyond transaction pricing and capital allocation. This information should treat risk as a dynamic entity that changes rapidly over time, using market prices to steadily calibrate exposure to:

- Market factors
- Credit factors, and
- Other critical risk factors (Chapter 9).

Traders and investors who are serious about risk management, and therefore about the job they are doing, concentrate on finding strengths and weaknesses in the market, and in the instruments in which they trade, as well as in the companies behind these instruments. 'Financial reporting is about more than just market pricing. We attach a lot of importance to stewardship and governance,' a senior analyst said.

Alert investors not only want to understand the facts affecting market behaviour, but also to appreciate future costs due to risks they have being assuming. Seen in this perspective, a financial reporting system that fails to capture the requirement of stewardship – documented through monitoring past transactions, positions and events – would not be forward looking.

No matter what their risk appetite may be, people who don't work hard enough to be ahead of the game find themselves among the losers. A surprising number of investors and traders dip in and out of the market, betting on just a 50:50 chance.

The worst possible investment mistake is the 'going bust' trade (section 5), which often results from a spur of the moment decision. There is probably no class of trades and investments with a higher failure rate than those presented as 'intuitive' – for instance, committing to an unplanned position because somebody just recommended it. In contrast to a hit-and-run approach, the right homework in risk management means following clear enough guidelines:

- *Assess and reassess one's risk tolerance.* The assessment of one's own risk appetite and risk tolerance must be accurate not precise, since it is not possible to kill two birds with one well-placed stone, and it must be properly documented. While the market is going north, it is easy to think one can handle riskier investments. But little by little the assumed level of exposure may be more than the investor wants to take, or actually needs, and much more than he or she knows how to handle.
- *Lower short-term expectations to meet market reality.* During the go-go 1990s, and similar periods in the past, many investors became accustomed to annual returns of 15–20% or higher. Not only is this well above the S&P 500's historical average of 11% (from 1926 through to 2000), but it also translates into huge risk – hence *future cost.*
- *Focus on the longer term and put a level of confidence on your projections.* This closely relates to choice of an investment horizon. It is always wise to keep an investment period, and the market uncertainty associated with it, in perspective. Volatility may be unpleasant, but it is not unnatural. Investors who have the time, patience and discipline to do their homework with their investment programme and the positions they have taken, are rewarded in the longer run.

7. Risk of ruin

The 21st century economy has three unprecedented characteristics that speak volumes about the risk appetite of investors and speculators. The first is a large amount of *leverage.* Even if banks hold 8% for regulatory capital adequacy (which they often don't because they play the system), this means 1250% leverage. LTCM had 35 000% leverage, and the average leverage with hedge funds is estimated to stand at about 5000%.

The second unprecedented characteristic of this century is the large and growing dependence on *derivative* financial instruments. In the early 1980s, only a few billion dollars were written off-balance sheet (OBS). With IFRS and GAAP,

OBS merged with on-balance sheet exposure, with off-balance sheet instruments now accounting for $300–400 trillion in notional principal.

- This means more than $60 trillion in real money at a time of major crisis,[5] and
- A sword of Damocles as the notional amount is growing by some 30% per year.

The third crucial characteristic of the modern economy, which can hit financial stability like a hammer, is the *in-transit credit risk* unloaded on third parties (Chapter 6). Credit risk mitigation was at the level of a few billion dollars in the early 1990s; it stood at $2 trillion on 1 January 2003, and by growing at 30–35% per year it is estimated to stand in excess of $6 trillion on 1 January 2007.

Is there an economic justification for taking such mega-risks? The theoretical answer usually found in textbooks is *return on capital*. Standard deviations of return and Sharp ratios (the latter being unstable) are commonly presented as measures of risk-and-reward profile.

However, as applied to some players like hedge funds, these metrics substantially understate the true risk assumed by the entity that puts in its block highly leveraged assets. And because there is no structure that cannot be subverted, the practical answer to the 'mega-risks' query is: lust and greed.

An issue many hedge funds, banks and investors don't seem to contemplate is that an ever growing risk appetite is subject to the law of *risk of ruin*. This is not reflected in the standard deviation of returns, but finds itself in spikes at the very long leg of the risk distribution. The only measure of *risk of ruin* is provided by stress testing at at least 15 standard deviations. Among the reasons for such an outlier are:

- Complex derivative instruments in which many players trade
- Liquidity characteristics of traded instruments
- Use of derivatives with non-linear sensitivities
- Wrong hypotheses and plain model error
- Non-representative historical data for estimating standard deviations
- Bad judgement or misconduct, creating the possibility of sudden, dramatic unexpected losses.

An error hypothesis most frequently found is that risk and return are almost linearly related, leading to the equally misplaced assumption that the bigger the risks one assumes, the greater will be the returns. Quite to the contrary, risk and return are proportional only up to a point. After that, the greater the risks one takes:

- The less will be the returns
- But the more likely becomes the ruin.

By going beyond the so-called efficiency frontier, the inverted U-curve in Figure 8.2 dramatizes what was stated in the preceding paragraph. Among the reasons for this inverted U-curve are: over-optimistic calculations of expected profits; biased interpretations of value-based tests; misjudgement of risks; use of too many volatility smiles in pricing; growing risk concentrations (sections 2 and 3); wrong distributions of risk-based capital; and ineffective supervision by the board and CEO.

Precisely for these reasons, there is plenty of scope for rethinking and revamping exposure control, and for emphasizing detail. A senior Barclays executive put it this way: 'If you take value management to transaction level rather than whole entity, you may increase deliverables from value-based management by 25%.'

There is much more to be gained from risk control at a high level of detail, because risk of ruin is a material exposure that does not respond to classical tests, and for which companies are not ready to proceed with stress tests. The September 2006 loss by Amaranth Advisors, a hedge fund, of 65% of its capital (a cool $6 billion, by speculating on volatile gas prices) is an example of risk of ruin.

Optimists say that as long as overall financial stability is not affected, the risk of ruin can be seen as part of *creative destruction and rebirth*, as happens in electronics and among internet companies. This particular concept is borrowed from Silicon Valley, where the organizational secret of stress is:

- Intentional creative destruction, and
- Rebirth, through imagination and innovation, as Apple Computer has shown.

Pragmatists answer that Silicon Valley is of interest to financial institutions as the birthplace of brilliant investment opportunities, but not as a model of corporate governance, because banks and financial institutions are not only operating entities, but also guardians of other people's wealth.[6] (Research done by Nasdaq in the 1990s has shown that, to survive, a Silicon Valley company has to reinvent itself every two and a half years. In that innovation-intense environment, old companies die and new ones emerge, allowing ideas, people and capital to be recycled.)

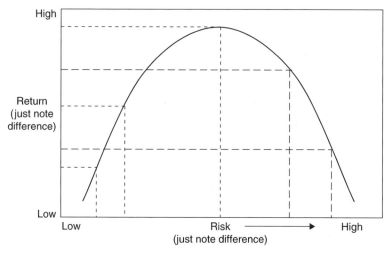

Figure 8.2   Risk and return are non-linear and are often negatively correlated

In banking, air transport, utilities and energy, new business vistas have been opened with *deregulation*, which started in the late 1970s. But in case some people hadn't noticed, a new wave of re-regulation has started – particularly in banking and insurance. Examples are:

- Basel II in 1987
- Market Risk Amendment in 1996
- Basel II in 1999–2007, and
- Solvency 1, Solvency 2 in the insurance industry.

GAAP and IFRS (including IAS 39) are also part of re-regulation – and for good reason. Enron tells us why. In 1986, Kenneth Lay became the head of a company just formed by the merger of two natural gas pipelines. In a manner characteristic of Silicon Valley thinking, the new CEO figured that there was plenty of business opportunity in changing the entire way gas pipelining was done.

Soon, however, by promoting deregulation as a way to bypass government controls, Enron became an energy hedge fund with a gas pipeline on the side. By merging risk in finance with risk in energy, the firm rode on the wave of derivatives and of high leverage. There has been no evidence of limits to this policy of risk of ruin.

One thing that distinguished Kenneth Lay from other gas company executives in a positive way is that he viewed the national map of gas pipelines differently than everybody else. He also recognized that by pushing deregulation, Enron could leverage itself. Another mark of distinction, this one most negative, has been that risk factors and their impact were ill-studied, and there were no limits to risk taking. Eventually, this proved to be Enron's and Lay's undoing.

Notes

1 Basel Committee on Banking Supervision, Working Paper No. 15, 'Studies on Credit Risk Concentration'. BIS, Basel, November 2006.
2 This is a real-life case, though some minor details have been changed.
3 *Business Week*, 13 February 2006.
4 *International Herald Tribune*, 8/9 May 2004.
5 D.N. Chorafas, *Wealth Management: Private Banking, Investment Decisions and Structured Financial Products*. Butterworth-Heinemann, London, 2005.
6 D.N. Chorafas, *Alternative Investments and the Mismanagement of Risk*. Macmillan/Palgrave, London, 2003.

Beyond Credit Risk and Market Risk

1. Liquidity risk

Liquidity risk arises from a variety of sources connected to a financial institution's day-to-day operations and longer-term commitments, including: lending and trading activities; business strategies (Chapter 3); potential damage to a firm's reputation (Chapter 12); and major changes in the macroeconomic environment. Liquidity risk correlates with credit risk, market risk, operational risk and other exposures. Though solvable, at a given moment of its life an entity:

- May not have the financial resources needed to face its current obligations, or
- Might be unable to secure them at reasonable cost, thereby putting creditworthiness and its future solvency in peril.

The probability of default is both influenced by and impacts on liquidity. Ratings downgrades lead to a loss of market confidence, influencing the firm's ability to refinance its current debt obligations. Liquidity risk also arises from events external to the entity, though in the majority of cases assumed exposure is the determining factor.

'In the short run,' (Gerald) Corrigan (then president of the New York Fed) argued, 'there was no way to tell the difference between just short-term liquidity problems and outright insolvency.'[1] Liquidity crises are often tail events, and therefore they must be stress tested. A May 2006 survey by the Basel Committee indicated that, in financial groups, the primary transaction- and product-driven sources of liquidity risk involve:

- Derivatives
- Other off-balance sheet instruments, and
- On-balance sheet insurance contracts with embedded optionality.[2]

The same study presents the fact that in the financial industry the most significant sources of liquidity exposure are over-the-counter (OTC) derivative transactions and stock-borrowing transactions. This is particularly true in cases where sharp and unanticipated market movements or events, such as a sudden bankruptcy, default or ratings downgrade, cause demand for additional collateral from counterparties.

Aware of the many origins of liquidity risk and of the perils embedded in liquidity exposure, banks and other financial firms use a variety of metrics to monitor their liquidity condition and challenges that they confront. Three approaches dominate the quest for sustained liquidity:

- Liquid assets
- Cash flow, and
- A hybrid of these two.

Under the liquid assets approach, the institution maintains liquid instruments on its portfolio that can be drawn upon as needed. For instance, management may keep close to its chest a pool of G-10 government securities that can be used to obtain secured funding through repurchase agreements and other facilities. Assets that are most liquid are typically counted in the earliest time buckets, while less liquid assets are counted in later time buckets.

Under cash flow matching, the institution attempts to match cash outflows against contractual cash inflows, doing so across a variety of near-term maturity buckets. The hybrid approach combines elements of cash flow matching and liquid assets, including a combination of contractual cash inflows plus inflows that can be generated through the sale of assets, repurchase agreement or other secured borrowing.

Liquidity comes under stress because of commitments that are being and have been made. Off-balance sheet exposures can contribute significantly to liquidity risk in banking firms during times of stress, and as the same Basel Committee study pointed out: 'Key off-balance sheet products that can give rise to sudden material demands for liquidity at banking firms include:

- Committed lending facilities to customers
- Committed backstop facilities to commercial paper conduits, and
- Committed back-up lines to special purpose vehicles.'

Financial institutions have adopted different organizational solutions for managing liquidity risk. Structural approaches range from highly centralized to highly decentralized, with the degree of centralization itself varying rather widely. Whichever the solutions may be, they encompass a domain from policies and procedures to structural issues, all the way to content of management reports.

In 'The Management of Liquidity Risk in Financial Groups', the Basel Committee points out that there are at least two aspects to be considered with regard to centralized and decentralized approaches to funding liquidity management:

- The extent to which liquidity may or may not flow to certain parts of the group, and
- The level(s) at which, within a financial organization, management policies and procedures, tools, metrics and/or limits are designed and applied.

Companies with a more centralized approach to liquidity risk management mention the advantages derived from a common approach language and methodology throughout the organization, along with the ability to add central management resources and expertise to local expertise of liquidity control.

By contrast, banks choosing a decentralized approach comment that they prefer to hold adequate liquid reserves at the local or subsidiary level. This generally helps to mitigate the liquidity risk, and also has the advantage that the person on the spot is better positioned to take appropriate action than somebody at headquarters.

An interesting finding of the same 2006 study by Joint Forum is the existence of a strong relationship between a firm's inclination toward central management of liquidity risk and the conduct of liquidity stress testing on an enterprise-wide basis. Given the importance of information provided by liquidity stress testing, such testing is also conducted by geographical region and at subsidiary level.

Financial institutions that may not conduct liquidity stress testing at subsidiary level tend to perceive all liquidity risk as residing in the main corporate unit. Contrary to this, in decentralized stress testing subsidiaries are often given considerable autonomy to devise experiments and scenarios specific to them, particularly if they are expected to stand alone in a crisis (without parent support, as often happens in the insurance industry).

Still another interesting finding of the same study on liquidity test methods and scenarios was the view taken by certain institutions that lack of group-wide stress testing may expose firms to intra-group contagion of liquidity risk. Global firms tend to state that failure to stress test at holding level may not take into sufficient consideration:

- Important group effects of local illiquidity
- Limits on accessibility of any parent support
- Operational and timing constraints that impede the movement of funds across national borders and currencies.

Last but not least, the type of stress tests varies between banking and insurance entities, as well as within the banking sector. In their liquidity stress tests, many credit institutions assume that they will roll over loans as they mature to protect their franchise. Also that repo and securitization markets may not remain open, and currencies of some developing countries will not remain convertible.

For their part, securities firms perceive as liquidity risk under stress conditions the inability to continue to obtain unsecured long-term debt to support the illiquid portions of their balance sheets. A basic assumption is that the entity will not be able to access unsecured funding markets at all, or it might do so on favourable terms for a period of time. Consequently, it will need to rely on government securities in its liquidity pool to meet cash needs.

2.   Event risk

The term *event risk* covers unforeseeable risks that suddenly reduce the credit quality of corporate borrowers and the value of their fixed-income securities, or have other unwanted effects. Event risks are hard to predict because they are often not necessarily related to the fundamental credit quality of the issuer. They also come in a variety of guises:

- Buyouts
- Buybacks
- Acquisitions, and
- Outsourcing.

Each can bring with it a number of shocks and complications. Many are linked to the apparent conflict that exists within companies simultaneously seeking to deliver value to shareholders, through buybacks, keep their bondholders happy and reward their management in the most extravagant way. This is a thankless task, with event risks hidden in:

- Leveraged buyouts (LBOs) in the aftermath of a bidding war (Reynolds Nabisco)
- Getting a big loan to buy back shares and prop up the equity value (a swarm of companies in 1999 and 2000)
- Stock swapping and high debt acquisition of companies with inflated equity (JDS Uniphase)
- Outsourcing real estate, information technology and other core business to improve the balance sheet (Sainsbury).

For bond investors, RJR Nabisco's mammoth leveraged buyout was a watershed. Since then, virtually no blue-chip company has been safe from debt meltdown. A factor contributing to over-leveraged LBOs has been the ready availability of junk financing, which encourages takeover artists to overpay, causing bid premia to soar.

'High-yield bonds are converted into junk bonds overnight,' John J. Creedon, Chief Executive Officer of Metropolitan Life Insurance, said at the time. 'We think that management has a duty to all constituents of the company, including bondholders.'[3]

Met Life was suing RJR in a New York State Court, charging that its LBO plan enriched a handful of executives at the direct expense of debtholders. The insurer wanted RJR to set aside money covering in full the $340 million in A-rated bonds it owned, bonds that plunged in value by some $40 million. ITT's insurance subsidiary also filed suit in federal court, alleging that RJR violated federal disclosure laws. ITT wanted its money back.

When that event took place, RJR was the biggest case of bond investor expropriation without representation. Federated Department Stores' senior debt also went from AA to B junk after Robert Campeau's debt-financed takeover. Campeau had disregarded the fact that credit markets are based first and foremost on trust.

As far as investors in debt instruments are concerned, one hedge against event risk is to buy bonds that include *event risk language* in their indentures. Two types have emerged into the foreground:

- *Poison put*, which allows an investor to put the bonds back to the issuer at par if a certain designated event and rating downgrade to below investment grade takes place. Designated events typically include LBOs and other changes of control, financial restructuring, recapitalization, a large stock repurchase, a large dividend payment, or other radical action that reduces assets or adds liabilities to the issuer's balance sheet.
- *Credit-sensitive notes*. These adjust the coupon if their rating changes up or down, whatever the cause.

Poison puts offer the advantage of taking the bondholder out of the investment if the outstanding paper suddenly becomes a 'high-yield' junk. Credit-sensitive notes offer considerable compensation in case of eroding quality. While both provide comfort, no fail-safe solution exists to fully offset event risk and resulting bond price volatility.

Some investors are sceptical about the value and effectiveness of event risk language. The pros answer that while this type of protection may not be ideal, the value of event risk covenants is not to be discarded. The system works both ways: issuers can lower funding costs significantly by including such covenants in the indentures of new issues, while investors receive protection against one of the major threats to their fixed-income portfolio positions.

Equities, too, are affected by event risk. On 22 July 1998, Computer Associates International (CAI) shares fell by nearly 31%. Analysts attributed the trashing of CAI stocks to one item in its first-quarter report: a $675 million after tax charge taken to pay three top executives, including the chairman and chief executive officer, an extravagant amount of money:

- Before the charge, CAI earned $192.4 million
- After the charge, it lost $480.8 million.

It is quite remarkable how this could happen, and even gain shareholder approval. The pay package had originally received a nod from 78% of voting shareholders in their 1995 proxies. This plan entailed awarding the CEO, the president and one of the executive vice-presidents more than 20 million shares *if* the company's stock closed above $53.33 for 60 days in a 12-month period.

In essence, the shareholders decision put a totally mispriced option on the company's stock. The trigger event was established without due consideration to the general trend in the stock market. Based on this decision, Charles B. Wang, the CEO, was handed more than 12 million shares, then worth $670 million, while his two subordinates got the remainder, worth $447 million.

Thus far at least, this charge has been the largest ever declared by a public company for executive pay. Its level equalled 43% of Computer Associates' entire net income for the three previous years – an event that took shareholders to the cleaners and at the same time wounded the company almost beyond repair.

3. Legal risk

The origins of legal risk are infinite, and each case has its own characteristics. Basically, legal risk is an operational risk[4] that amplifies credit and market risk, and has assumed king-size dimensions over time. As Figure 9.1 shows, legal risk is integral to counterparty risk:

- As manifested in judicial and extrajudicial disputes, legal risks have always been an integral part of any business, and
- At increasing pace, not only malpractice but also aggressive strategies in competing for customers and high profits can generate legal risk.

Even if the precise extent of risks arising from legal disputes and the associated reputational risks are very difficult to quantify, it can be said that during the last 20 years these risks have increased considerably. This is particularly true when taking on new types of business and when operating in areas that are prone to conflicts of interest, or may lead to abuse of customer confidence – alternative investments being an example.[5]

Legal disputes may result from conflicts with individual counterparties, business partners (customers or suppliers), disputes with employees, lack of regulatory compliance, complexity of instruments developed and sold, and other reasons. Both judicial and extrajudicial disputes may be very costly.

The internationalization of business has increased the opportunities for legal risk, as well as its complexity. Owing to the fact that no two jurisdictions have the same laws, the risks of legal disputes grow along with an institution's increasing

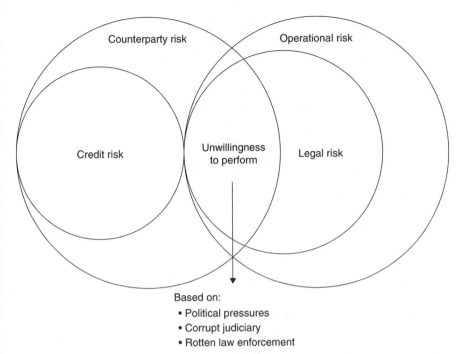

Figure 9.1   Stress testing should focus on the grey area where counterparty risk and legal risk merge

cross-border activities. Banks and other companies are exposed to considerable indemnity claims owing to the legal instrument of punitive damages.

Andersen risk is a legal risk whose origin has been *deception*. In the aftermath of losing its reputation, the company went down the tubes. Notice that the risk of deception may have more than one origin: incompetence, conflict of interest, repeated errors, lack of transparency and more.

Additionally, the growing importance of technology in banking harbours not only settlement and reputational risks, but also legal exposures. For instance, the intrusion by hackers into bank customers' accounts is an issue that has increased in severity. Three factors – laws, jurisprudence and the legal system – are critical in defining legal risk.

- In the USA there are plenty of class actions, judgement by jury, unlimited liability and high environmental liability
- In the UK there are no class actions, the judges decide, there is a liability cap and environmental liability is not that high

- In France and much of continental Europe, where Napoleonic law applies (which is different from Anglo-Saxon law), a major role is played by the spirit of the law, which reflects the intent of the legal clause.

In most jurisdictions, however, the danger of legal disputes increases in line with the growing complexity of modern financial instruments, a wave of malpractice, and the ongoing trend of reinforcing consumer and investor protection in legislation. During the past few years, European legislators have deliberately strengthened the position of consumers and investors through, for example:

- The Markets in Financial Instruments Directive (MiFID) of the European Union, and
- The Act improving investor protection (*Anlegerschutzverbesserungsgesetz*) under German law.

In an age of innovation, another origin of legal risk is *product exposure*. Merck's Vioxx provides an example. According to Benedict Lucchesi, a pharmacologist at the University of Michigan, Vioxx encourages dangerous blood clotting that can lead to heart attacks and strokes. In his testimony at a court in Atlantic City, New Jersey, Lucchesi stated that Vioxx and other similar drugs, known as COX-2 inhibitors, can cause blood clots or thromboses that break loose and plug blood vessels.[6]

The issue the pharmacologist raised is that the probability is very high that products like Vioxx and COX-2 inhibitors can lead to the development of thromboembolic events. And there is a significant likelihood, the pharmacologist added, that Vioxx poses a risk to patients with underlying disorders. On these and similar grounds, Merck faced about 5000 Vioxx suits, with billions of dollars in liability if it lost several early trials.

Legal risk can indeed be very costly. In May 2004, Citigroup agreed to pay $2.65 billion to settle a lawsuit brought by investors in WorldCom, and set aside a further $5.2 billion for the pending lawsuits, including Enron. In June 2005, it agreed to pay $2 billion to settle a class-action lawsuit filed by Enron investors who sued the world's largest financial services group for its alleged role in fraudulent deals at the collapsed energy company.

Led by the University of California, investors have been seeking tens of billions of dollars from banks that they claimed helped Enron hide billions of dollars of debt. By 10 June 2005, the date of Citigroup's payment, they had already won more than $2.7 billion from J.P. Morgan Chase, Lehman Brothers and Bank of America.

In mid-June 2005, J.P. Morgan Chase agreed to pay $2.2 billion to settle its part in a class-action lawsuit, also led by the University of California, that accused several banks of aiding Enron in defrauding investors before the energy trader went bankrupt in December 2001. And the investor group continued its legal action against other banks, including Merrill Lynch, Crédit Suisse First Boston, Barclays Bank, Deutsche Bank and Royal Bank of Scotland, which it alleged were involved in fraudulent transactions. It also pursued Goldman Sachs for its role in underwriting Enron securities.

In September 2005, as the new Parmalat, the restructured Italian dairy group, prepared to relist on the stock exchange, investors tried to pin a value on the many lawsuits that Parmalat's bankruptcy administrator had filed against those that helped cause its bankruptcy in December 2003. These cases, too, were filed against major international banks.

Parmalat shares were 'guestimated' to be worth around 2.40–2.50 euros on the grey market, suggesting an equity value of around 4.4 billion euros, or an enterprise value of 4.8 billion euros, including debt. Of this, the dairy business accounted for about 2.7 billion euros, some 7.5 times this year's earnings before interest, taxes, depreciation and amortization (EBITDA), leaving 2 billion euros or more to be gained from lawsuits.

This estimate of legal proceedings made up just over 10% of the total of 18.5 billion euros that Parmalat had been seeking. The optimistic estimates on legal gains were based on the fact that legal suits connected to Enron had recovered around 30% of the $30 billion they sought from the courts. Moreover, Morgan Stanley and Nextra, the asset management unit of Banca Intesa, had already settled with Parmalat, paying more than the firm claimed. But precedence is not a fail-safe yardstick.

The challenge in valuing lawsuits highlights what a complex job investors face on both sides of a settlement. In Parmalat's case, one solution that was considered, but not adopted, was to spin off the legal suits into another company, thereby allowing the dairy arm to attract shareholders interested in food products. Then, the legal arm could attract hedge funds who earn their money valuing exotic assets.

Not to be lost from P&L estimates is the fact that what one company pays as an after-effect of a court decision is not necessarily what is gained by those who brought it to court. In 2003, for example, Lucent Technologies, the telecoms equipment maker, agreed to a $517 million settlement. Of this, $100 million plus expenses went to plaintiffs' lawyers. The rest was split among shareholders who could satisfy numerous conditions and use various formulas to calculate an applicable loss. By the time the cheques arrived in 2004, this turned out to be as little as a cent on the dollar.[7]

4.   Longevity risk: a case study

The financial staying power of an insurance firm typically starts with premiums earned and invested to cover claims occurring at a future date, sometimes many years later. Insurance management involves limits to risk – for instance, through reinsurance, being in charge of financial market risks associated with assets and liabilities, and controlling claims.

Asset accumulation by insurance companies results predominantly from premiums being paid earlier than claims are settled. Time differences, which may exceed 50 years for annuity business, have major implications for risk management. Also crucial in terms of after-effects are three key steps characterizing good governance in the insurance business:

- Risk to be assumed, and sums insured, must be properly selected
- Funds have to be invested in such a way that they generate cash flows in line with the anticipated cash outflows in the liability structure, and
- Product-specific characteristics, such as maturity and inflation-dependent insurance claims, must be treated appropriately.

Non-life insurance risk relates to claims that may be more frequent or larger than forecast, and/or that may have to be paid earlier than expected. To be in charge of such risks, premium levels are examined in full consideration of the expected frequency and amounts of claims resulting from insured risks. Moreover, if adequate reinsurance protection is not in place, substantial losses could be triggered by a single natural catastrophe.

Non-life insurers usually hold a diversified portfolio with respect to geographic and industry structure, because better diversified insurance portfolios tend to imply smaller differences between expected and actual claims. Still, even a well-diversified insurance portfolio with many business lines spread over many policyholders might be vulnerable to natural hazards, resulting in a significant accumulation of risk of exposure.

In *life* insurance the basic risk characteristics are similar to those in non-life, but insurance risk also includes deviations from expected mortality. This includes the *longevity* challenge (more on this later), disability and other risks. Life insurance risk management involves:

- Product profit testing
- P&L monitoring
- Product portfolio diversification, and
- Reinsurance solutions.

One of the accounting practices is that contracts providing for indemnity against loss or liability relating to insurance risk are accounted for as reinsurance. By contrast, reinsurance contracts that do not transfer significant insurance risk are accounted for as deposits. Gains on retroactive reinsurance ceded are deferred and amortized over the estimated settlement period.

Among well-managed firms, the provision for future benefits for policyholders participating in traditional life products is computed using the net level premium method. This represents the present value of future policyholder benefits less the present value of future net premiums. Net level premium uses assumptions for mortality and interest rates that are:

- Guaranteed in the contracts, or
- Employed in determining dividends.

Assumptions are based on the insurance company's experience and industry standards, including provision for adverse deviations that were in effect as of the issue date of the contract. The provision for future policyholder benefits also includes liabilities for non-traditional life products for which the assets cannot be legally segregated.

When the provision for future policyholder benefits, plus the present value of expected future gross premiums for a product, are insufficient to provide for expected future benefits and expenses for the line of business, deferred policy acquisition costs are written off to income. A premium deficiency reserve is established by charge to income.

While all this is established practice in life insurance, several important assumptions have to be made in performing actuarial valuations. These assumptions require a significant amount of judgement and estimates of longevity risk. The expected long-term rate of return on assets is determined on a plan-by-plan basis, taking into account:

- Asset allocation
- Historical rate of return
- Benchmark indices for similar type pension plan assets, and
- Longer-term expectations of future returns associated with investment strategy.

Accounting policies, however, change with new regulations and the behaviour of markets. Risks evolve over time and estimating the level of exposure by means of a methodology established years ago may well be inaccurate. An example from the life insurance industry is that, in Western countries, insurers are now exposed to *longevity risk* – a systematic type of exposure that is:

- Beyond the control of the insurer, and
- As a generic characteristic of our society, cannot be minimized.

Longevity risk is a relatively new challenge for insurers, and many companies study it through their experience with mortality risk. The payback of a bond for mortality risk varies depending on mortality dynamics. If this is lower than was assumed when pricing the bond, the payback will be accelerated; if higher, payback will be slowed.[8] If mortality experience is adverse:

- It will first deplete the economic reserves of the life insurer, and
- Then, it will use the redundant reserves of the special purpose vehicle (SPV).

Not only life insurance companies but also other providers of annuities, like pension funds, face the risk that the duration of their assets can become mismatched from that of their liabilities, and that mortality rates of policyholders could fall at a faster rate than anticipated in their pricing and reserving calculations. Added to this are the facts that:

- Because of competition, profit margins in the provision of annuities tend to be low, and
- The profit margin of annuity providers is further squeezed if mortality assumptions built into the prices of annuities turn out to be overestimated.

In fact, a growing number of life insurance companies are claiming that their annuity businesses have been producing losses because people have been living longer than expected. Some insurers have sought to cover themselves against this longevity risk by only quoting prices for annuities on uncompetitive terms.

A first significant step towards developing a methodology specific to longevity insurance took place in December 2005, when Crédit Suisse launched the CS Longevity Index. This provides an objective mortality and longevity index for insurers, institutions and investors exposed to longevity risk. Based on such an index, securities designed to offset longevity risk are supposed to have lower overall longevity risk.

Some experts suggest that the most effective way of addressing longevity risk would be for governments to issue *longevity bonds*, but the role of governments in providing such bonds is highly debatable. Governments can only spread longevity risk across future generations. Reinsurers have a role to play. Swiss Re, for example, issues mortality-linked securities to manage adverse mortality risk. But altogether the insurance industry is still perplexed by the risk. In conclusion:

- Longevity exposure is a new risk difficult to diversify
- But financial markets might provide an alternative way for institutional risk pooling.

One of the mistakes currently made in the study of longevity, and of its after-effects, is that it is approached as a mass problem, which it is not. Rather, solutions should be *customer centred*, putting the insured person at the centre of the longevity challenge because each person has their own life cycle. It is therefore important to come up with alternative plans that are parametric and can be customized.

5. Payments risk

Several types of exposure are associated with payment and settlement operations, as well as to systems supporting them. These include, but are not limited to, credit risk (Chapter 5), liquidity risk (section 1), legal risk (section 3), technology risk and other operational risks. Among the latter are payment system disruption and the likelihood that the inability of one market player to meet their obligations would snowball.

In March 1996, the Bank for International Settlements (BIS) published its key findings on how banks could improve their controls to reduce settlement risk, including how to deal with large liquidity requirements without moving market prices. Financial institutions that get into trouble in connection with their payments and settlements sometimes need to sell large amounts of currency or other assets quickly.

- Liquidity in settlements presents an amount of risk that the market must absorb at any one time
- Without liquidity, major payments can move prices against the settler.

As far as major transactions and their settlements are concerned, several trends combine to erode liquidity. One is the growing popularity of electronic brokerage systems in deals involving foreign exchange. Electronic brokerage is popular because it permits small banks, which previously had to channel forex trades through larger ones, to deal directly with each other.

- Electronic trading makes the market more transparent, as electronic brokers publish details of trades immediately

- But the more information other banks have about prices, the harder it is for money centre banks to execute big trades without the market moving against them.

Another issue playing havoc with banks is the after-effect of foreign exchange derivatives, in particular the growing use of currency options that give their owners the right to exercise on an underlying currency at strike price. Some options can produce sharp swings in currency prices, and these can create short-lived pockets of illiquidity.

Because such events can threaten the stability of the global system, they have to be addressed beforehand in their details. In January 2001, the governors of the G-10 central banks approved the 'Core Principles for Systematically Important Payment Systems',[9] which address:

- Legal certainty
- Management of financial risks
- Security
- Operational reliability, and
- Criteria for participation in cross-border multi-currency netting.

Other principles that were not among the Lamfalussy standards are minimum requirements for efficiency (for assets used for settlement and for the governance arrangements) and statements on the responsibilities of central bank in applying the Core Principles as well as their oversight.

According to the 2001 Core Principles, the payments system should have a well-founded legal basis under all relevant jurisdictions. Its rules and procedures must enable participants to have a clear understanding of its impact, in regard to each of the financial risks occurring through participation in it. Moreover, the payments system should clearly define procedures for management of credit risks and liquidity risks, specifying the respective responsibilities of:

- The system operator, and
- Participants in the system.

A system in which multilateral netting takes place should, at a minimum, be capable of assuring timely completion of daily settlements in the event of an inability to settle by the participant with the largest single settlement obligation. Assets used for settlement should preferably be a claim on the central bank. Where other assets are used, they must carry:

- Little or no credit risk, and
- Little or no liquidity risk.

Another Core Principle stipulates that the payments system should ensure a high degree of security and operational reliability, including contingency arrangements for timely completion of daily processing. It must also provide a means of making payments that is practical for its users and efficient for the economy.

Additionally, to minimize payments and settlements risk, the system should have publicly disclosed objective criteria for participation, and these criteria must permit fair and open access, with operations executed in an:

- Effective
- Accountable, and
- Transparent way.

An example on effectiveness is that while being safe and secure settlement systems, and most particularly securities settlement systems, should be cost-effective in meeting users' requirements. Accountability has many aspects, including able governance, operational reliability, secure access and protection of customer files.

Payments and settlement systems should be subject to transparent and effective regulation and oversight, with central banks and securities regulators cooperating among themselves and with other relevant authorities. Implicit in this requirement is that the payments and settlement system should have a well-founded basis in all relevant jurisdictions.

Taking securities settlement as an example, sound governance should fulfil public interest requirements, promoting the objectives of both owners and users. Technologically speaking (see also section 6), the systems should be reliable and secure, with adequate but scalable capacity. Contingency plans and back-up facilities must be established to allow for:

- Timely recovery of operations, and
- Completion of the settlement process.

It is also essential that customers' securities are protected against the claims of a custodian's creditors. Furthermore, in a globalized economy, settlement systems must feature links permitting the settlement of cross-border trades – which are designed and operated in a way to swamp risks classically associated with cross-border settlements.

6.   Risk must be controlled intra-day

Many banks, brokers and corporate treasurers have systems in place to monitor and accumulate *daily* information for risk management. This is a solution that would have been great in the 1980s but not in the 21st century, where *intra-day* tick-by-tick financial data streams, interactive data mining and models must be online, permitting exposure to be judged in real time for:

- Any instrument
- Any trader
- Any transaction
- Any counterparty
- Anywhere in the world.

Intra-day market valuation of all transactions and positions (Chapter 8) is the best practice for banks, dealers and investors. A corollary to this is to always understand *what* the bank, its traders and its counterparties are trying to accomplish with their deals and investments. What senior management needs to have at its fingertips in order to react firmly and quickly are:

- A virtual balance sheet
- A virtual income statement, and
- Accurate answers to ad hoc queries.

Virtual financial statements are based on accounting books, but they are part of the institution's executive information system, not of regulatory financial reporting. In exchange for the ability to provide a global position in B/S, P&L and risk management terms, in a matter of minutes, they work by order of magnitude. This is acceptable for management decisions because speed with accuracy is more important than slow response.

The reason why virtual balance sheets are not yet as popular as they should be is that today very few companies have the know-how to capitalize on what high-technology currently offers. The majority is still living in the past with legacy systems that grew like wild cacti and find it difficult to satisfy basic requirements – even if their cost is enormous.

'Chance favours the prepared mind,' said Louis Pasteur, and many institutions are simply not prepared. Therefore, they fail to capitalize on the fact that virtual financial statements can be called up with a mouse click, permitting:

- Full view of *intra-day* values for assets and liabilities
- Comprehensive evaluation of current exposure, and
- Critical plan/actual evaluations regarding ongoing operations and deadlines.

Sound governance requires critical *plan versus actual* evaluations, which bring deviations into perspective. This can be obtained by analysing the latest figures interactively online, comparing them with plans and limits. This is important to all enterprises.

Companies that wish to be ahead of the competition develop and use online experimentation in every field of product design and testing, and for management reasons. This has happened in the aerospace and motor vehicles industries for many years. Now, it has entered the pharmaceutical industry, because leading firms see it as the future of pharmaceutical research – and of company survival.

In Britain, GSK is working with a faculty from Imperial College and the Hammersmith Hospital on a radical new approach to testing and funding drugs. Scientists are studying *in real time* how humans respond to microdoses by means of molecular imaging.[10]

In business, for more than a decade, Sears exploited online two years worth of detailed budgets and plans using *interactive computational finance*. Since the mid-1990s, at Sun Microcomputers the CFO takes only a few hours to close the books and deliver a virtual financial statement to the chief executive officer – spending more time managing forwards instead of backwards.[11]

Among the better-run companies, the pace of this sort of interactive real-time application is accelerating. In one of the better known financial institutions, a former CIO, who became executive vice-president, developed a pattern analysis programme that allows:

- Critical evaluation of intra-day activity, and
- Comparison of the pattern of one timeframe to that of any other timeframe.

Johnson & Johnson is one of the companies whose senior management has been revolutionized through modern financial information technology. Since the mid-1990s, Johnson & Johnson reinvented itself by thoroughly restructuring its information technology. The revamped system:

- Allows the CFO to concentrate on analysing financial information to boost revenue, and
- Does away with the need to spend time on fire-fighting approaches to rush out financial reports.

The strategic aspect of assets and liabilities modelling is a direct consequence of the fact that a company's balance sheets present successive financial states that are important to all stakeholders: shareholders, bondholders, members of the board, senior management, employees and regulators. Intra-day financial data are mainly of a tactical nature, helping in developing theoretical models of risk and return.

Many people fail to appreciate that, like it or not, they use theoretical models to help themselves understand a given situation, expose inconsistencies in their inputs, make possible rethinking of variables and patterns, and contribute to determining likely implications of potential, actual and future exposures at transaction by instrument position and counterparty, along a framework shown in Figure 9.2.

- *If* this simulated behaviour represented by the theoretical model fits the real world well enough
- *Then* we can have confidence with regard to insights derived from this model.

Knowledge, information and the right conceptual modelling are instrumental in understanding opportunities that come along and in appreciating their risks. Without full comprehension of the purpose for which one enters into a trade or investment position, it is nearly impossible to assess risks in terms of potential exposure, actual exposure and future exposure.

Potential exposure, or expected exposure, is the proactive estimation of current and future risk taken when undertaking a financial transaction. Mathematically, it is equal to the sum of actual exposure and future exposure.

To estimate potential or *time-to-decay* market risk, banks quantify future market movements and their impact. For instance, in forward rate agreements (FRAs) they simulate the after-effect of a change by 5, 10 or 20 basis points in their FRA portfolio – as well as the impact this exposure will have on the more important counterparties.

Actual exposure, also known as replacement cost, is the actual market risk and credit risk. It represents the amount of exposure inherent, for instance, in a derivatives transaction, a loan or any other banking operation. By and large, *future* (or fractional) *exposure* – also known as deemed risk and pre-settlement risk – represents market risk.

Mathematically, this market risk is the amount of future exposure inherent in a financial transaction, and it can be estimated through modelling and simulation. This brings our discussion back to the intra-day control of exposure assisted through technology. The notions of potential, actual and future exposure are not new – what is new is that algorithmic and heuristic solutions:

- Help to keep a rigorous check on exposure, and
- Permit significantly improvement in the personal productivity of managers and professionals.

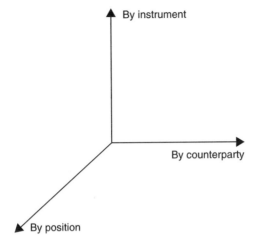

Figure 9.2   Frame of reference for identifying risk and return at each individual transaction level

Making knowledge work productively is the great management mission of the 21st century. The growing body of experience in knowledge-enriched system solutions suggests that the best approach to risk management is to:

- Provide the necessary infrastructure – networks, data mining, expert systems, training programmes
- Enable people to find for themselves what they need to know to improve their effectiveness, and
- Track individual performance in mental productivity, as IBM does by profiling its consultants.

At the company's research centre in the USA, data miners, statisticians and knowledge engineers are scrutinizing personal profiles of 50 000 IBM employees.[12] This is an example of the application of the science of *stochastic analysis*. Mapping the random behaviour of humans into mathematical models, the analysts build models of their colleagues.

Then, using the profiles developed in this way, expert systems[13] can pick the best team for every assignment and track each consultant's contribution to the project's progress. Because organizations are made up of people, this is the next frontier in risk management.

Notes

1   Bob Woodward, *Maestro: Greenspan's Fed, and the American Boom.* Simon & Schuster, New York, 2000.

2 Basel Committee, The Joint Forum, 'The Management of Liquidity Risk in Financial Groups'. BIS, Basel, May 2006.

3 *Business Week*, 5 December 1988.

4 D.N. Chorafas, *Operational Risk Control with Basel II: Basic Principles and Capital Requirements*. Butterworth-Heinemann, London, 2004.

5 D.N. Chorafas, *Alternative Investments and the Mismanagement of Risk*. Macmillan/Palgrave, London, 2003.

6 *Sunday Telegraph*, 18 September 2005.

7 *The Economist*, 21 January 2006.

8 *Sigma*, No. 7. Swiss Re, Zurich, 2006.

9 These date back to a report published in 1990 by the Committee on Interbank Netting Schemes of the Central Banks of the Group of Ten Countries, known as the Lamfalussy Committee.

10 *The Economist*, 27 January 2007.

11 *Business Week*, 28 October 1996.

12 *Business Week*, 23 January 2006.

13 D.N. Chorafas and Heinrich Steinmann, *Expert Systems in Banking*. Macmillan, London, 1991.

Part 3

Risk, Regulation and
Management Control

Basel II and the Accountant

1. The Basel II framework

The new capital adequacy framework by the Basel Committee on Banking Supervision, known as Basel II, is a set of regulatory standards. Its objective is not only a sound capital ratio for credit risk, market risk and operational risk, but also a host of subjects relating to good governance, and therefore to accounting policies and practices. The setting of standards is important because it brings:

- Improvement in *financial staying* power
- Reduction in the variability of financial results, and
- The possibility of localizing reasons for existing variations.

Together with IFRS, whose target is sound financial reporting, Basel II affects a wide area of activities from corporate strategy to risk management, and the technology put in place to assist in better governance. Top-tier information technology is necessary to provide the infrastructure necessary for factual and effective allocation of financial resources, as well as the monitoring and control of exposure (Chapter 9).

Basel II has followed in the steps of Basel I, the 1988 Capital Accord, which was the first to set international standards. Basel I addressed credit risk, setting *a minimum* 4% capital standard for national banks and 8% for international banks. In 1996, it was complemented by the Market Risk Amendment.[1]

These 4% and 8% capital ratios were flat ratios all banks had to observe, with a distinction made between Tier-1 and Tier-2 capital (section 4). Tier-1 is equity and, as originally defined, it had to be more than 50% of the total capital reserve. (Over the years, however, commercial banks engaged in *regulatory arbitrage*.)

A very interesting aspect of evolution in regulatory thinking, which came with the 1996 Market Risk Amendment, has been the idea that modern technology permits marking to model (Chapter 7). Within a couple of years, the more technologically advanced banks marked to model credit risk. In 1998, this became known as *pre-commitment*. The sense of it has been that:

- Commercial banks could calculate in advance the capital *they* think they needed, and
- Regulators would control post-mortem if they did a good job, applying a penalty if they did not.

Pre-commitment was promoted by the big American banks, who were ahead in technology, but in Europe regulators were not convinced. In mid-1998, I was talking to a senior director of the Bank of England who found the concept wanting, and the idea of penalizing a wounded bank post-mortem absurd. Quite similar was the response of a senior director of Banque de France, with whom I met at that time.

In spite of this initially adverse reaction, in 1999, only a year later, the first version of Basel II was born along similar principles, but without the post-mortem penalty. Along with it came the concept of *risk-based pricing*, which brings into perspective the critical question of what the real cost of an instrument or commitment is (Chapter 11).

Modelling and testing are keywords in Basel II. A pragmatic view of pre-testing is that it permits assessment of a credit institution's exposure with a higher degree of accuracy than ever before – provided, of course, that all hypotheses, risk weights and coefficients are right. Mathematically assisted risk analysis requires a lot of:

- Skill and time
- Pragmatic models
- Rich and reliable information, and
- Management understanding.

Other prerequisites also exist, like a fine grade scale of creditworthiness (Chapter 5). It is widely acknowledged that credit rating now plays a critical role in the definition of regulatory capital – whether a counterparty's creditworthiness is evaluated by independent rating agencies or by the bank itself – but not everyone is tuned to the requirements of accuracy and of steady update.

A similar statement is valid in terms of appreciating what is needed for realistic modelling of credit risk. Prerequisites for modelling under the Foundation Internal Ratings-Based (F-IRB) approach and the Advanced IRB approach (A-IRB) still need to seep down the organization. The same is true of the need for databases with more than ten years historical data and for online interactive data mining, which add to the sophistication of required solutions.

An even greater challenge exists with the understanding that vital modelling factors like *correlation coefficients* (Chapter 4) cannot be set by board decisions – as is often done with banks adopting A-IRB. Either the rules of mathematics governing eigenmodels are respected throughout or risk-based capital adequacy is wrong throughout.

Another important challenge related to Basel II is the high degree of attention to be paid by senior management, loans officers, traders, investment experts and accountants to *unexpected losses* (UL). Before the rules of Basel II were unfortunately twisted in 2006, they clearly stated that:

- *Expected losses* (EL) should be covered through regulatory capital
- While the role of economic capital is to address unexpected losses and extreme events.

This distinction is extremely important on account of the fact that a globalized economy increases many times over the risk of unexpected losses, as well as the event risk (Chapter 9) that contributes to them. (The thin red line separating EL and UL was very clearly outlined in Basel II's early versions, but in mid-2006 the Basel Committee did away with it and turned off the lights on UL.[2])

The recent confusion between regulatory capital and economic capital, as well as between EL and UL, is evidence that over the years the original aims of Basel II have changed, and the whole business may turn into an accountant's nightmare. Just as worrisome is the fact that pre-committed capital requirements may be shrunk at will, by cherry-picking the correlation coefficients.[3] This has been one of the main reasons why American regulators:

- Have so far allowed only a handful of big banks to implement Basel II, and
- They insist that capital requirements for credit risk must be 8%, no matter what the models say.

The United States has over 9000 banks, of which approximately 20 are expected to use the Basel II framework. This evidently poses a problem as Quantitative Impact Study 4 (QIS 4, section 5) has indicated that Basel II would allow the banks adopting it to have a substantial competitive capital advantage over their smaller US counterparts, which must apply Basel IA – a newer American version of Basel I.

Correctly, the US Congress and US regulators have sought to restore competitive equality and to ensure the safety and soundness of the US banking system. They did so by tempering the capital reductions of Basel II's models. They have also maintained a leverage ratio, developed Basel IA and put limits to capital arbitrage by US banking institutions that adopt Basel II. For obvious reasons certain large US banks have resisted these changes as 'contrary to the spirit of Basel' – an argument that is simply nonsense.

2.   Competitive impact of Basel II

In its 30-year history, the Basel Committee on Banking Supervision has acted as a clearing house of ideas on how to strengthen the banking sector through capital adequacy and better governance, and how to establish a policy of handholding among G-10 regulators. It also performed the mission of a standards setter, its strength being based on consensus. This consensus no longer exists.

It is not only that US regulators are deeply concerned about huge capital reductions by marking-to-model credit risk, but also the fact that China and India have not adopted Basel II. At the same time, other countries apply a number of exceptions – not only to Basel II, but also to IFRS – which further reduces hand-holding and the impact of standards. Many experts look at the fact that in a global economy capital standards are not universal as:

- Disquieting, and
- Sure to lead to future tensions.

One of several reasons behind this statement is the fact that there is already significant competitive tension between large US banks and smaller US banks because of A-IRB, as well as the challenge of keeping large US banks competitive with their foreign counterparts, given the limits applied to marking-to-model capital reduction:

- This has put accountants in the eye of the storm of a developing controversy, as capital requirements are subject to international patchwork, and
- The patchwork that was introduced by the central bank of Spain, to provide banks in its jurisdiction with additional business cycle reserves, has turned into an accountant's nightmare.

In connection with the first bullet, the Federal Deposit Insurance Corporation (FDIC) estimates that Basel II banks can expect their capital requirements to fall sharply over a business cycle. *If* so, this will drag the Basel II minimum below the level needed to keep equity ratios above the 8% level for most of a typical economic cycle.

This unwarranted capital reduction comes at a time when, to strengthen banks' capital, American regulators require them to comply with *Prompt Corrective Action* (PCA) requirements (originally introduced in the early 1990s). Indeed, to be called *well capitalized*, a bank must have *Tier-1* capital of at least 5% of its unweighted assets; below 4%, it is considered undercapitalized (the balance to 8% is provided by Tier-2 and hybrids). Some of the questions experts pose have far-reaching consequences:

- With lower weighted average cost of funds, will Basel II A-IRB banks become more capital efficient and generate returns at tighter pricing?
- Would such differences threaten the US banking system and, by extension, the global banking system?

- Will they accelerate or decelerate consolidation in the banking industry?
- Will lower capital requirements lead to more rapid growth or to higher dividends and buybacks?
- Or will the downsized regulatory capital lead to greater exposure and eventually to systemic risk?

Nobody is able to answer such queries in a factual manner at present. What many people say is just guesswork. There is, however, one quantitative estimate of which it is wise to take notice. The way one study had it, 50 basis points (bps) of additional capital headroom for HSBC would support a 50:50 cash and stock acquisition of roughly $12 billion.

Thinking aloud, and only thinking aloud, innovations in risk-based capital estimates affect risk management and therefore, theoretically at least, they should hold a promise. At the negative end, however, are two factors: model risk and the policy of many Basel II banks that artificially 'decide' their correlations of exposure – which is synonymous with creative accounting.

On the positive side, an Ernst & Young study found that 80% of 300 responding banks felt the risk management capabilities developed in the course of Basel II compliance will improve their competitive position. This is reasonable, provided that:

- The whole risk management culture of the bank is revamped from board members and CEO to lower management, and
- There is no regulatory arbitrage, which promotes short-term profits at the expense of creditworthiness.

In the USA, there is evidence that regulatory agencies will not allow capital to drop materially; but this will not necessarily happen in other jurisdictions. Rather, the hope is that rating agencies will downgrade firms that drop capital 'significantly', this being a term still awaiting definition.

Other signs, however, are negative. With Basel's EL and UL mix up, in conjunction with the fusion of economic capital and regulatory capital, a bank's capital will not be aligned with risk taking. Adding to the prevailing leverage ratio actually encourages more risk taking. Leverage capital and risk-based capital are not the same thing:

$$\text{Leverage capital} = \frac{\text{Capital}}{\text{Assets}} \tag{10.1}$$

$$\text{Risk-based capital} = \frac{\text{Capital}}{\text{Risk-adjusted assets}} \tag{10.2}$$

As the Federal Deposit Insurance Corporation (FDIC) points out, there is no evidence that the limits placed on US banks' leverage requirements have created for them a competitive disadvantage. American banks have had to follow leverage requirements since 1991, yet their growth and profitability have substantially outpaced growth in the broader economy, and this is true in every country. Rather than constituting a competitive disadvantage, strong capital has contributed to the strength and resilience of the US banking system.

3. Accounting-based indicators

One of the negatives of Basel II, and most particularly of IRB, is that it has failed to account for *model risk* in the way that VAR does with back testing. However, the risk that model-based estimates can be 'off the mark' is always present. An ISDA study showed that there is reasonable convergence of the banking industry's internal credit models when applied to simple hypothetical credit portfolios.

- The fact that different models behave similarly when parameters and calculation choices are controlled is good news
- The bad news is that a key reason when results of internal models do not converge is the arbitrary choice of parameters, which might be accidental but also intentional.

'The free choice of model parameters is the 21st century's version of creative accounting,' said a banker. This is true, and it is creating major unanswered questions (and regulatory concerns) about Basel II's advanced approach, including:

- The true level of regulatory capital requirements
- Unwanted dispersion of economic capital
- Potential competitive effects, and
- Likelihood of systemic risk.

A sound way to assess the performance of an individual bank is to compare its accounting data and share price with similar indicators computed for a peer group. Comparisons based on both accounting-based and market-based information can be aggregated to form a peer group distribution with expected value and standard deviation of dispersion.

Today, there exist several accounting-based indicators attempting to gauge various aspects of banking sector performance, including overall profitability, asset quality, efficiency and compliance to regulatory capital rules. To arrive at a more comprehensive assessment, this information should be complemented with data extracted from market indicators like stock prices, price/earnings ratios and more:

- Accounting data is based on actual outcomes reflected in financial reporting
- Market data is based on investors' expectations of future bank performance, formed by adding up all available information on a bank's outlook.

Moreover, credit risk and market risk factors should be aggregated. Market risk capital rules have broader coverage, bringing together trading assets and liabilities. They are also affected by liquidity risk (Chapter 9) and business risk (Chapter 3) considerations. Credit risk capital rules are more focused but, as of recently, subject to uncertainty and controversy.

Andrew Carnegie, the 19th century's great industrialist and 20th century philanthropist, had a rule that Basel II violated: 'Don't begin a new departure without first testing fully upon a small scale.' The eight years from 1999 to 2007 were horse trading rather than testing – as the dismal results of Quantitative Impact Study 4 (QIS 4) and QIS 5 document; they were not the 'small-scale' testing Carnegie aptly recommended.

Because of this, banks and regulatory authorities that go wholesale on Basel II are sure to encounter many surprises in the coming years. My guess is that commercial banks are wrong in their fear that without bending the rules they would be facing huge capital requirements. Carnegie's dictum should have been religiously applied with:

- Correlation coefficients, and
- Risk-weighted assets (RWAs).

In many cases, risk-weighted assets expanded due to organic growth in loan books and in other exposures, and in some specific instances they could have increased due to mergers with other banks. At the same time, the loss of goodwill from core capital also tends to reduce Tier-1 capital.

If experience from European banks is used as a proxy, due to a general increase in RWAs the weighted average Tier-1 ratio declined slightly, from 8.1% in 2005 to 8.0% in the first half of 2006.[4] Basel I's 8% capital ratio is in no way outrageous. It was a compromise that made possible the 1988 Capital Accord. It is an average and, by itself, an average does not mean much. More meaningful is a system that:

- Computes risks and determines exposures to be covered by eligible funds
- But also keeps in perspective historical precedence, which helps in establishing the lower limits of prudential capital.

Between 1840 and the late 1870s, among European banks the average ratio of capital over assets fluctuated between 24% and 36%, with a mean value slightly above 30%. In the subsequent 20 years, however, it dropped steadily and by 1900 it dipped below the 20% level.

In the inter-World War I/World War II years, the capital ratio stabilized in the 12–16% range (way above Basel's 8%), with a much smaller volatility than in the mid-19th century. Then, during WWII, it again took a dive. In the post-WWII years, and prior to the 1988 Capital Accord, the *average* capital ratio held within a narrow 6–8% band. This has been:

- Less than a quarter of what it was 100 years earlier, and
- Only half of the capital ratio featured by the banking industry in the inter-war period.

If capital ratios have varied so widely over time, *then* we should find a way to calibrate them. One of the better ways for enriching the information content of accounting-based indicators is to relate them to *volatility*: of the bank's income sources and of the market at large. Raw accounting data may not fully incorporate the risks incurred by credit institutions. Given the fact that if individual banks take on different levels of risk, returns will not be strictly comparable.

A way of risk-adjusting accounting return measures is to normalize them with the standard deviation of net bank income in an attempt to adjust for risk. When risk-adjusted indicators reflect similar aspects of bank performance, they would tend to correlate, provided the necessary care is taken to assure reasonable homogeneity among institutions included in the peer-to-peer test.

An example is provided from US banking. A new notion in US regulation connected to Basel II's scope of implementation is the class of *core banks*. To this class belong credit institutions with assets equal to or more than $250 billion, and/or consolidated total on-balance sheet foreign exposure of equal to or more than $10 billion. (Back in the mid-1990s, the Swiss Banking Commission had instituted a class of *big banks*, roughly corresponding to the US core banks.)

Core bank holding companies are those of consolidated total assets (excluding assets held by an insurance underwriting subsidiary) of equal to or more than $250 billion, or consolidated total on-balance sheet foreign exposure equal to or more than $10 billion, or a subsidiary depository institution that is a core bank or opt-in bank (any qualified institution may opt in).

In the USA, core banks must use the Advanced IRB method to calculate and report capital ratios, unless their primary Federal supervisor determines in writing that this requirement 'is not appropriate in light of the bank's asset size, level of complexity, risk profile and scope of operations'. This is still a proposed guideline, but its application in other jurisdictions that adopted Basel II can help in streamlining some of the rough edges.

4. Tier-1, Tier-2, Tier-3 capital and the hybrids

From section 1 the reader will remember that the Basel Capital Accord of 1988 addressed exposures arising from credit risks. It also specified that these must be backed by the bank's own funds (Tier-1) and some other eligible funds (Tier-2). With the 1996 Market Risk Amendment, the algorithm became:

$$\frac{\text{Own funds} + \text{Other eligible own funds}}{\text{Risk-weighted exposures from credit risk} + \text{Charges for market risk}} \geq 8\%$$

$$(10.3)$$

Independent credit rating agencies, however, are not happy when a credit institution bets its future only on regulatory capital, and this affects the level of creditworthiness they assign to an institution:

- *If* a bank has only regulatory capital to cover credit risk
- *Then* it may be a BBB institution, at the edge of investment grade or even lower.

Self-respecting banks are targeting 'AA' credit rating, which is an imaginative business but not an easy one. As 'AA', and even more so as 'AA+' or 'AAA', the bank must have more economic capital than otherwise – at the 99.97% level of confidence (Chapter 4). It should also appreciate that *target rating*:

- Has global perspective, and
- It can be a financial burden.

A basic characteristic of high credit rating is that it constitutes a moving target, since it is a lagging indicator depending on assumed risks (credit, market, operational), transfer risk(s), credit cycle, quality of management and, evidently, economic capital beyond regulatory capital requirements.

Other constraints regard the *quality* of regulatory capital. The capital each bank puts aside has its own profile, but there are limits to what management can do in gaming the system.

Regulatory capital principally consists of *Tier-1* (T-1), or *core capital*, and *Tier-2* (T-2) capital as defined by the 1988 Capital Accord. Around the year 2000, two other categories were introduced: *Hybrid Tier-1* (HT-1) and *Tier-3* (T-3) capital. Independent rating agencies don't buy HT-1. 'We don't consider hybrids as core capital,' said Walter Pompliano of Standard & Poor's. Regulators, however, permit HT-1 to constitute up to 15% of Tier-1 – which amounts to a T-1 discount.

Discounts go against good sense because the purpose of banks' core capital is to absorb major losses in order to safeguard the solvency of the institution and enable it to continue operating as a business. That's why regulatory core capital originally consisted of mainly equity, which belongs to the bank and is used at the board's discretion when the need arises.

- HT-1 is hybrid in the sense that it has some characteristics of equity, some of debt and much of leveraging
- T-3 capital comes from trading profits and, because it arises mainly from derivatives trading, it is very volatile.

For instance, one type of hybrid capital may pay a regular dividend based on a par value, treated in a way similar to equity for regulatory purposes. The pros say that expansion of risk-weighted assets (RWAs) made it necessary for banks to find additional sources of longer-term capital. Critics answer that hybrids are destablizers, not pillars of the financial system.

- The characteristic of equity is that in an adversity it finds itself in the front line, and management can use it without constraints
- The opposite is true with debt, which management cannot dispose freely for solvency reasons, since it constitutes other parties' assets.

After 2000, declines in long-term interest rates, coupled with increasing investor appetite for junk bonds, supported a growing number of hybrids. Moreover, according to the pros, banks welcome these instruments because they provide a cost-effective way of raising loss-absorbing capital. Cost-effective they may be, but how secure are they when a crisis hits?

Critics say that the pros' arguments about hybrids don't hold water because they take no account of risk factors, which can wipe out hybrid capital. The only argument that holds water is the hybrids' use of current tax laws. Dividends on equity are paid out of post-tax profit, whereas the coupon payments on bonds are tax deductible. Therefore, banks and plenty of other companies have an interest in structuring security transactions so that, for tax reasons, they are treated as debt.

Many of the worries associated with hybrid instruments concern their loss absorption capacity and their permanence. Equity is permanent, hybrids are not. Their inclusion depends on the decision of the local regulator, and this dents the assumed universality of Basel II. Even the interpretation of a hybrid is not universal:

- If the hybrid is deemed to be equity, it may be included in Tier-1
- If it is deemed to be more debt-like, it will be placed in Tier-2.

Some regulators say that, from a financial stability viewpoint, it is preferable that these hybrid securities behave like equity, by being capable of absorbing losses and providing a practically permanent source of capital. But that's a pipe dream. In the case of financial turbulence, hybrids will not be sufficiently strong to keep a bank out of distress:

- The pros say that hybrids could do so by deferring payments (subject to regulatory approval) for several years of dividends on trust-preferred securities
- Critics respond that deferral of payments can have a very negative impact on a bank's reputation and an adverse bearing on its future ability to raise funds in debt markets.

Furthermore, when evaluating hybrids, the reader should bear in mind that all forms of regulatory capital are there to help the credit institution face *expected losses*. In terms of good business practice, the safe bet is that neither expected risks nor unexpected risks are instantaneous. Like business cycles and economic downturns, an entity's downs take years to develop and correct. Therefore:

- One of the challenges is the computation of the holding period of return
- This computation must be seen as a management requirement rather than a regulatory issue.

What the supervisors require is that, within the medium- to longer-term perspective, the board must not only assure compliance to regulatory capital, but also have enough additional reserves to cover the bank's business risk, liquidity risk and other channels of exposure.

The top three major contributors to exposure, shown in Figure 10.1, are closely followed up by supervisors. By contrast, the bottom two big risk factors are left at management's discretion – and the way in which they are watched speaks volumes about the bank's governance.

In conclusion, rather than trying to reduce regulatory capital requirements through hybrids and model risk, the board, CEO and senior managers should remember that financial power can quickly turn to ashes. In 1989, at the apogee of the Japanese banks' brief rise in the world's financial capitalization, the Japanese financial industry had an impressive $400 billion in unrealized profits.

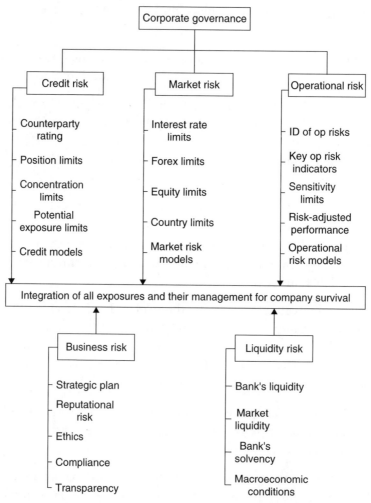

Figure 10.1   A global view of risk control and capital allocation in financial institutions

Suddenly, this turned into a $1.2 trillion torrent of red ink, which has been very serious because:

- Japanese banks were never strongly capitalized, and
- Their special reserves have been negligible or completely non-existent.

Not everybody appreciates the importance of special reserves, which go well beyond regulatory capital, and in some countries they are even illegal. Yet, they can be life-savers. On 15 November 2002, after injecting another $1 billion into

Winterthur, Crédit Suisse exhausted its special reserves. In Wall Street, some experts said that this completely changed its risk profile.

5. The high risk of too little capital: a lesson from QIS 4 and QIS 5

In theory, greater sophistication in doing something provides better assurance in terms of end results. In practice, this might happen only if the new solution does not weaken the safeguards. Until the 1980s, the control of market risk was fully manual. In the early 1990s, analytics were enriched by tools collectively known as 'the Greeks'.[5] Today, technology allows market risk control to be exercised in real time, using models and simulators, but:

- The 99% level of confidence is used with VAR still in place and is utterly inadequate, and
- VAR itself is an obsolete model doing an average job, which becomes more irrelevant as the complexity of financial instruments increases.

With Basel II's IRB methods for credit risk control, the notional limits of credit risk become dynamic and credit risk evaluation is ratings driven. Both are positive developments, and the same is true of the fact that expected default frequency (EDF) and individual counterparty analysis have become 'musts', as well as companies having started using finer-grain time buckets for credit rating. However, something has gone wrong.

In brief, the method has failed, as the results of two Quantitative Impact Studies – QIS 4 (in the USA and Germany) and QIS 5 (in the rest of Europe, published in July 2005) – demonstrate.[6] Even more vehemently criticized by experts has been the rush with which the Basel Committee and national regulators (with the exception of the USA) have implemented an untested Basel II.

Released in February 2005, the QIS 4 results have alarmed American regulators because risk-based capital requirements were significantly and materially reduced. This changed the dynamics of the reform process the Basel Committee had targeted in 1999, and in September 2005 it led to US congressional hearings where top priority has been given to:

- Safety, and
- Soundness.

The huge capital reductions QIS 4 and QIS 5 have shown were achieved by gaming the system (and the models' input). Ironically, it comes at a time when the quality distribution of G-10 financial institutions is loaded on the BBB side – barely investment grade.

Research project after research project shows that the creditworthiness of banks is deteriorating. The trend in the 1990s was particularly disquieting, as Figure 10.2 shows. More recently, as Table 10.1 shows, research by the Bank of England indicates that credit rating of the world's top financial institutions is almost normally distributed with BBB as mean, while A and BB (non-investment grade) have practically equal weight on two sides of the mean:

- This is hardly a situation to warrant less regulatory capital, and
- *If* the models said so, *then* the models are plainly wrong.

The message the preceding paragraphs convey is that no matter what the models say, First World banks' balance sheets are weak and this poses challenges in regard to their solvency. Regulatory capital resources are not there for their own sake, but to absorb those risks that cannot be covered by current earnings. Solvency is a major determinant of risk-bearing capacity, but somehow it seems to have been left along with other skeletons in the closet.

It would be superfluous to explain that it is always necessary to retain a capital base that is commensurate with *potential risk*. Therefore, the results of QIS 4 have created concern among US regulators about capital requirements and their fulfilment by different Basel II models. The whole issue of undercapitalization is counter-productive:

- Avoiding substantial reductions in capital requirements was part of the original Basel II agreement, and
- Substantially reducing capital requirements could harm the safety and soundness of our banking system.

Some bankers say that the results of QIS 4 should not have been surprising, because most of the capital drop was attributed to the cycle, and anyway rating agencies would downgrade firms that dropped capital greatly. This argument has little merit.

Credit downgrading is a lagging indicator and pre-commitment through IRB is an early indicator – these two should not be confused. Additionally, as Table 10.2 demonstrates, QIS 4 has shown a very substantial difference in capital requirements for fairly similar exposures, in the same business cycle. Among the most likely reasons are:

- The IRB model needs considerably more fine-tuning than was originally thought, and
- Many different parties are carrying out *mathematical model arbitrage* through correlations and risk-weighting factors.

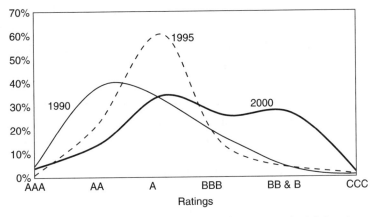

Figure 10.2   Ratings distribution of global banks according to Standard & Poor's. (By permission of Walter Pompliano, Standard & Poor's)

Table 10.1   G-10 quality distribution in the financial industry – Bank of England research using 1990–92 credit risk transition*

Rating	Percentage
AAA	3.0
AA	5.6
A	26.9
BBB	29.8
BB	26.2
B	5.6
CCC or less	0.9
Defaulted	2.0

* Statistics presented at the 'Capital Allocation 2003' Conference of the IIR, London, 21–22 January 2003.

Table 10.2   Large reductions in risk-based capital requirements shown in QIS 4 estimates

Percentage change in	Weighted average (%)	Median (%)
Total capital requirement	−15.5	−26.3
Tier-1 capital requirement	−21.8	−30.8

Source: QIS 4 in the USA.

Based on FDIC calculations, which reflect QIS 4 findings, Table 10.3 shows that 20 of 26 participating banks – or 77% – think that IRB allows them to have *less than 3% Tier-1 capital* (half of them with less than 2%). This is 'computed' at a time when the minimum Tier-1 capital requirement for well-capitalized banks is 5% of risk-weighted assets in the USA and at least 4% internationally.

To make a bad situation worse, QIS 4 shows that there have also been large reductions in capital requirements for derivative financial instruments, like counterparty credit risk charge for OTC derivatives and securities financing transactions:

- With securitizations the capital reduction indicated by QIS 4 was 18%, and
- For all off-balance sheet exposures, excluding OTC derivatives, capital requirements showed a decrease of 19%.

Credit risk weights, too, got the haircut of their life. The credit risk weight for small business loans, which is 100% under Basel IA, decreased to 61% under Basel II/QIS 4. That of high-volatility commercial real estate dropped from 100% to 70%, and for other commercial real estate loans descended even further to 48%.

The results of QIS 5, conducted with credit institutions from 31 countries, were even worse in terms of capital adequacy. Participating in this test were 56 Group 2 banks in G-10 countries and 146 Group 2 banks from countries other than G-10. (Group 1 includes those fulfilling all of the following criteria: T-1 capital of more than 3 billion euro ($3.9 billion), diversification of assets and international banking business.)

For various reasons,[7] a comparison between QIS 5 and previous quantitative impact studies (with the possible exception of QIS 4) is unwise. But even if looked at in isolation:

- The results of QIS 5 are an unmitigated disaster, and
- If these are compared to QIS 1, 2, 2.5 and 3, the whole process of marking-to-model capital requirements looks strange.

Indeed, as several cognizant people remarked, the results of QIS 5 are simply a laughing matter. According to them, Group 1 G-10 banks will *reduce* their capital requirements by 7.1%(!), Group 2 G-10 banks will *reduce* them by 26.7% (!!) and non-G-10 banks will *reduce* them by 29.0% (!!!). And why not by 100%?!

In November 2006, the Financial Stability Review of the Deutsche Bundesbank (a very serious publication from a very serious central bank) noted that data collected from over 100 participating banks during QIS 4 and QIS 5 made it possible to carry out a stress test using an approach that allows direct assessment of the

Table 10.3 QIS 4 minimum Tier-1 requirements of US banks, as percentage of on-balance sheet assets

Ratio	Number of entities in range
<2%	10
2–3%	10
3–4%	4
4–5%	0
>5%	2
Total QIS-4 banks	**26**

Source: FDIC calculations based on QIS 4.

Table 10.4 Capital ratios depending on stress intensity

	Average capital ratios (%)		
	No stress	Moderate stress	Severe stress
Group 1	12.2	11.4	10.8
Group 2	14.2	13.4	12.8

Source: Deutsche Bundesbank, Financial Stability Review, Frankfurt, November 2006.

impact of changes to the input parameters on capital ratios. Two different stress scenarios were studied:

- Moderate, and
- Severe.

For all exposures, *probabilities of default* (PDs) were increased by 30% in the moderate stress scenario and *by 60%* in the severe stress scenario. As the cyclical fluctuations of the PDs are likely to be lower for this asset class, lower add-ons were applied to the PDs for retail exposure:

- Moderate scenario 15%
- Severe scenario 30%.

The assessment showed a reduction in the average capital ratio for a range of banks, from large internationally active ones to those of small and medium size. But, as shown in Table 10.4, capital adequacy ratios were clearly above the required minimum of 8% of risk-weighted assets. Stress scenarios, the Bundesbank suggests, can be enhanced by increasing the loss-given default (LGD), as is likely to be the case in a cyclical downturn.

6. Innovation in risk management: market discipline and operational risk

The trend towards hybrid capital, the dismal results of QIS 4 and QIS 5, and the fact that Basel II institutions will find further incentives to hold high risk-weight assets in non-bank or off-balance sheet structures are significant negative factors as regards risk management. Experts say that these three issues present plenty of new *regulatory arbitrage* opportunities, whose consequences are difficult to predict.

Contrary to these developments, Basel II features three positive innovations: *stress testing*; capital for *operational risk*; and *market discipline*. To appreciate the notion underpinning market discipline, it should be kept in mind that different groups of investors in a bank have different approaches and incentives in valuing:

* Its management, and
* Its financial results.

These different ways of valuing management policies and practices extend all the way from strategic choices to capital structure, capital adequacy, credit risk, market risk, operational risk, risk appetite and risk control.

As a group, shareholders expect, on average, higher yields for riskier investments. Therefore, they tend to be less sensitive to a bank's higher risk taking than depositors and creditors. Contrary to equity holders, depositors, lenders and holders of subordinated debt have an incentive to monitor a bank's risk taking because they have no stake in the upside from greater profits, but are fully exposed to an institution's risk appetite.

Along with creditors and bondholders, the interbank market (used by banks for short-term refinancing) reacts negatively to higher risk appetite – and is capable of exercising effective market discipline. Given that relatively large amounts are traded on the interbank market, its participants have a considerable incentive for acting as watchdogs, particularly so as banks are well positioned to obtain and evaluate information about their peers.

It is no less true, on the other hand, that despite the fact that market participants can exercise discipline, its effect may wane whenever a bank is under the threat of insolvency, particularly when the heavy hand of the state interferes with market action. Market discipline, in other words, is not a linear process.

Many companies have operational risks that tend to overlap, at least partly, with market risk and credit risk. Operational risks are present whether the business is regulated or deregulated, centralized or decentralized, old technology or high technology, local, nationally based or international, characterized by simple or complex products, or trading through a single or multiple channels. In general, operational risk:

- Is causal
- Event-oriented, and
- Its consequences are loss and damage.

Many operating risk problems have so far escaped management's attention because they are elusive. Normal tests do not necessarily reveal them. We have to do *stress testing*. Three different types of stress tests are relevant:

- *Scenario writing*, like the Delphi method
- *Sensitivity analysis*
- *Statistical inference*, under normal and extreme conditions.

A prerequisite to the monitoring of operational risk events is the clear definition of primary and secondary indicators. Key indicators for operational risk include: outstanding risk claims; number of errors, by channel; frequency of other incidents; impact of each class of incidents in economic terms; legal issues (Chapter 9); level and sophistication of staff training; staff turnover; and the way in which jobs are organized and supported – including information technology (IT) support.

Operational risks often result in reputational damage and they are characterized by a certain synergy with each other. Basel II's definition of operational risks goes beyond the more classical cases of external fraud and internal fraud. Additionally, since 1999, when it first came into the public eye, this list has been extended to include, among others, management risk and technology risk. Figure 10.3 gives a bird's eye view of classical, modern and IT-oriented operational risks.

'*Management risk*,' according to the senior executive of one of the global banks, 'is *our* No. 1 operational risk. It represents one of six or seven operational risk cases [confronting us].' Next in importance is *event risk*, followed by technology risk. Included in the latter are:

- System reliability
- Analysis/programming, and
- Model risk.

As an example of the third bullet, the executive I was talking to made reference to value at risk (VAR), saying that: 'VAR has clean parameters. But how do you value somebody's incompetence?' 'A challenge is that we don't have enough data to model information technology risk,' commented another banker.

As my research has documented, a salient problem in operational risk control is that the staff is not fully trained, and some of the work being done lacks focus because of a lack of clear directives. To be in charge of these issues, staff training should include an understanding of what drives people to obey or break the rules put in place to keep operational risk under control. It should also deal with the four reasons reinforcing operational risk:

- People don't know *what* is being targeted
- They don't understand *how* to be in charge
- They don't *want* to do it in a rigorous way, so as not to offend other people's sensibilities, and
- They don't *like* to be controlled in what they are doing.

Experience from other fields of endeavour also demonstrates that headway will not be made by attacking all operational risks at once, but rather by selecting the top operational risk issues as salient problems and bringing them to senior management's attention.

With the implementation of Basel II, bank supervisors require individual credit institutions to have in place operational risk management policies and processes to identify, assess, monitor and mitigate operational risk. These policies and processes must be adequate for the size and complexity of the bank's operations. Another requirement is that policies and processes for the management of operational risk must be approved, and periodically reviewed, by the board.

According to the rules of Basel II, national supervisors review the quality and comprehensiveness of the institution's operational risk control, as well as its contingency plans, to satisfy themselves that the bank is able to operate without undue exposure to operational risks, including those that may arise from disturbances to the payment and settlement system (Chapter 9) in the event of severe business disruption.

With Basel II, national supervisors also determine that banks in their jurisdiction have established appropriate information technology policies and processes that address areas such as information security commensurate with the size and complexity of their operations. Figure 10.4 presents, on a log–log scale, results of a Monte Carlo simulation of probability of exposure due to operational risk.

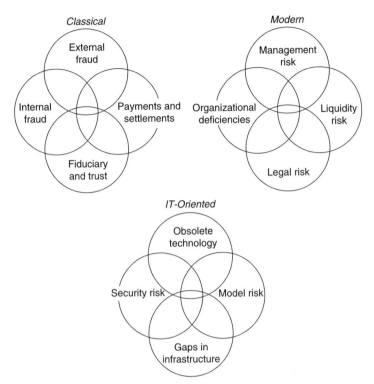

Classical

External
fraud

Internal
fraud

Payments and
settlements

Fiduciary
and trust

Modern

Management
risk

Organizational
deficiencies

Liquidity
risk

Legal risk

IT-Oriented

Obsolete
technology

Security risk

Model risk

Gaps in
infrastructure

Figure 10.3   Three different groups of operational risk present in practically every organization

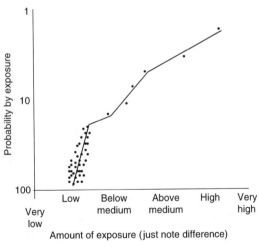

Figure 10.4   Results of a Monte Carlo simulation presented on a log–log scale of probability of exposure due to operational risks

7. Return on investment from Basel II would be better governance

Responses to the query on the cost of implementing Basel II vary widely with the institution. An early 'guestimate' was 'more than Year 2000 (Y2K)'. It was followed by an estimate of £100 million ($194 million) made by a large British bank, and more recently by an expense between $50 million and $100 million for every 100 billion of assets, which is a great deal of money.

Confronted with that expense, one may ask: 'How much business capability is acquired with the required investment?' A short answer to this query is that greater business capability should be found in areas such as:

- Better governance
- Focused analytics
- Real-time simulation
- Risk-based pricing (Chapter 11), and
- The kind of scientific experimentation that can be found in R&D labs.

Yes, but how many commercial banks have the culture and technology to benefit from these bullets? *If*, and only if, it is properly implemented, high-technology is making it possible that: risks are measured in real time; not only mean value, but also confidence intervals are computed (Chapter 4); and correlation assumptions as well as all types of weights are tested against real-life statistics, and appropriately corrected. But is this being done?

The necessary cultural change was supposed to be promoted through Basel II, but the results of QIS 4 and QIS 5 put this in doubt (section 5). Moreover, several structural issues must be revamped to help in the necessary transformation of an institution's risk management culture. Some of these changes should have taken place prior to Basel II, but they are yet to be made. Therefore, in evaluating cost and benefit, it is advisable to differentiate between:

- Mandatory costs associated with Basel II, and
- Gaps in the bank's risk management armoury that should be closed anyway, as shown in Table 10.5.

Beyond that, the level of costs of Basel II is closely associated with project organization, leadership and effectiveness. Some organizational issues are defined by regulators. For instance, in the USA, after meeting the criteria for a *core bank*, a credit institution must adopt a written plan to comply with Basel II within a start date of no more than 36 months.

Table 10.5   Measuring the cost of implementing Basel II

Mandatory Basel II costs	Gaps that should be closed
	Cultural change
	Risk models
	Rocket scientists
	Correlations of exposure
	Steady management training, including board and CEO
Bought models (RAROC, MKMV, others)	Granular rating system
Methodology for SPD	Methodology for PD, DP
Methodology for SLGD	Methodology for LGD
Methodology for SEAD	Methodology for EAD
Methodology for UL	Methodology for EL
Operational risk control	Reliable and rich DB
Risk-based pricing	Any-to-any network
Economic capital allocation	Real-time IT solutions
Closer scrutiny by regulators (Pillar 2)	Expert systems
Transparency, market discipline (Pillar 3)	Rigorous risk control methods and measurements
	Better than haircut measures of collateral
	Reliable financial reporting (Sarbanes–Oxley)
	Steadily improved governance

There also exist costs of Basel II associated with mergers and acquisitions. A Basel II bank that acquires a non-Basel II bank may continue to use the acquired bank's Basel IA rules for its exposures for up to 24 months after the calendar quarter in which the acquisition was completed. Then, an acquired entity must comply with Basel II.

A cost item, but also a major contributor to Basel II's return on investment, is the *use test*, which is a polyvalent proposition. Systems, processes and procedures used by a Basel II bank must be consistent with the bank's internal risk management processes and executive information reporting solutions. Assuring such consistency requires ongoing validation, including:

- Outcomes analysis
- Back testing, and
- Senior management appreciation of the obtained results.

Return on investment is highest if this understanding and appreciation of results from analytical studies associated with Basel II characterizes all levels of management of the credit institution. Experimentation may involve simulation exercises replicating crisis scenarios that will help the institution's managers and professionals understand how they should act and react in a real-life crisis situation.

Based on stress testing and other methods, crisis simulation exercises can be instrumental in developing the organization's preparedness for crisis management. An effective solution would integrate different disciplines into one well-knit system that can serve in a polyvalent manner not only classical style risk control, but also modern approaches to management of complexity that employ scientific experimentation.

Another cost item is expenses associated with a methodological approach requiring the best available skills. A rush to solutions has been the Achilles heel of Basel II. The concept underpinning IRB is not wrong. What is wrong is that it has not undergone thorough laboratory testing, and this led to the QIS 4 and QIS 5 snafus. Moreover, instead of applying the brilliant original idea of treating unequal losses – expected losses (EL) and unexpected losses (UL) – in different ways, risk control details have been squashed by merging them, after unwisely adding to their joint effect operational risk and whatever else could be found around – ending with much less regulatory capital than credit risk alone.

It goes without saying that this is the antithesis of better governance. Therefore, the best hope to recover Basel II costs has been thrown away. There is an American saying that a camel is a horse designed by a committee. That's where we are now with Basel II and it is, indeed, a pity. Models and computers should be used to:

- Act as a microscope on risk, and
- Expand the horizon of our vision.

Instead, the whole business has been poorly managed, with more attention paid to gaming the system than to bringing scientific management into banking. This has done a disservice to the banking industry. Time has been lost, but one can always hope that the current improvisation will fade away in the rear-view mirror, and new leadership at the Basel Committee will deal with the real problems and put Basel II back on the right lines.

Notes

1   D.N. Chorafas, *The 1996 Market Risk Amendment: Understanding the Marking-to-Model and Value-at-Risk*. McGraw-Hill, Burr Ridge, IL, 1998.
2   D.N. Chorafas, *Stress Testing for Risk Control Under Basel II*. Elsevier, Oxford, 2007.

3 D.N. Chorafas, *After Basel II: Assuring Compliance and Smoothing the Rough Edges.* Lafferty/VRL Publishing, London, 2005.
4 European Central Bank, Financial Stability Review, Frankfurt, December 2006.
5 D.N. Chorafas, *Advanced Financial Analysis.* Euromoney Books, London, 1994.
6 D.N. Chorafas, *Stress Testing for Risk Control Under Basel II.* Elsevier, Oxford, 2007.
7 D.N. Chorafas, *Stress Testing for Risk Control Under Basel II.* Elsevier, Oxford, 2007.

Risk-based Pricing

1. Counting the odds

> 'Buffett said: "What do you think the odds of this thing making it are?" I said, "Pretty good. One out of two." He said, "Do you think that's good? Why don't you go in an airplane with a parachute that opens one out of every two times and jump?" '[1]

Counting the odds is a cornerstone of risk-based pricing, but it is not easy because the financial world in which we live is so complex and there is a tendency to confuse apples and pears, like the case of EL and UL with Basel II (Chapter 10). The good news is that science and technology provide us with tools that allow us to count the odds in a fairly dependable way:

- From science, particularly physics and engineering, banking inherits a wealth of analytics, and
- Technology provides any-to-any networks and computers to be used for simulation and experimentation.

Clear minds have seen this. In the early 1950s, Dr Robert Oppenheimer prophetically suggested that the computer is much more than a glorified accounting machine, and it can offer a totally different level of insight and foresight than previously possible. But then he added that it would take two or three decades to realize the difference.

At the heart of Oppenheimer's hypothesis was the fact that with a programmable general-purpose computer we can simulate any real-life system. This paralleled the original thoughts of Dr Alan Turing and his 'Turing machine', a hypothetical device widely considered as the conceptual forerunner of modern computational procedures.

Whether in banking or in science, what really matters in attacking the problem of complexity and of risks associated with instruments and processes is the notion of *computability*. This can be expressed in two bullets:

- By following a programmable course, a man-made device can perform what are normally regarded as mental manipulations
- This is the algorithmic computational process that accountants and financial experts have been using all along in their professional duties.

The concept of computability, which by counting the odds enables risk-based pricing of financial instruments, has underpinned many of the developments in engineering and physics. Most significantly, it constitutes the foundations on which lie the edifice of mathematical models – from simple algebraic equations to nonlinearities, stochastic processes, heuristics, simulators and fuzzy engineering.[2]

As many successful implementations in finance and industry document, mathematical models provide a structural quantitative approach to the freedom of expression while a verbal description offers the qualitative complement. As with accounting, every structured procedure must be thoroughly studied *ex ante*:

- Accounting programmes are designed primarily to prevent unauthorized tinkering with financial information
- Whereas modelling programmes are designed to encourage tinkering with the data, which is the sense of counting the odds.

The notions behind these two bullets complement one another. Luca Paciolo, the man who laid the foundations of accounting, was a mathematician and his seminar work required a comprehensive view of models and modelling. What professionals from all walks of life have in common is the drive to simplify the complexities confronting them in their daily work:

- Abstraction and idealization underpin both accounting and the art of management
- Whether consciously or unconsciously, by abstracting we simplify and model the real world.

The first challenge in risk-based pricing is this power to abstract and simplify – which permits us to identify, qualify and quantify exposures associated with each type of transaction. This needs to be done before the transaction is concluded. This real-time response is the cornerstone of risk-based analysis (see also section 6 in Chapter 9):

- *If* we don't know the risks
- *Then* we cannot price our product in a way that covers assumed exposure(s) and leaves a profit.

Risk-based pricing, however, raises a second challenge: that of selling the properly priced product to the counterparty. Risk-based pricing will be a theoretical exercise if the product does not sell, and it may not sell because embedded risk may see to it that the price becomes too high. This case confronts top management in all pricing issues, and in extremis it can be phrased in these terms:

- Will the company cut the price and risk bankruptcy?
- Or will it stick to risk-based pricing and lose business?

The answer will most likely fall between these two bullets. Even when it is not fully observed, risk-based pricing serves as both benchmark and warning. When deviations from it occur, the salient problem is: Shall we use risk-based pricing only as a discovery mechanism or as pricing rule?

Both options have merits. For instance, risk-based pricing might lead to exiting some markets or to shifting bad risks from one bank to another, less sophisticated and with poor knowledge of assumed risks. Therefore, both in the short and the longer term, risk information must be available:

- At all times
- For any product
- In every channel
- In regard to every counterparty.

Within an expanding global market and growing interdependence between financial institutions through 24-hour trading, both opportunities and risks oblige banks to rethink in a rigorous manner the nature of their pricing methods, along with the ways and means of re-evaluating their exposures and capital requirements.

Prior to its merger into Chemical Banking, the Manufacturers Hanover Trust Company (MHTC) had found that, day in and day out at about 14.00 hours, it had on its books $2.5 billion in exposure with only one counterparty: General Motors. This risk was not accounted for in pricing its services.

Controlling the pricing of financial instruments means analysing and sizing up their risks, keeping them under surveillance in *real time*. But in most financial institutions, today, effective intra-day *risk tracking* is practically non-existent. 'If one big customer company goes belly up,' a cognizant banker said during our meeting in London, 'the bank can go out of business.'

2. Primary and consequential risks

While many risks are inherent in business activities, not all of them are of equal importance. To help them with the choice of salient exposures, on which they should be concentrating their attention, many banks differentiate between primary, or first-order, and consequential, or second-order, risks. *Primary risks* are the exposures deliberately entered into through transactions:

- *Credit risk*, including credit spread risk
- *Market risk*, including interest rates, currency exchange rates, equities and other commodities, and
- *Liquidity*, including funding risk and mismatch risk.

Funding risk is the likelihood that our bank may be unable to fund itself in order to meet assumed obligations at a reasonable price or, in extreme situations, at any price. Liquidity risk does not come directly under Basel II (Chapter 10), but its importance is such that it must be studied by risk factor for all operations by instrument, currency and market.

To confront liquidity risk, some banks establish *liquidity limits* based on two levels of reference: one first order, the other second order. Liquidity risk *per se* is first order. By contrast, *liquidity volume* by open position and by individual security is usually classified as second-order risk.

Consequential (second-order) *risks* are mainly, but not necessarily exclusively, operational. They consist of exposures that are not actively taken, but which are incurred as a consequence of business being undertaken. *Transaction processing risk*, for example, is consequential, arising from errors, failures or shortcomings at any point in the transaction process, and from deal execution and back-office work.

Similarly, settlement risk is consequential and so is *compliance risk*, which may result in financial loss due to regulatory fines or penalties, restriction or suspension of activity, business risk, reputational risk (Chapter 12) and so on. Some banks expand the notion of second-order risk to include factors such as:

- Yield curve
- Interest rate basis risk
- Cross-currency basis risk
- Swap spread, and
- Option delta, gamma, meta, kappa, rho.[3]

We can study through simulation *yield curve risk*, in connection to non-parallel shift in yield curves. We can also analyse interest rate basis risk arising from movements in the spread between, say, LIBOR and non-LIBOR indices. Other study themes include cases influenced by cross-country curves, as contrasted with single-currency curves.

Swap spread risk arises from the spread between swap rates and rates on underlying government bonds. Movements in the option's underlying bonds are at the origin of option delta and option gamma. *Delta* is the first derivative of the underlying bonds and *gamma* is the second derivative. Option volatility risk arises from volatility changes, which are reflected in *kappa*.

Theta measures the loss of computed value for each day that passes with no movement in the price of the underlying bonds. *Rho* is the change in the option price per 1% change in the interest rate. This is a significant statistic that also has an impact upon carrying cost.

The message presented to the reader by these examples is that the nature of second-order risk varies widely. In fact, the definition of consequential risk varies by institution. Exposures connected to transaction processing and payments are operational risk, but *legal risk* is also consequential, resulting in financial loss from malfeasance or inability to honour a contract due to:

- Inadequate or inappropriate contractual arrangements
- Failure to adhere to applicable laws, rules and regulations
- Violation of local or international best practices.

Both first- and second-order risk must be appropriately measured and monitored. Metrics and measurements are subject to Dr Werner Heisenberg's *Uncertainty Principle*, which states that the act of studying a problem, let alone attempting to correct it, can fundamentally alter the nature of the problem itself. This is true throughout science, and it is just as valid in banking and finance.

Moreover, primary and consequential risk share among themselves the fact that they do *not* have a well-defined or sure outcome, which is of course at the origin of the possibility of loss. For each of them, the outcome may be: possible and even probable – but *not* certain.

The fact that several primary risks correlate among themselves and with secondary risk is also very important. An example is the synergy between interest rate risk and currency exchange risk. In the 1970s, an Italian financier bet on the devaluation of the lira, but also made the bet that interest rate volatility would be relatively low:

- The lira indeed fell like a stone, and this meant significant profits
- But the two oil shocks created a wave of inflation, with the result that interest rates rose, wiping out profits and leaving significant loss.

In Hemingway's novel *The Sun Also Rises*, one of the characters was asked how he had gone bankrupt. 'In two ways,' came the response. 'Gradually and then suddenly.' To avoid the 'suddenly' disaster, one of the better-known Swiss banks has assigned the responsibility of quantitative and qualitative risk analysis to its internal audit department.

Quantification is based on 12 major categories; the first is internal control and it has a weight of 10, while the weight of others, like asset management and quality of transactions, is lower. The higher weight assigned to internal control arises from the estimated risk and reward results associated with each of the primary risks. This is followed by a risk and reward analysis of secondary risks.

To obtain pragmatic answers, these categories are studied by departments in the bank – treasury, derivatives, brokerage and so on – as well as by subsidiary companies. Bar charts are established by department and controlled entity, on which are mapped the risks associated with the auditing categories. According to company policy, these charts are interactively available to the risk control unit and senior management, with emphasis placed on deviations that become the subject of exception reporting.

3. Pricing risk

As for practically all other exposures, *pricing risk* results from uncertainty about the likelihood, extent and timing of market changes and losses that may be incurred in the bank's products, positions and obligations. Pricing risk may also be the outcome of pricing approaches being too competitive, trimming the margins and leaving the bank exposed in the longer run.

Apart from cut-throat pricing, which is a bad policy often promoted through volatility smiles, pricing risk is affected by the quality and availability of historical information, as well as by erroneous assumptions made about future conditions, such as low-default frequency (see examples on mispricing credit risk in section 4).

Whether the product is a loan, a call or put option, or other derivative instrument, mispricing is often amplified by intense competition in a market that quite frequently tempts its participants into accepting uneconomic pricing in order to obtain (or maintain) market share.

An excellent programme for the control of pricing risk in lending is Risk-Adjusted Return on Capital (RAROC), developed in the mid-1980s by the Bankers' Trust. RAROC uses an operating characteristics curve (Chapter 4) to classify counterparties in terms of their creditworthiness. Every time the bank is confronted with a borrower's greater credit risk, the model increases the interest rate of the loan – emulating a reinsurance policy.

Subsequently more sophisticated knowledge engineering artefacts were developed for loans, confronting loans officers with queries to which they must provide factual answers: Are our credits to this counterparty diversified by country of operations? By currency? By maturity? Other knowledge artefacts are designed to improve the bank's internal control, providing senior management with information on:

- The pattern of credits by credit officer, by branch and by foreign subsidiary
- Abnormal numbers of 'weak credits' and the likelihood of negative consequences based on historical evidence
- Whether the same credit officer is always dealing with the same counterparty and what conditions he/she makes

- Whether the same trader is repeating the same or similar pattern in deals with the same counterparty, and the risks assumed.

The information contained in these responses forms a *risk pattern* that is revealing of each loan officer's and trader's behaviour, as well as how well the bank's internal controls operate: Is *this* party dealing in billions of dollars in swaps? Is the counterparty a steady user of OTC or do they balance the deals they do with *our* bank with exchange traded products? (See the case study of the Dutch bank in Chapter 4.)

Pricing risk is reduced with this knowledge engineering-based methodology, because senior management has at its fingertips answers to critical questions regarding lending and trading behaviour, including what the net and gross exposure with any major counterparty is. Well-managed banks have developed systems that:

- Integrate credit risk and market risk by important counterparty, and
- Based on historical evidence, project *if* the customer is likely to break assigned limits.

By adopting approaches that are sensitive to risks, banks can establish risk control policies that are more in line with their risk appetite. As a consequence, a credit institution becomes better able to manage its exposure through periods of stress, and this makes the banking system not only safer and sounder, but also more efficient.

As the case with the Bankers' Trust RAROC has shown, credit institutions must realize that they have to become proactive. Not only is the amount of effort required to modify existing systems and procedures important, but also speed of action is crucial and it can be achieved only when the whole organization moves forward as one, without reservations and with a concentration of effort.

Risk-based pricing is a proactive method that not only helps in sizing up future exposure, but also assists in computing capital needs. The pattern is shown in Figure 11.1. Self-respecting managements don't misprice their financial products to gain market share or just do a deal. Instead:

- They encourage risk-based pricing, and
- Prompt all their departments and subsidiaries to use high-technology in fine-tuning the pricing of their products and services.

This should be done as basic policy, with risk control, profit and loss, return on investment (ROI) and future competitive position in mind. Crucial questions

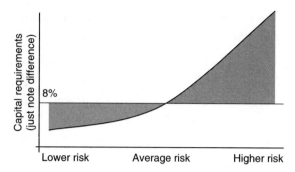

Figure 11.1   Risk-based pricing ensures that exposure is controlled proactively and capital requirements are dynamic

are: Will *our* bank remain a going concern in five years? In ten years? How much better off are we going to be in terms of financial staying power compared to our competitors if we properly price our risks?

The best indicators of real price competitiveness are those that capture risk and return in every product and area of operations as comprehensively as possible. *Cost* and *risk* information is instrumental in indicating not just a company's but also an economy's staying power and competitiveness. Return is influenced by variables such as:

- Market acceptance
- Product quality
- Customer satisfaction
- Capacity for innovation, and
- Flexibility in customer relationships.

Risk analysis provides information both on the entity's survivability in the longer term and on its competitiveness in the short term, as perceived by the market. Moreover, while risk-based pricing reflects assumed credit risk and market risk, it also maps into itself factors affecting an entity's business risk (Chapter 3). Cost base, margin and volume constitute the company's *operational leverage*, which is influenced by both internal decisions and external events.

4.   Mispricing credit risk

One of the challenges in the implementation of a risk-based pricing policy lies in the fact that a wave of innovation in debt markets has produced sophisticated and complex products, with risk factors that are not well known. For example, while the use of credit derivatives has exploded, giving investors in debt great flexibility, unknowns associated with novel debt products are leading these same investors to ever-higher levels of:

- Exposure, and
- Financial leverage.

Additionally, because these instruments are pumping up global liquidity further and further, a growing number of economists and financial analysts have doubts about their macroeconomic effects. For instance, they doubt a new credit downturn will be softened by the apparently changed structure of the debt market.

Contrary to views that prevailed in the first years of the 21st century, today several economists raise the question of whether the next downturn could be even worse than on previous occasions, because of *mispriced credit risk*. In their opinion, a growing amount of exposure is driven by the unusually high proportion of failure-prone companies rated CCC or lower, which means non-investment grade and just a few notches above default:

- In 1990, in the USA this rating category accounted for just 2% of junk-rated debt
- Today, it makes up almost 20%, and the prevailing opinion in the market is that nothing short of a crisis will stop it from growing.

What particularly worries economists, analysts and regulators is that the market is not pricing the *CCC* risk into its demand for higher interest rates due to misinterpretation of default signals. The likelihood is that, in an average low-default year, the market would experience between three or four junk bond defaults. However, because 2006 saw no such defaults, investors are widely and wrongly assuming none will come in 2007 – which is no sure bet.

Experts suggest that all this is flagrant mispricing, because if only one default occurs over the next six months, a spread of just 150 basis points would be just sufficient to cover the associated loss. By contrast, more than one default would see many investors losing out. The mispricing of debt instruments takes no account of the fact that the extra basis points of bonds – junk, BBB, A and AA compared to AAA – is in effect a cushion to absorb any marking-to-market losses linked to spread widening:

- *If* spreads widen, sellers of protection in the credit market will lose money, and
- *Then*, after this cushion is eaten away, investors will be in the front line with their capital.

A risk scenario (but by no means a worst case one) suggests that if equities begin to be sold off due to a macroeconomic problem with inflation-led interest rate rising, the outcome for low-quality/high-yield credit is likely to be very negative, and eventually disastrous.

American and European regulators are, moreover, expressing concerns that banks may be allowing hedge funds to increase their borrowing capacity, without a proper measure of assumed risk – for instance, by using collateral that could lose its value rapidly in a financial crisis. An additional factor is that, given the lower risk premiums in credit markets, it may no longer be prudent to assume credit default swap contracts will be liquid when a credit risk adjustment occurs.

Some regulatory authorities and central banks have also found that certain firms have been extending credit on less liquid instruments. Because of these and similar facts, American regulators are now asking questions about offshore leverage vehicles that allow US-based banks to extend credit to hedge funds beyond the limits imposed by American law.

The fear among some regulators and knowledgeable market observers is that, in a big market dislocation, hedge funds and other speculators investing in junk debt might be unable to sell those securities. This will increase the likelihood of widespread defaults. In fact, not only is there a possibility that risk is being seriously underpriced, but also much trading in credit derivatives assumes that liquidity will remain when an adjustment in credit markets takes place – which is not at all true.

Questions connected to the ongoing mispricing of credit risk concern every bank and every investor. They are also part of a broad new effort by the New York Federal Reserve, Securities and Exchange Commission (SEC), Office of the Controller of the Currency (OCC), Britain's Financial Services Authority and European regulatory bodies to understand better and more accurately:

- How much exposure large banks have to hedge funds, and
- Whether that could present a significant risk to the financial system, in the event of market disruption.

As an example, experts worry about a spike in junk bond default rates that is not priced into current instruments. In the late 1980s/1990s, the global default rate on junk bonds leapt to almost 13%. At present it is estimated that even a less severe downturn could send defaults to nearly that level. In fact, several analysts believe that a recession similar to the one that occurred in the early 1990s could push US junk-rated default rates as high as 17%.

One of the problems with credit derivatives' credit risk transfer mechanism (Chapter 6) and similar instruments currently confronting central bankers is *embedded leverage* – where one's exposure is multiplied many times compared to the same investment in the underlying conventional security. Experts suggest that embedded leverage has expanded phenomenally, while at the same time:

- It does not appear on balance sheets, and
- Therefore, it is impossible to quantify it across the financial system.

However, its effect is felt, and this is the reason why no one can be sure how much capital must be set aside as insurance against such embedded leverage going wrong. Additionally, mathematical models of risk, which are currently used to stress test derivatives, give too much weight to the low volatility of recent times, even though experimenters and risk controllers should know that it is incorrect to use the recent past as a guide to predicting the future.

According to Gerald Corrigan, former President of the New York Federal Reserve and currently a partner in Goldman Sachs, there is a virtual consensus among leading investment banking practitioners and central bankers that the statistical probability of a major financial shock with systemic features has got lower. But at the same time, there is also agreement that another major shock is likely and the potential damage could be greater than in the past. Corrigan gives three reasons for this increased toxicity:

- Speed
- Complexity, and
- Tighter linkages across institutions and markets.

'The trouble,' says the former President of the New York Fed, 'is that we do not have the capacity to anticipate the timing and triggers of such a shock.'[4] Neither is it possible to ascertain that if we could anticipate the timing and triggers, the shocks wouldn't happen, because there are so many unknowns involved with complex financial instruments and historical evidence suggests shocks do happen.

Central bankers and regulators are right to be watchful. Tim Geithner, the President of New York Fed, emphasizes that credit risk in the over-the-counter derivatives market is large relative to more traditional forms of credit, as well as relative to the capital cushions and earnings of the major commercial and investment banks. These thoughts, expressed at the World Economic Forum, Davos 2007, are seeping into the minds of economists and financial analysts. A policy of doubt is a basic ingredient in the management of risk.

5. Marking to market

Dr John Maynard Keynes is the first on record, in the mid-1930s, to bring attention to how crowds impact market prices. The stock market, the derivatives market and any other market is a crowd consisting of anyone buying, selling or even only analysing prices and risk factors at any one time. This crowd:

- Makes up the global market
- Resets prices every minute, and
- Its decision is not negotiable or subject to appeal.

Moreover, this crowd's action, reaction or inaction impact upon, if not create outright, what we call *market volatility*, which characterizes every commodity traded in the market. It also underpins the very notion of what we call a 'free market' and constitutes the most important component part of market discipline (Chapter 10).

In the market economy in which we live, any financial product at any time is worth whatever the market thinks it is worth at that particular time. This statement, of course, does not exclude mispricing. Marking to market is so important because this price can be negotiated between a willing seller and a willing buyer, even if this is not necessarily the product's true value. Typically:

- Price is what you pay
- Value is what you get
- Cost is what you have incurred, and
- Risk is what you assume by acquiring the product.

As the reader will recall from Chapter 1, not only do risk and cost correlate, but also risk is a big chunk of the cost. Unless they have computed the risk in advance and factored it into their cost structure, buyers could find themselves like a rat in a trap who no longer wants the cheese, but the only thing left to do is to eat it.

In the general case, with the exception of panics, there is no problem in marking-to-market instruments that are regularly dealt with, like shares, bonds and exchange-traded commodities. Indeed, quoted market prices are used for most investments whether they are equities or liabilities, such as securitized debt. But the more complex the instrument, the greater the pricing uncertainty.

The counterpart to this statement is that as Jean-Claude Trichet, the President of the European Central Bank, said at the January 2007 World Economic Forum in Davos: 'The rapid growth of structured financial products and derivatives make it increasingly difficult to weight risk.'[5] (More on this in Chapter 12.)

Trichet also advised that investors need to prepare for repricing of some aspects because of unstable conditions. In his words:

'There is no such creativity of new and very sophisticated financial instruments ... that we don't know fully where the risks are located. We try to understand what is going on but it is a big, big challenge.'

Whenever it is done, marking-to-market valuation should be executed against the concept of prevailing market liquidity. If the market is illiquid, this should be factored into the equation; illiquidity is a major risk and we must account for it. Additionally, account must be taken of currency exchange risk and interest risk volatility.

One of my professors at UCLA taught his students that there is no such thing as a bad risk. There are only badly computed product prices. If banks don't properly price risk into the products that they sell (or buy), the market will do it for them, albeit in a rather coarse and often painful manner. That's what *marking to market* is all about.

Accountants have a good deal of work to do in this regard. The simplest approach is that – for those instruments which have a market – actual exposure is evaluated on a regular basis, at pre-agreed time-points – intra-day, daily, weekly, monthly – depending on the product's dynamics and regulatory compliance. Alternatively, the marking may take place once a marking trigger is reached.

The effect of higher frequency of marking to market, which imposes important prerequisites, is to protect the bank from acquiring too much exposure in what may be higher risk instruments, lower-rated counterparties or transactions that tend to exceed set risk limits.

Of course, not all financial instruments have a market. For performing loans, where no quoted market prices are available, contractual cash flows are discounted at quoted secondary market rates, or estimated market rates if available. Otherwise, sales of comparable loan portfolios or current market origination rates for loans with similar terms and risk characteristics are used for pricing purposes.

For loans with doubts as to collectibility, expected cash flows are discounted using an appropriate rate considering the time of collection and a premium for the uncertainty of the flows. The value of collateral is also considered. For liabilities such as long-term debt without quoted market prices, market borrowing rates of interest are used to discount cash flows contractually – which is essentially marking to model (section 4).

Last but not least, accountants should be aware that it is unwise to use both marking to market and accruals within the same instrument class and under the same management intent guidelines. This practice can give results that are uncoupled. Take, as an example, a balance sheet which shows:

Assets	Liabilities
100	10 Equity
	90 Debt

Over time, accruals still show 100 in assets. But marking to market may show 90 in assets, using capitalization as proxy. Because the debt has not changed, the equity is gone. This poses problems in accounting, and it brings into perspective the need for recapitalization.

6. Marking to model

Marked-to-market valuations are often difficult because for many instruments there is no current market, or if there is one it only handles very small volumes and there is uncertainty about the effect on prices from buying or selling a large amount of instruments or wares.

With derivative financial instruments, for example, including futures and options, less than 30% are traded in exchanges. The other 70%, however, are over-the-counter (OTC) deals that have a market value only twice in their life cycle:

- When they are contracted, and
- When they come to maturity.

The objective of *marking to model* is to estimate, within a certain margin of confidence, the fair market value of a financial instrument. *Fair value* is the price that will be paid by a willing buyer to a willing seller under conditions other than fire sale. In the general case, but not necessarily in every instance:

- Fair value incorporates market value concepts, and
- It might extend them to situations where products are not sold in traditional markets and where markets are not sufficiently liquid or transparent.

The work actuaries are doing provides a proxy on how to go about fair value calculations. Embedded value, the main valuation concept used by actuaries, is classically computed by employing fixed or effective interest rates and deterministic scenarios. Fair value and embedded value are not equal. For example:

- The fair value of a firm is calculated as the difference between the value of its assets and liabilities

- By contrast, embedded value is the sum of the firm's discounted net cash flows.

Their conceptual similarities are, however, important. At least theoretically, these two approaches should yield almost identical results when applied to the same firm or product, but in practice this is not always the case. On the other hand, because actuarial practices have begun to incorporate market risk techniques in their models, this might lead to convergence between fair value and embedded value.

American insurers, for example, were the first to use, in marking to model, full-term structures of interest and Monte Carlo simulation.[6] The increased attention to fair valuation techniques in Solvency II and financial reporting characteristics of IFRS accounting (including IAS 30 and IAS 39) is also considered to be a stimulant towards further convergence between fair value and embedded value.

Another factor is the growing trend among supervisors to actively encourage the development and use of marking to model, as it recognizes the challenge of implementing fair value in the case of products for which clear indications of market value are unavailable, or basic fair values concepts may not be relevant.

To be able to develop realistic mathematical models for pricing its products, assigning fair value to its portfolio positions and controlling risk, an institution needs the skills and services of *rocket scientists* (Chapter 1). However, their models must be steadily tested to assure that:

- They are able to continue to deliver reliable results, and
- They are not only accurate, but also compliant with rules and regulations.

At the heart of marking to model is analogical thinking and its constraints. The Heisenberg principle states that if something is closely observed, chances are it is going to be altered in the process. If an equity is in a tight consolidation and then breaks out the day financial analysts in known brokerages upgrade this stock to strong buy:

- The odds of a price move upwards are high
- But the likelihood this breakout will be sustained is small.

By contrast, if everybody believes there is no chance of this equity breaking out, and it suddenly does, the chance that there exists an important underlying cause is much greater. In other words, the more a price pattern is observed by speculators, the more likely it is to give false signals, and the more a market responds without speculative activity, the greater the significance of breakouts.

Modelling, of course, is not risk free. Model risk is not only due to mathematical errors and poor data, but also to misinterpretation of results. An example is that regulators require credit institutions to report value at risk (VAR) at the 99% confidence level. As we have already seen on a couple of occasions:

- This still leaves 1% of all cases out of risk accounting, and
- The safe bet is that this 1% lies in the queue of the risk distribution, where the impact of events is greatest.

Model risk is a new risk; it is part of technology risk and therefore of operational risk. It is also an integral part of modern financing because design, trading and risk control of derivative products largely depend on models. Moreover, several banks employing models fail to appreciate that they have locality and their use in alien domains is total nonsense. Credit VAR is an example.

7. Beyond valuation models

While analytics, simulation and experimentation are necessary to every modern financial enterprise, they are not enough. Of primary concern is a policy to control exposure that is concerned both with risk pricing and with concentrations of risk. Taking credit risk as an example, the maximum exposure in a bilateral agreement results when a counterparty defaults. Losses include all claims on this counterparty, actual and potential, which would arise from outstanding credit lines:

- Revocable or irrevocable
- Conditional or unconditional

that the bank has committed itself to provide, and claims that the bank has committed itself to purchase or underwrite, contingent liabilities arising in the normal course of business, and those resulting from the drawing down in full of undrawn facilities. In the same class fall assets that the bank has committed itself to purchase or underwrite, whose value depends wholly or mainly on a counterparty performing its obligations, or whose value otherwise depends on that counterparty's financial soundness, even if they do not represent a claim on the counterparty.

A bank's approach to large exposures should also account for the particular characteristics of individual counterparties, including the nature of their business, the markets in which they operate, and the experience and decision-making ability of their management. Figure 11.2 provides in a nutshell the structure underpinning a holistic risk control methodology. The role of the board's Risk Management Committee is explained in Chapter 12.

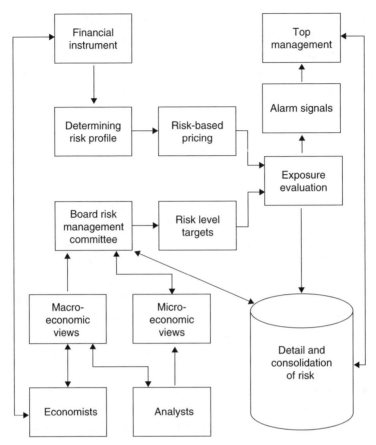

Figure 11.2   Structure of a risk management organization with a risk-based pricing facility

In terms of underwriting commitments, regulatory authorities imply that in cases where a bank has underwritten an issue of securities (equity or debt) the amount at risk should be measured as its credit equivalent amount. This includes interest rate contracts: interest rate swaps; forward rate agreements; interest options purchased; cross-foreign currency swaps; forward foreign-exchange contracts; and foreign-exchange options purchased.

The basis of measurement of exposure connected to the above instruments may vary by jurisdiction and regulatory authority, but in its fundamental constituents a risk-based pricing methodology can be valid across borders, in connection to issues such as: loans, advances and overdrafts, net investment in finance leases, discounted bills held, bonds, acceptances, promissory notes and other paper held.

Other exposures may result from margin deposits with futures, options and commodities paid to brokers, investment exchanges and clearing houses. Also, claims arising from similar transactions entered into through bilateral agreements, including claims on the counterparty. For instance, claims and other assets sold forward resulting from foreign-exchange and interest rate contracts:

- In the case of interest rate contracts, the exposure is the interest payments due from the counterparty
- With foreign-exchange contracts, the exposure is the amount to be received in settlement.

Other amounts subject to exposure regard commitments to: purchase claims outstanding under sale and repurchase agreements; forward purchase agreements; buy-back agreements; underwriting commitments; and similar transactions. The risks involved in underwriting differs substantially from those connected to lending.

The likelihood of a bank experiencing a loss from an underwriting commitment is related to the risk of actually having to take up the securities, possibly leading to a subsequent forced sale. For these reasons the amount at risk on an issue is more reasonably measured in the context of a large exposures policy by some proportion of the amount underwritten rather than by the full amount of the issue, provided regulators allow this approach.

Different reserve banks look at this issue in different ways. The Bank of England, for example, stipulates that where the credit equivalent amount of an underwriting exceeds 10% of the reporting bank's capital base, the bank is required to report it as an exposure in the same way as for other forms of exposure. Where the credit equivalent amount of a proposed underwriting exceeds 25% of the capital base, the exposure is required to be notified to the central bank before the commitment is entered into.

An important class of capital at risk is that of *contingent liabilities*, including amounts outstanding in the form of guarantees, standby letters of credit, bills accepted by the reporting bank but not held by it, endorsements, claims sold with recourse, undrawn documentary letters of credit issued or confirmed, tender and performance bonds. It also includes retention money guarantees, import and export excise duty bonds, and those arising from similar transactions entered into by the bank.

Technology contributes a great deal in automation of the aforementioned procedures. The counterparty-by-counterparty evaluation of risk, assumed with every one of these product lines and with each individual instrument, can be assigned to knowledge artefacts designed to monitor intra-day assumed exposure anywhere in the world. Knowledge artefacts that act as the risk manager's agents should be an integral part of any sound methodology.[7]

A similar statement is valid in regard to risk monitoring of assets like equities, equity warrants and options, as well as instruments classified as assets whose value depends, as we have seen, on the issuer's financial soundness. Knowledge artefacts designed to substantiate an exposure control policy also address market risk, position risk and all other material risks emphasized in this text.

This and similar system solutions are prerequisites to effective control of global risk, as banks are trying harder than ever to push into foreign markets – racing to expand their network with cross-border links that are evolving into a global system that virtually eliminates the boundaries of time and distance.

Notes

1 Roger Lowenstein, *Buffett, The Making of an American Capitalist*. Weidenfeld & Nicolson, London, 1996.
2 D.N. Chorafas, *Risk Management Technology in Financial Services*. Elsevier, Oxford, 2007.
3 See D.N. Chorafas, *Advanced Financial Analysis*. Euromoney Books, London, 1994.
4 *Financial Times*, 30 January 2007.
5 *Financial Times*, 29 January 2007.
6 D.N. Chorafas, *Risk Management Technology in Financial Services*. Elsevier, Oxford, 2007.
7 D.N. Chorafas and Heinrich Steinmann, *Expert Systems in Banking*. Macmillan, London, 1991.

Board of Directors and
Risk Management

1. Risk control requires unconventional thinking

'We never do anything bold,' Walter Bedell-Smith, Eisenhower's Chief of Staff in WWII, complained in a conference. 'There are at least 17 people to be dealt with, so [we] must compromise, and compromise is never bold.'[1] Bedell-Smith's dictum describes in the most imaginative way many (albeit not all) deliberations of the board of directors, as well as of military alliances and of the United Nations.

Given proper schooling, wide reading, a varied career exposed to risks, power of observation and a gift for analysis, theoretically board members should approach any new problem with an open mind and a penetrating view. Theirs should be the Socratic method, the art of asking the simple and devastating question: 'What exactly are we trying to do?' – to be followed by 'Why?' and 'How?'

This is not what happens in practice. Not only have board members very little time to devote to any of the many companies where they are directors, but also their minds are often absorbed in the routine of industry, they lack expertise in risk management and are often set in their ways. Yet deregulation, globalization and rapid innovation require departures as well as the power to eliminate 'accepted courses of action' and start afresh *as if* one has never before seen a financial institution.

Another handicap to taking bold initiatives and reaching 'out of the ordinary' decisions is that, from university lectures to books and newspapers, there is often a call for 'practical approaches' to deal with a current problem – whatever it may be. In contrast, really difficult problems call for an 'unpractical' not a practical beaten path solution:

- The greater the difficulty, the more unconventional should be the approach to a sought-after answer, and
- The only way to find the right answer is to ask tough questions that go outside and beyond conventional wisdom.

This is true whether the problem confronting a board of directors is that of elaborating and approving new business strategies, establishing major policies relating to the management of risk, assuring that the bank's senior management takes the steps necessary for innovation in instruments and products, or deciding on the sophistication of a new system that needs to be established for monitoring and controlling exposure.

Figure 12.1 provides a snapshot on the board's and CEO's duties in establishing an effective risk management organization. The importance of cultural change has been brought to the reader's attention throughout this book; section 2 explains why microeconomic evaluation is part of the board's responsibility and section 3 presses the point that the board needs a devil's advocate in risk control. The role of the board's risk management committee is the theme of section 5.

Because the board of directors has ultimate responsibility for understanding the nature and level of risk taken by the institution, its members should be in a position to appreciate and analyse all risks being assumed, as well as all inventoried risks (Chapter 8). Moreover, risk oversight must be the responsibility of a subcommittee of the board (section 5), which:

- Approves objectives, strategies and policies governing credit risk, interest rate risk, currency risk, derivatives risk and other outstanding exposures
- Reviews accounting procedures, auditing policies and risk limits, and periodically assesses compliance with board-approved policies, as well as regulatory rules and guidelines
- Provides guidance to senior management regarding the board's tolerance for risk, while assuring that the right deals are done at the right time, accompanied by steps to measure, monitor and control assumed risk.

How are board members responding to these requirements and to the company's business objectives? Legend has it that Dr Peter Drucker was once called in as a consultant by a company that manufactured glass bottles. At his first meeting with the board he asked the simple question, 'Well, gentlemen, what is your business?' Surprised at his ignorance, the chairman replied, 'Our business is in the manufacture of glass bottles for soft drinks and beer.' To this, Drucker replied, 'No, I don't agree. You are in the *packaging* business.'

With this challenge to their long-held notions and convictions, the directors began to think in unconventional ways, repositioning their firm against market forces. A similar statement is valid in the banking industry. The notions directors have inherited from their predecessors may be obsolete and unfit for the current market's dynamics.

For its part, senior management should assure that: the bank's operations are effectively managed; appropriate risk control policies and procedures are available to conduct the institution's business in a safe and sound manner; and information flows are regularly evaluated in respect to accuracy and timeliness to allow all managers and professionals to understand and assess the institution's risks.

While the board establishes the direction, sets the limits and controls the effectiveness of execution, senior management has the responsibility for daily execution and oversight of the institution's activities, including the implementation of

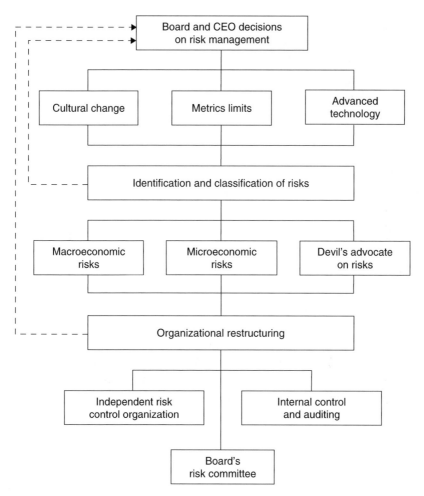

Figure 12.1   Framework for unconventional decisions by the board on risk management

the board's risk management policies. An integral part of this responsibility is the assurance that there is in place a state-of-the-art system that provides:

- Ways to measure risk and value positions
- Tick-by-tick tests of risk limits, and
- Open channels for effective internal control, immediately reporting on deviations (Chapter 11).

Earnings at risk (EAR) and *capital at risk* (CAR) are two examples where deviations are relatively easy to track, identify and report to the board. *Earnings at risk* (EAR) measures the discounted pre-tax earnings impact over a specified time horizon of a given event – for instance, a defined shift in interest rate yield curve, for a given currency. Typically, but not always, the yield curve shift is statistically derived as a two-standard-deviation change in a short-term interest rate over the period required to decream the position, usually four weeks.

Earnings at risk must be calculated separately for each currency and reflect the repricing gaps in the position, both explicit and embedded. It should be part of the annual planning process, plus other exercises connected to risk and return. Limits may be set for earnings at risk on a business, country and total entity basis, with exposures regularly reviewed in relation to:

- Limits, and
- Interest rate environment.

Capital at risk is a concept based on the aggregation method, which simulates allocation of financial resources among competing objectives in loans, investments, trading and so on; it also tracks changes in the value of the bank's portfolio with predefined extreme moves and correlations in market forces.

Modelling and experimentation are the best ways to pre-evaluate EAR and CAR. Capital at risk modelling helps to compute the maximum simulated loss. To be done effectively, this requires inputs from product design, marketing and trading, which have to be integrated through sophisticated software and made available interactively to all authorized persons.

2. The board's responsibilities in macroeconomics

One of the foremost challenges confronting the board of every major company is that of fully understanding macroeconomic conditions and developments, as well as the way in which they will most likely impact on the business of their firm and that of its competitors. The duty of the chief economist is to explain, and that of the board members to appreciate, plausible but not certain events and take decisions.

Macroeconomic projections are crucial for every product policy and every market policy, and for tuning the firm's appetite. One of the opinions to which many economists subscribed at the January 2007 World Economic Forum, in Davos, Switzerland, was that the prevailing conditions in global financial markets look potentially unstable. Therefore, investors need to prepare themselves for a significant repricing of some assets (Chapter 11).

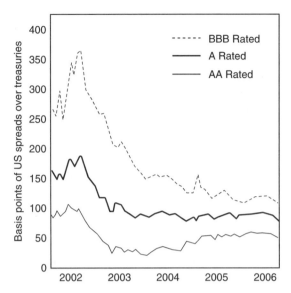

Figure 12.2   The ever-shrinking corporate bond spreads – US spreads over treasuries (in basis points)

In the background of these concerns is the ongoing explosion of structured products and derivative instruments, which has made it more difficult for regulators (and investors) to judge the current risks in financial systems. 'We are currently seeing elements in global financial markets which are not necessarily stable,' said Jean-Claude Trichet, President of the European Central Bank.[2]

Other central bankers and regulators also pointed to risks embedded in a number of variables that, among themselves, create a pattern. These include very-low-level real interest rates, spreads and risk premiums that have become factors that could trigger a repricing. Figure 12.2 shows how much room the ever-shrinking corporate bond spreads have left for this to happen. As a quotation from the Monthly Central Bulletin of the European Bank explains:

> 'Consistent with an increase in market participants' general appetite for risk is the fact that the euro area BBB-rated corporate bond spreads were further compressed during December (2006) and early January (2007).'[3]

The reader has already been warned in the discussion on position risk, in Chapter 8, that credit risk and market risk concentrations can have disastrous results on the firm's ability to withstand adverse conditions. One of the arguments heard in Davos 2007, that firms which are well diversified have nothing to fear of such repricing because gains will rebalance possible losses, is definitely wrong.

There exist conflicting theories concerning the degree of diversification and, as has already been brought to the reader's attention, the recommendation of being 'as diversified as possible' is so vague and imprecise that it helps precious little in reducing risks, let alone in confronting conditions. Additionally, a research project by analysts of the Deutsche Bundesbank supports the thesis that:

- Each kind of diversification tends to lower banks' returns
- By contrast, focusing generally increases the profitability of credit institutions.

The analysts also point out that the impact of any diversification on banks' return changes in line with the risk level being assumed, with the effect that sectoral focus on return is declining monotonously with increasing risk.[4] Diversification significantly improves banks' profits only in the case of moderate risk levels, but current risk appetite is far from moderate.

Regarding exposure to counterparties, the belief expressed by Martin Fridson, publisher of *Leverage World*, is that though financial institutions and hedge funds are managing risks better than they did, complex new products only redistribute credit risk. 'Financial engineers want you to believe they have reduced the risk. That's preposterous,' Fridson suggested.[5]

Anecdotal evidence that hedge funds and banks have been staffing up and raising money in anticipation of the next wave of corporate defaults adds to these worries. According to some opinions, not only company defaults but also country defaults should not be excluded; neither are sudden measures to stem the tide of a crisis free from unexpected consequences.

A few days before Christmas 2006, Thailand's introduction of capital controls sent its stock market plunging. This revived memories of mid-1997, and some economists said: 'Here we go again.' As will be recalled, the 1997 Asian financial crisis devastated the so-called 'tigers', and capital flight on a huge scale caused:

- Financial markets, and
- Economies in the region to collapse.

In macroeconomic terms, the problem that Thailand and other Asian countries face today is the exact opposite of that of 1997. Their challenge is how to stop capital from flowing in because of worldwide abundance of liquidity, which lures investors into riskier assets in search of higher returns. Capital controls, however, scare the market because no economy can simultaneously:

- Control domestic liquidity
- Manage its exchange rate, and
- Have an open capital account.

An opinion to which investors should be paying attention is that the macroeconomic factors behind the 2006/2007 challenges are the unstoppable worldwide liquidity glut and leverage through derivative financial instruments. These challenges and the practice of pumping up the balance sheet correlate, and they lead to risks well beyond the limits we have known so far. The cheap cost of money and excess liquidation can create crises that hit:

- Several of the more exposed firms, and
- Some of the larger national economies.

According to certain sources, in Washington Henry Paulson, US Treasury Secretary, reactivated a team for crisis management. Its mission is to watch over and help to deal with the likelihood of systemic risk from financial meltdown. Allegedly, Paulson is concerned about 8000 unregulated hedge funds that have $1.3 trillion in capital and $370 trillion (!) in outstanding credit derivatives – a leveraging of 285.[6]

The way an article in the *Washington Weekly Standard* had it, Paulson fears a death blow for the US economy.[7] Other ministers of finance and central bankers have similar fears, a reflection of the fact that over the last 15 years innovative financial instruments have radically changed the rules of the game.

A debate is now raging among central bankers, regulators and other policymakers about the implications of the accelerating use of derivatives products, which has reached an astronomical level. In Davos 2007, several central bankers, regulators and economists argued that the growth of the $450 trillion derivatives market may have helped to reduce market volatility so far, but these instruments may now be raising high levels of:

- Leverage, and
- Risk taking.

In retrospect, keeping the cost of borrowing at artificially low levels has brought the financial system to a dangerous stance. Moreover, some senior policymakers admit that it has become hard for them to track the risks created by these products because the sector is opaque, hedge funds are unregulated, and products shift rapidly across markets and between the boundaries of central banks' jurisdictions.

During Davos 2007, Stanley Fisher, governor of Israel's central bank, pointed out that it remained unclear 'who takes responsibility for the [financial] system' at a time of crisis. This is true of the globalized economy as a whole. By contrast, in the case of every institution the answer is unambiguous: the 'who' is the board of directors and the CEO.

This responsibility is shared by the CEO and senior management. US supervisors, like the Office of Thrift Supervision (OTS), require that institutions under their authority identify individuals and committees responsible for risk management, and assure there is adequate separation of duties in key elements of the risk control process to avoid potential conflicts of interest. Additionally, the institutions should assure the supervisor that:

- The risk management unit is sufficiently independent of position-taking functions, and
- This unit reports directly to both senior management and the board's risk management committee.

Smaller institutions with limited resources and personnel are permitted to provide oversight by outside directors, to compensate for the lack of a formal risk management committee structure. But larger banks should have an independent risk management unit, particularly if the Treasury also works as a profit centre.

3.   A devil's advocate in risk management

Paraphrasing Dr Ben Gurion, risk management must have some brilliant operators assigned to a permanent doubting role of devil's advocate. The mission of these experts should be to challenge possibly wrong hypotheses and assumptions, search for what is wrong in risk control, and criticize other inefficiencies.

'I don't believe in the single God but believe in the single devil,' says Professor Urs Birchler, of the Swiss National Bank, adding that: 'Market discipline does not bring us to paradise, but can prevent us from going to hell.' This single devil, the challenger of everything – from ideas to decisions, systems and practices – is what Socrates called his *demon*.

In every institution the board of directors needs a *demon* who challenges optimistic reports on macroeconomic developments on risk and return characteristics of instruments, and on position exposure, bringing attention to failures in the control of risk. The reasons may be many:

- Lack of a global concept
- Incomplete or inconsistent top management directives
- Obsolete, incompatible or even contradictory rules on exposure
- Guidelines that can be easily bypassed or lack of dynamic cut-offs
- Wanting technology that provides a coarse filter
- Failure to account for risk correlations that can turn management plans on their head.

Even the best hedges can turn sour, as Hirokazu Nakamura, Chairman of Mitsubishi Motors, once admitted:

> 'Mitsubishi has been long and wrong on the direction of the yen. While the yen passed the 100 bar to the US dollar Mitsubishi Motors had hedged at 90 yen to the dollar, till 31 March 1996. Hence, the dollar's appreciation would not show in the bottom line for another seven months.'[8]

As I have found in over 50 years of practice in the financial industry, many people believe that once they have identified the main risks they can attack them individually one by one. This is utterly wrong. As Chapter 4 showed, exposures are usually characterized by co-movement as they impact upon one another. Account should therefore be taken of:

- Volatility correlations in equity and debt prices
- Cherry-picking of correlations by the risk model being used, and
- The board's individual decisions on hedging unmatched positions and the way these are executed.

The co-movement of credit risk and market risk factors can harbour both unwanted consequences for the institution itself and systemic risks that may strike in the event of tensions in financial markets anywhere in the globalized economy (section 2). In my experience, there are few board decisions that account for this fact.

Experts who have acted as devil's advocates suggest that the risk co-movement problem has two faces. It may occur within the banking system *if* banks that are active in the market have similar market positions. In this case, a shock event would adversely affect the trading result of these banks simultaneously and put their liquidity position in peril.

Alternatively, in the event of a more general crisis, co-movement in the positioning of market players in the global financial market may have repercussions for individual banks. This may happen, for example, in the aftermath of liquidity shortages, suddenly changing risk correlations or other events.

Precisely for these reasons, Chapter 4 pressed the point that challenging risk correlations has become very important to every market risk and credit risk analysis. Due to the fact that correlation of trading results demonstrates remarkable similarity to the increasing co-movement of hedge fund returns, particularly since the beginning of the 21st century, co-movement in trading results of banks active in the market has started to show a marked increase.

Optimists say that, from time to time, this is reversed, as diversification effects among the banks' various proprietary trading portfolios are instrumental in rebalancing risk. But as we have seen in Chapter 8 and in section 2 of this chapter, diversification is quite often a good intention rather than a real-life event. The potential systemic risks emanating from a possible co-movement of market positions is always present.

It is part of the mission of the devil's advocate to show that diversification is more often a wish rather than a fact, and that there is no alternative to maintaining a carefully controlled risk balance – on a steady basis. We must continuously assess not only the risk involved on an instrument-by-instrument basis, but also analyse existing correlations and evaluate, on an enterprise-wide basis, assumed correlation of risk.

Stress tests, with which the reader is by now familiar, can provide plenty of evidence to the devil's advocate. They help to predict an increase in default risk in the credit portfolio, depreciation of assets in the trading book, and possible decline in operating income due to changed interest rates or falling demand for loans. As a reminder, in the domain in which they apply, stress test scenarios assume events that are:

- Very unlikely to materialize in the short and medium term
- But plausible because of market development or historical precedence that has repeated itself.

For instance, macroeconomic stress tests analyse the impact of cyclical and interest rate developments on loss provisions and net interest received; credit risk stress tests investigate the effect of changes in the creditworthiness of individual borrowers; market risk stress tests evaluate the impact of extreme market events on portfolio positions.

These rigorous tests at the long leg of the risk distribution provide the devil's advocate with, for extreme simulated losses, an insight into the ability of a given capital ratio to withstand shocks. This allows us to see how far the shocks appear to be manageable by the institution – forming an opinion that is based on quantitative assessments and on qualifying opinions of experts.

4. Risk management is like pre-trial preparation

The role of the devil's advocate is by no means an easy one. Since organizations are made up of people, he or she can be sure to have opponents who would contradict their theses and prepare counter-evidence. That's why playing the role of devil's advocate in risk management requires a lot of homework, which is like pre-trial preparation by criminal law attorneys. Discovery calls for thorough investigation, including:

- Detailed analysis of facts and hypotheses
- Examination and cross-examination
- Distillation, testing, counter-testing and summation.

This summation, substantiated by plenty of detailed evidence, will be the subject of a presentation to the board, CEO and senior management. This job must be done in a convincing manner, which not only explains and answers queries, but also prompts corrective action. In a way, this mission is similar to auditing, but with two essential differences:

- The devil's advocate looks at transactions and positions from a management accounting viewpoint, and
- His or her presentation involves qualitative assessment over and above hard numbers, the way certified public accountants are now required to work.

Furthermore, such detailed investigation will only be worth its salt if it looks at all different types of exposure, including those with longer-term maturity, and if it is able to analyse their impact within a pre-established level of confidence (Chapter 4), suggesting to the board the future consequences of both:

- The risks that have been currently assumed, and
- Corrective steps necessary to control them over the timeframe under investigation.

One of the money centre banks has looked at dividends paid by investigative risk management and found that, for every $1 invested in this activity, the benefit has been $6 in terms of reduction in losses. Among the findings has also been the need to thoroughly analyse expected benefits from business activities, whether or not:

- They are too optimistic, and/or
- Have miscalculated assumed exposure.

For instance, overestimating net present value (NPV) is a frequent way to gain personal credit, but in the process the portfolio accumulates risks and becomes filled up with pockets characterized by concentration of exposure. A devil's advocate study that concentrated on relationship managers established that 80% of them had never delivered on their mission.

Another interesting finding of the same discovery study concerned banks' weak defences in combating the penetration of their business by organized crime. Yet, this is a very important issue whose impact has been demonstrated time and again, one of the better-known cases being the $10 billion scam at the Bank of New York in August 1999.

This case illustrated legal risk and reputational risk in one act. Billions of dollars were channelled through the Bank of New York in the 1998/99 timeframe, originating from what had allegedly been a major money-laundering operation by organized crime. Some $4.2 billion were laundered in more than 10 000 transactions, passed through one account that was kept open to help continuing investigation by the US federal authorities.

Investigators said the transactions seemed to add up to one of the largest money-laundering operations ever uncovered in the USA, with vast sums of money moving in and out of the bank in a day. A US official who followed money laundering and Russian organized crime said, 'What we have here is the penetration of a major US organization by Russian organized crime.'[9]

Since the collapse of the Russian financial system in August 1998, the flight of money out of the country accelerated, and investigators have been on the lookout for activities suspected to be money-laundering operations. This sort of risk is best analysed as a pattern of activities, rather than by looking at each one individually. A good example on the necessary methodology can be learned from engineering science.

The traditional way to evaluate emissions is to measure waste gases at tailpipes while a burner, a car or some other engine is running. An improved approach is to calculate not one incident (such as exhaust at a given point in time), but the pattern created by the net environmental load of the engine –

for instance, a motor vehicle. This is sometimes divided into two parts, known as:

- *Well-to-pump* efficiency, and
- *Pump-to-wheel* efficiency.

The measurement described by the first bullet counts the cost of extracting and processing the fuel. The second bullet reflects the environmental impact of different engine systems. Several studies demonstrate that results can be revealing. For instance, gas engines are about 84% efficient from well to pump, but just 15% efficient from pump to wheel. Combine the two, and the overall efficiency is about 13%.

As far as environmental pollution is concerned, pump-to-wheel efficiency matters a great deal. It is expected that by 2010 there will be more than 1 billion automobiles in the world. Because cars last longer, it will take decades to completely replace the existing base of low-efficiency cars and the aforementioned value of 13% is indeed very low efficiency.

Along the same lines as engineering thinking, the latest generation of burners for house heating deliver much better results. High-quality burner-boiler systems can reach up to 93% *pump-to-heating* efficiency, though this drops to about 63% with lower quality systems, or less if the quality is below average.

By extension to this engineering line of thinking, consider the bank capital channel theory. It states that poorly capitalized banks subject to capital regulation may cut their loan supply after monetary tightening *if* the market for *bank equity* is imperfect. Analogous to the case of engineering efficiency we have just reviewed, banks face maturity transformation costs that:

- Reduce their interest income, and
- Impact upon their capital position.

Because of this, as a Deutsche Bank study pointed out, poorly capitalized banks may have to cut lending. This possibly generates real economic effects if the credit institution's customers do not have efficient substitutes for bank loans (as happened in the 1990s in Japan). A Deutsche Bank discussion paper has tested the hypothesis of whether a bank capital channel type of transmission mechanism exists (in the German banking system), and whether monetary tightening leads to costs for banks with a time-to-maturity mismatch between assets and liabilities.[10] The answer is that it does lead to such a mismatch.

The message the reader should take from these examples is that a successful investigation is based not only on hard data but also, if not mostly, on a questioning methodology that challenges the 'obvious'. Without such a methodology, the discovery process is handicapped and therefore fails to unearth the most critical information that allows investigation of successive thresholds of adverse conditions.

5. Helping board members to understand risk and return

In August 1939, Albert Einstein, Leo Szilard and Eugene Winger drafted two versions of the famous letter Einstein sent to President Roosevelt on the need for a race to beat Germany in the development and delivery of the atomic bomb. One version was shorter and the other longer, on the premise that, as far as they could see, it was difficult to judge how many words were necessary to explain the issue to the President.[11]

This principle of two versions of the same document fits amazingly well the need for risk control information to be provided to the chairman and board members. Many details are vital, but if included in the daily report on exposure, or intra-day when necessary, there may be a case of not being able to see the wood for the trees.

The *virtual balance sheet* is an example of the short version Einstein, Szilard and Winger chose to submit to President Roosevelt. It can be supplemented with short statements of total recognized but not realized gains or losses, and of realized profits and losses – all of which should be steadily updated and interactively accessible. Interactivity can provide more detailed information by instrument, branch and counterparty. For instance, making available to board members for every relationship:

- *Cost* – cost of capital, discounts, trading and other losses, as well as cost of risk being assumed, and
- *Benefit* – interest income, fee income, trading benefit and other benefits that result from the client relationship.

This type of more analytical report may be a burden to some members of the board, but hold necessary information for others, particularly directors who want to know how much the institution gives away under different agreements, or accepts in advance to lose under thresholds of adverse conditions, and how many profits it makes in return.

Up to a point, but only up to a point, greater detail makes possible a better appreciation of business opportunity and of assumed exposure; it also permits factual and documented management decisions. Beyond that point, however, for many people 'more information' becomes a burden and esoteric explanations become incomprehensible. Therefore, it is time to personalize risk control information in a way that befits the recipient.

For risk managers and line executives, gains and losses must be determined by marking-to-market positions *intra-day*, since technology makes it feasible to account for *microseasonality*. (Microseasonality is *intra-day* seasonality. This contrasts with the better-known term 'seasonality', which is inter-day and usually extends over a one-year period.)

For the majority of board members, though not for all, microseasonality is not important except in the case of panics. In contrast, changes in the current phase of the business cycle and the seasonality underpinning them are very important. The greater sensitivity provided by intra-day data contrasts with the tendency of economists who realize that there is a recession (technically defined as two consecutive quarters of negative economic growth) when we are actually in the middle of it. And something similar often applies to a recovery.

Stress tests on macroeconomic conditions can be revealing. The Deutsche Bundesbank uses them for assessments of the prevailing economic situation, based on major economic risk factors that are simulated. The shocks affect banks through a subdued growth in gross domestic product (GDP). In two model scenarios interest rates were assumed to remain unchanged and the hypothesis of a decline in GDP with likewise constant interest rates characterized a third scenario. The crucial factors were:

- *Scenario 1* – oil price shock
- *Scenario 2* – abrupt adjustment of global imbalances
- *Scenario 3* – deep recession, modelling a maximum of cyclical shock.[12]

Among monetary policy institutions, the Deutsche Bundesbank is among the *avant-garde* of simulation and experimentation, whose output helps in readiness to confront future shocks, and in the implementation of knowledge engineering. Notice that this technology is available to every central bank, commercial bank and investment bank, but only those best managed to use it.

The members of the board should be enabled to read tomorrow's newspaper today, thanks to simulation and experimentation. This has become a 'must', given the increasing complexity and diversity of financial operations, which has changed the nature and magnitude of risk. Even credit institutions whose mission has been deposits and lending now rely much more on financial trading.

Additionally, the bigger players' competitiveness is measured by the standards of:

- Globalization
- Rapid product innovation, and
- Sophisticated technology.

The effects of this polyvalent evolution, which is still in a phase of acceleration, have to be fully understood at board level and managed proactively. This is expressed in the understanding that with many organizations the bottleneck is at the top – as in every bottle.

Globalization makes it mandatory not only to have a first-class risk control system, but also that top management frequently visits the overseas offices where trading is being done, and talks to: traders, risk controllers, accountants and other staff about their activities and challenges that they face. Barings is far from being the only bank that suffered an absolute failure of management controls because the people at headquarters were living in an ivory tower.

For instance, Barings' treasury and settlements department in London seem to have done nothing to clarify whether the large sums sent to the bank's Singapore office were for client trading or Barings' proprietary trading. In fact, much of the industry's criticism of the venerable bank's bankruptcy was concerned with:

- Management failures, and
- Non-existence of internal controls.

Furthermore, with Barings' default, the so-called matrix management, in which individuals have both regional and functional reporting lines but can give their undivided attention to neither, came under attack. This tends to dilute responsibility and accountability by creating alibis. It also blurs the lines segregating front-desk and back-office functions.

Another lesson from the Barings case is that top management should be wary when one individual fields all questions about a specific business activity, particularly when this person seems to have presided over extraordinary performance. At Barings, Nick Leeson appeared to be generating large profits from activities like arbitrage, with feedback information suggesting that his transactions were essentially free of risk. This is tunnel vision and it goes against the rule in investment banking that risk and reward are inextricably linked.

6. The risk management committee of the board

The Basel Committee on Banking Supervision defines the role of the board's risk management committee as being that of providing oversight by senior executives in managing credit, market, liquidity, operational, legal, compliance, reputational and other risks of the institution.[13] According to the supervisors, this role should include receiving from senior management periodic information on:

- Risk drivers
- Risk exposures, and
- Risk control activities.

Section 5 suggested that this is better done through *interactive computational finance*, using a system solution that has no geographic limitations and no time-zone constraints. The solution to be chosen must be instrumental in informing the board's risk management committee on all elements vital to its decisions. The example in Figure 12.3 concerns the allocation of an institution's financial resources, the end result of an effort that started with identification of risk drivers.

Well-managed banks define and use a variety of key risk indicators, which, as underlined on several occasions, address both quantitative and qualitative issues related to exposure. It is advisable that these indicators are forward looking, like the *Windows on Risk* employed by one of the better-known global financial institutions. Through them, the board's risk management committee reviews not only exposure, but also the entity's risk tolerance.

The adopted solution has been tested regarding its ability to provide top-down examination and review of material corporate-wide risks, covering all primary and several consequential windows of exposure. These include:

- Credit risk ratings and trends in client creditworthiness
- Pre-settlement risk on foreign exchange, interest rate and derivative products
- Industry concentrations, globally and within regions
- Limits assigned to relationship banking and consumer programmes
- Instrument concentrations in areas characterized by important risk drivers
- Price risk, evaluating earnings at risk resulting from changing levels of implied volatility
- Liquidity risk, focusing on funding assumed exposures
- Equity and subordinated debt investment risk
- Exposures associated with distribution and underwriting
- Commodities risk, resulting from changes in commodity prices

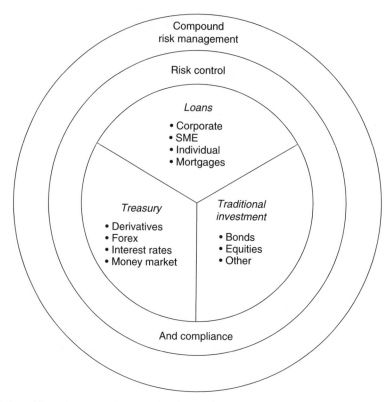

Figure 12.3   Risk control over the allocation of an institution's financial resources

- Country risk, encompassing political and cross-border exposures
- Dependency risk, linking and evaluating specific industry and consumer product exposure to external environmental factors.

This committee is chaired by the vice chairman responsible for risk management, and includes the CEO and other senior officers. The definition of Windows on Risk is kept dynamic through steady observation, and exposure in it subjected to rigorous assessment, evaluating and measuring defects in the institution's business processes:

- Legal, evaluating vulnerability and business implications
- Technology risk, assessing the vulnerability to rapid changes in technological developments.

Three major components characterize the overall Windows on Risk process. The first is assessment of the global external environment, drawing on the bank's own acquired knowledge and understanding, but also bringing in experts on specific subjects. A characteristic of this process is that it promotes contrarian views. The review of the external environment integrates the outlook for:

- Major country and regional economies
- Significant consumer markets and global industries
- Potential near-term critical economic and political events, and
- Implications of potentially unfavourable developments as they relate to specific business activities.

The second key component is assessment of the company's exposures in terms of different Windows on Risk, looking for potential large material exposures that are now confronting or are likely to confront the institution. Specific decisions and follow-ups constitute the third component. Their objective is to assist in adjusting overall exposure to dynamically identified risks.

The steady process of risk assessment involves both qualification and quantification of dangers, permitting bank officers to decide if a particular risk is worth taking. Quantification is supported through models. For instance, in lending, every time the customer's risk level changes (more precisely, worsens), the system calculates the insurance necessary to cover such risk and ups the premium. Keeping the premiums interactively adjustable:

- Permits the expansion of loans and derivatives trading activities, while keeping a tap on exposure, and
- Makes it feasible to build up market share in terms of financial services, in the knowledge of the exposure being assumed.

Models can be instrumental in profit and loss evaluations, and their results are more valuable when computed at a specific level of confidence. An interactive presentation, like the example presented in Figure 12.4, increases management's ability to appreciate levels of exposure, and it facilitates the understanding of risk and return by members of the board.

Several other banks have developed a similar approach but have few co-involved board members – yet a firm policy that is closely followed up is a prerequisite to sound risk management. A focused solution requires maintaining and selectively enhancing the risk factors associated with financial services, but also in getting senior management's attention, including the time of directors and of the chief executive officer.

Invariably, the board has to consider *risk-based* strategies that, apart from other exposures, have an impact on business risk (Chapter 3) and on reputational risk (section 7). Crucial questions include: Can we make risk selection a central

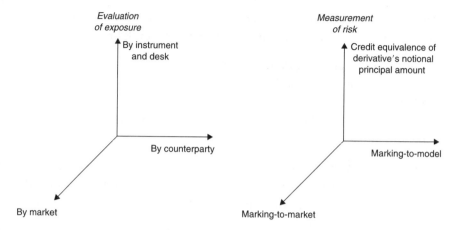

Figure 12.4   Two interactive frames of reference for total risk management

part of our strategic planning? Can we comprehend the bank's overall risk profile, to rethink our strategy? Do the results being projected justify reliance on our risk capital models? Can we assure regulators that our risk strategies and risk control are evidence of our quality of management?

7.   The board's responsibility for reputational risk

Good managers are not always chasing after facts. From time to time, they step back from day-to-day operations and take a more relaxed philosophical look at the way business is being conducted, customer relations are managed, human resources are developed, products are innovated, costs are swamped and risks are controlled. If this is true for line executives, it is even more so for board directors and CEOs.

Another characteristic of excellence in management is the ability to develop alternatives, evaluate their strong and weak points, and develop dissent so all aspects of a decision are examined prior to commitment. 'All' also means those issues that are negative and not only those that seem to be the more favourable. In doing so, much can be learned from old masters.

Alfred P. Sloan Jr once said at a GM board meeting: 'Gentlemen, I take it we are all in complete agreement on the decision here.' When the assembled executives all nodded their assent, Sloan added: 'I propose further discussion of this matter is delayed until our next board meeting, to give yourself time to develop disagreement and perhaps gain some understanding of what the decision is all about.'

When elaborated at board level, answers responding to this specific requirement are instrumental in accounting for the fact that even the best organization, as well as the best risk management system, have weaknesses. Appreciating this fact is important inasmuch as in the world of credit risk, market risk, liquidity risk and operational risk we often work with imperfect data. Only through questioning everything we do can we do better than our competitors.

In risk management parlance, for example, it is important to appreciate that even the 99.97% level of confidence leaves an unlikely but plausible adverse event out of our calculation. That's why a culture of experimentation has an important place in banking. 'We have experience in reducing every operation to loans equivalent in conjunction to risk-based pricing,' said a senior executive of one of the major banks. But not every financial industry executive can make this statement.

In a significant number of cases, credit institutions don't quite know: how to integrate risk analysis into their pricing of new products; how to use predictive analysis for risk-based pricing (Chapter 11); how to control pricing tools to better match price with relative risk assumed; or how to meet both the market demand and the requirements of rating agencies and regulators – since their criteria tend to conflict with one another.

Many cognizant people who participated in the research that led to this book suggested that perhaps the greatest current weakness lies in the management of *reputational risk*, which so often morphs into business risk, and vice versa. Its management requires what many people call an 'appropriate balance' between:

- Enhancing core business
- Observing the interests of all shareholders
- Implementing suitable internal controls, and
- Adhering to a strict policy of regulatory compliance.

But is that enough? To answer this query we need to define what is meant by *reputation*. A rather near-sighted approach looks at reputation as a comprehensive set of enduring stakeholder perceptions, opinions and expectations. A broader definition will definitely include market discipline – where reputation takes years to develop and can be destroyed overnight.

Some institutions tend to include in reputation their ability to innovate by launching new tailor-made products. Also, their readiness to pay attention to shareholder value and handhold with stakeholders that directly interact with the firm. A wider view of reputation will also consider in the list of issues to watch:

- Name
- Trustworthiness

- Standing, and
- Stature.

Contributing to reputation is the way in which a company stands by its name, associates risk analysis with human resources training, develops risk profiles and rigorous management practices, keeps its policies transparent and avoids creative accounting as a way to beautify its financial statements.

Mounting stakeholder vigilance, and an increasing activism, make the business environment much more exposed to reputational risk than it used to be. At the same time, however, opportunities abound for senior management to promote and positively influence the firm's reputation as a provider of products and services that are higher quality and more cost-effective than those of the competition.

Experts suggest that in a globalized and dynamic business environment the effectiveness of reputation management ultimately determines the degree of strategic alternatives with which a company is able to shape its future. In turn, reputational risk management makes it even more important to develop and apply both state-of-the-art:

- Risk control systems, and
- Reputation promotion skills and policies.

Part of reputational risk is the so-called *headline risk*, where a company's internal and more general market problems are aired by the media – because of 'this' or 'that' scandal or because the company underperformed relative to its competitors. This type of exposure entails that the risk manager should be chosen not only for organizational skills and knowledge of detail in risk control, but also for a fertile mind and ability to take action averting headline risk.

Risk management and intelligence services share a common characteristic: they both require conceptual skills and a great deal of imagination. As we have seen on several occasions in this book, often risk information is scant and incomplete. This is not surprising since the notions of risk and uncertainty strongly correlate, and therefore increase the responsibility boards, CEOs and risk managers share for the firm's reputation and its future. This is a task that must take precedence over other responsibilities, no matter how important they may be.

In conclusion, very effective and responsive management of exposure, as well as control over reputational risk, are the board's and CEO's true friend. A true friend not only warns of what he sees to be dangers, but also ventures to counsel his friend as to what he should do in a crisis that is imminent. Risk management is not child's play but an activity whose outcome reflects the maturity of the people performing it.

Notes

1   Max Hastings, *Armageddon: The Battle for Germany 1944–45*. Pan Books, London, 2004.

2   *Financial Times*, 29 January 2007.

3   ECB, Monthly Bulletin, Frankfurt, January 2007.

4   E. Hayden, D. Porath and N von Westernhagen, 'Does Diversification Improve the Performance of German Banks?', Discussion Paper No. 05. Deutsche Bundesbank, Frankfurt, 2006.

5   *Financial Times*, 30 January 2007.

6   When it virtually collapsed in September 1998, LTCM had a leveraging of 350.

7   *EIR*, 5 December 2006.

8   *Asian Wall Street Journal*, 12 September 1995.

9   *International Herald Tribune*, 20 August 1999.

10 W. Merkl and S. Stolz, 'Banks Regulatory Buffers, Liquidity Networks and Monetary Policy Transmission', Discussion Paper No. 06. Deutsche Bundesbank, Frankfurt, 2006.

11 Albrecht Fölsing, *Albert Einstein*. Penguin Putnam, New York, 1997.

12 Deutsche Bundesbank, Financial Stability Review, Frankfurt, November 2006.

13 Basel Committee on Banking Supervision, 'Enhancing Corporate Governance for Banking Organizations' (Consultative Document). BIS, Basel, July 2005.

Index